It's Not
the Media

It's Not
the Media

The Truth About
Pop Culture's Influence
on Children

KAREN STERNHEIMER

A Member of the Perseus Books Group

Copyright © 2003 by Karen Sternheimer

Published in the United States of America by Westview Press, A Member of the Perseus Books Group, 5500 Central Avenue, Boulder, Colorado 80301–2877, and in the United Kingdom by Westview Press, 12 Hid's Copse Road, Cumnor Hill, Oxford OX2 9JJ.

Find us on the world wide web at www.westviewpress.com.

Westview Press books are available at special discounts for bulk purchases in the United States by corporations, institutions, and other organizations. For more information, please contact the Special Markets Department at the Perseus Books Group, 11 Cambridge Center, Cambridge, MA 02142, or call (617) 252–5298, (800) 255-1514 or email j.mccrary@perseusbooks.com.

Library of Congress Cataloging-in-Publication Data

Sternheimer, Karen.
It's not the media : the truth about pop culture's influence on children / Karen Sternheimer.
    p. cm.
Includes bibliographical references and index.
  ISBN 0-8133-4138-8 (hardcover)
1. Mass media and youth—United States. 2. Popular culture—United States. 3. Internet and children—United States. 4. Children—United States—Social conditions. 5. Children and adults—United States. 6. Teenagers and adults--United States. 7. Mass media and public opinion—United States. I. Title: Pop culture's influence on children. II. Title.
  HQ799.2.M35S84 2003
  302.23'0835—dc21

                                                              2003014599

The paper used in this publication meets the requirements of the American National Standard for Permanence of Paper for Printed Library Materials Z39.48–1984.

Designed by Reginald R. Thompson
Set in 10.5-point ITC Century Book by the Perseus Books Group

10   9   8   7   6   5   4   3   2   1

For my grandfather Henry Fettner,
gone but never forgotten.

Contents

Acknowledgments   *ix*

Part 1

Introduction: Who's Afraid of the Big Bad Wolf?
*The flawed logic of media phobia, past
and present*   *1*

1 Why Americans Choose to Fear Media
*It's not the media: What really changed
childhood*   *21*

2 Why Americans Choose to Fear Youth
The politics of youth-bashing   *41*

Part 2

3 Fear of Media Violence
Four fallacies of media-violence effects   *61*

4 Fear of Cartoons
Role models for bad behavior?   *85*

5 Fear of Video Games
The blamed games   *109*

6 Fear of Music
   Musical murder and misogyny?   *125*

Part 3

7 Fear of Advertising and the Young Consumer
   How much is that psyche in the window?   *147*

8 Fear of Sex
   Do the media make them do it?   *169*

9 Fear of the Internet
   Information regulation   *193*

Conclusion: Rethinking Fears of Media and Children
   Media: A sheep in wolf's clothing   *207*

Notes   *221*
Selected Bibliography   *251*
Index   *257*

Acknowledgments

This book could not have been written without the support and encouragement of dozens of people. First, I need to thank Westview Press for making my vision a reality, particularly my editor, Jill Rothenberg, whose enthusiasm was tempered with the perfect blend of constructive criticism. Jill championed this project from the beginning and I couldn't have asked for a better editor and friend in this process. I want to acknowledge the marketing team in advance for their excitement and dedication to this book. I also need to thank the department of sociology at the University of Southern California for the years of academic nurturing. In particular, Mike Messner, Barry Glassner, Jon Miller, and former faculty members Darnell Hunt, Cheryl Maxson, Malcolm Klein and Barrie Thorne have been incredibly supportive through the years. A special thanks to the department's office staff, Dora Lara, Pat Adolph, Stachelle Overland, and Monique Thomas for their daily assistance. Other colleagues and friends provided support and/or valuable feedback on the manuscript, including Sally Raskoff, Noel Riley Fitch, Christine L. Williams, David Altheide, Mike Males, Brian Chisling, Elizabeth Thoman, Doug Kellner, Rhonda Hammer, and Betsy Amster.

Many thanks to my wonderful undergraduate students at USC; a great deal of these ideas took shape in class discussions over the past few years. Several students served as research assistants on this project: Ryan Halfon, Heather Hutcheson, Jin Kang, Kourtni Kardashian, Lisa Schloss, Audra Thamrin, and Mark Yapelli spent many hours on Lexis-Nexis and doing library searches, and I am grateful for their hard work.

In addition to professional support, I am thankful to the many friends that encouraged me to keep going on the project, particularly my writing group friends Jean Summer, Antoinette Samardzic, Louise Everett, Sarah Clune, Carol Cyr, and Portia Cohen. Carmela Lomonaco, Monica Whitlock, Lynda Green, Laura Goldman, and Molly Ranney have been especially supportive over the years.

Finally and most importantly, my family has always encouraged me, no matter how ridiculous my endeavor. I am grateful for having such a wonderful extended family, including an aunt who has also been a professional mentor, Barbara Cohen. My grandmother, Frieda Fettner, has both encouraged me and helped me put things in perspective. Without the lifelong encouragement from my sisters, Laura and Linda Sternheimer, and my parents, Lee Sternheimer and Toby Sternheimer none of this would have been possible.

Part One

Introduction: Who's Afraid of the Big Bad Wolf?

The Flawed Logic of Media Phobia, Past and Present

April 20, 1999: I remember that Tuesday morning clearly. I was working at home, exhausted after teaching a Monday night class. When I turned on the television I knew that something horrible had happened because news programs had gone into crisis mode, with the "breaking news" banner underlining each station's coverage. There had been a shooting at a high school in Littleton, Colorado.

While the shooting at Columbine High School was discussed in context with other high-profile school shootings of the 1990s, it was clear that this one was different. The casualties were greater, the school larger and more affluent. Nonstop coverage ensued—I joined the news event as cameras were stationed at an off-site location where parents eagerly awaited the arrival of kids bused to safety. Parents hugged children, classmates held onto each other sobbing while telling reporters what it was like inside. As several students described crouching under tables in the library, I imagined myself in my own high school library, a place I went nearly every day after lunch for a little bit of quiet. I began to feel relieved that my high school days were long past. High school was hard enough without worrying about being shot.

1

Once the initial shock of the shootings ended, the commentators appeared to try to explain how something like this could happen. It didn't take long before pundits invoked the popular culture rationale. What music did the killers listen to? Why did they wear those trench coats? Wasn't the scene eerily reminiscent of the 1995 movie *The Basketball Diaries*, where Leonardo DiCaprio opens fire on his classmates and teacher and is met by the applause of his buddies? Did they learn to make bombs on the Internet? They sure seemed to play lots of violent video games where they could take virtual target practice at their classmates. The commentary appeared to point to mounting evidence: the media were guilty, and the public has had enough. Columbine seemed to tell us that violent media could create tragedy, as we had long suspected.

This book is not about the Columbine High School shooting, but the incident serves as a powerful example of American anxieties about our media culture and our fear of what it may have "done to" children in the years leading up to and following the tragedy. Although the Columbine killers were in their teens, the word "child" is frequently used to encompass all minors to heighten the sense of young people's vulnerability to media culture. Throughout the book I try to be clear about which age group I'm talking about, but keep in mind that others aren't. My intent in writing this book is to take a step back and think about exactly why it is that we fear the effects of popular culture. As we will see, a great deal of our concern about media and media's potential effects on kids has more to do with uncertainty about the future and the changing landscape of childhood. In addition to considering why we are concerned about the impact of popular culture, I also explore why many researchers and politicians encourage us to remain afraid of media culture.

The Flawed Logic of Media Phobia

Ironically, we are encouraged to fear media by the news media itself, because doomsday warnings sell papers and keep us so scared we stay glued to our TV sets. "TV is leading children down a moral sewer!" the late entertainer Steve Allen claimed in several full-page ads he purchased in the *Los Angeles Times*. Other headlines seem to concur— "Cartoon violence is no laughing matter," said the *Kansas City Star*. "Health Groups Link Hollywood Fare to Youth Violence," announced the front page of the *Los Angeles Times*. "Today's Youth Need to Learn to Care," *The Denver Post* reported. These and hundreds of other stories nationwide imply that the media are a threat to children, and more ominously, that children are subsequently a threat to society. Media *are* a central facet of American culture, but media culture is not the root cause of American social problems, not the Big Bad Wolf, as our ongoing public discussion would suggest. Instead, our anxieties about a changing world, uncertain future, and seemingly unsolvable social ills are deflected onto popular culture, which serves as a visible target when the real causes are harder to pin down.

The news media are central within American public thought, maybe not telling us what to think, but, to borrow a popular phrase, telling us what to think about.[1] The abundance of news stories similar to the ones listed above directs us to think about entertainment as public enemy number one for kids. This fear of media was not invented out of thin air, nor is it only fanned by news stories suggesting media culture is dangerous. There is a parallel groundswell of public concern about the larger role of media culture in contemporary American society. Let's face it: a lot of media culture is highly sexualized, is filled with violence, and seems to appeal to our basest interests. Many politicians and social scientists have made challenging popular culture central in their careers. Everyday citizens' letters to the editors of newspapers around the country reveal the widespread nature of the fear that media are ruining the next generation. The fear is everywhere.

Fear is a powerful force, especially when children seem to be potential victims, so it is understandable that the public would be concerned about our ubiquitous media culture. However compelling news reports are, with attention-grabbing visuals and the constant competition for our attention, the fear that media are a central threat to children and the future of America is a tempting explanation, but at best misguided. Dangerously misguided when we consider all the real, though not as sexy, issues that get pushed out of the headlines in favor of media fears. Poverty, family violence, child abuse and neglect, and the lack of quality education and health care are problems that merit public attention way before media culture. But these policy issues can seem dry and aren't what build big ratings, so they get pushed aside for stories that are more emotion-driven, where the "breaking news" or "live" banner can wave across the screen to excite us.

The explanation that media create a culture of violence is tantalizing. It diverts us from delving into the deeper questions, questions about how young people in overgrown, albeit well-funded, learning institutions may feel alienated and turn to violence. Focusing on the media only in a cause-and-effect manner fails to help us understand the connection between media culture and politics and power, as well as the ways in which the media are central to American culture, not merely an influence on individuals' behavior. An emphasis on media as the cause of kids' bad behavior prevents us from asking deeper questions about the use of violence to solve problems on a national and global level, for instance, or why boys are socialized to save face at any cost, to be tough and never vulnerable. But most ominously, the effects question crowds out other vital issues affecting the well-being and future of young people. These issues play out more quietly on a daily basis and lay hidden underneath the more dramatic fear-factor type headlines. This book uncovers these vitally important issues and provides a wake-up call for us to look beyond the hype to understand that it's not the media, but very real policy decisions that hurt children.

The Real Big Bad Wolves

Blaming media for changes in childhood and social problems has shifted our public conversation away from addressing the real problems that impact children's lives. The most pressing crisis facing American children today is not media culture but poverty. The National Center for Children in Poverty reported that nearly twelve million children (approximately 16 percent of Americans under eighteen) live in poverty, a rate two to three times higher than that in other industrialized nations.[2] Reduced funding for families in poverty has only exacerbated this problem, as we are now starting to see the effects of 1996 welfare "reform" legislation that threatens to take away the safety net from children. Additionally, our two-tiered health care system often prevents poor children from receiving basic health care, as 14 percent of American children have no health insurance.[3] These are often children with parents who work at jobs that have no benefits.

These same children are admonished to stay in school to break the cycle of poverty, yet many of them attend schools without enough books or basic school supplies. Schools in high-poverty areas are more likely to have uncertified teachers; for instance, 70 percent of seventh through twelfth graders in such schools are taught science by teachers without science backgrounds.[4] We worry about kids being in danger at school but forget that the most perilous place, statistically speaking, is in their own homes. In 1999, for instance, over 1,000 children were killed by their parents compared with thirty-five killed in school during the school year.[5] By continually focusing on media-made killers, we forget that the biggest threat to childhood is adults and the policies adults create.

I can understand why people are concerned about popular culture. Many of us find it to be distasteful at times and wonder what its impact may be. We don't like hearing foul language blasting from the stereo of the car next to ours and cringe when young girls want to emulate sexy pop stars. We hear the news report study after study by researchers from leading universities telling us that our fears have been confirmed, that kids who watch violent TV allegedly grow up to be more violent adults. Media culture has become very pervasive in the last few decades, and at times it feels like it bombards us—twenty-four-hour news streams, Internet pop-up ads, instant messaging, and other forms of media culture have reshaped our daily lives as well as how we interact with each other.

The media have come to symbolize society and present a clear picture of both social changes and social problems. Changes in media culture and media technologies are easier to see than the complex host of economic, political, and social changes Americans have experienced in the past few decades. Graphic video games are more visible and easier to target than changes in public policies we hear little about. We criticize irreverent cartoon characters or single mothers on television because it is difficult to explore the real and complex situations that impact people's choices and behavior. The point of this book is to expose that what lies behind our fear of media culture is anxiety about an uncertain future. This fear has been deflected onto children, symbolic of the future, and onto media, symbolic of contemporary society.

OK, Sometimes It *Is* the Media

While media culture may not be the biggest threat to childhood, it certainly merits criticism in other arenas. For one, the news media are often guilty of peddling fascination rather than information. This book serves as a critique of the press coverage of children's issues and why "the media made them do it" theme continually resurfaces. Aside from the news, media content is important too. Stereotypical images of women as sexual objects persist, as do narrow portrayals of racial, ethnic, and religious minority group members. Limited or absent representations of the elderly, the plus-sized, Asian Americans, and Latinos reflect the tendency of mass entertainment to focus on a limited portrait of American life.

The quest to get the biggest box office opening or Nielsen ratings leads to lowest common denominator storytelling, which explains the overuse of sex and violence as plot devices. Profit, not critical acclaim, equals success in Hollywood (and on Wall Street). Sex and violence create fascination and are sold in popular culture like commodities to attract our attention, if only for a little while. I think concerns about sex and violence in entertainment stem from fears that *real* sex and violence may become equally as meaningless as the multitude of empty images we often see.

So I understand critics who argue that graphic media depictions of sex and violence debase our culture. Hollywood's dependence on these tools often represents the failure to tell complex stories and the lack of courage to take artistic (and financial) risks. Rather than just ask for Hollywood for self-censorship, I think we should have more choices, more opportunities for our media culture to engage the complexities of life that the summer blockbusters seldom do. But business as usual often makes this impossible, when a handful of big conglomerates produce the lion's share of entertainment media and smaller producers have a difficult time getting attention. The 1996 Telecommunications Act, which eased media ownership restrictions, made it even harder for smaller media outlets to compete with the big studios like Disney, AOL Time-Warner and Viacom.

That said, I know that sometimes at the end of the day I prefer to be distracted and amused rather than informed or inspired. With the threat of terrorism, war in the Middle East, and a faltering economy, maybe superficial entertainment serves a purpose. But deflected anxiety doesn't go away, it just resurfaces elsewhere. And in uncertain times such as our own, it is understandable that our concerns would eventually focus on children and the media culture that both reminds us of our insecurities and distracts us from them.

Changing Times

The terrorist attacks of September 11, 2001, are a dramatic reminder that we are living in a time of flux and fear. Political allegiances and diplomacy have had to be reconsidered. The Cold War logic that shaped American foreign policy for nearly forty years is now obsolete, and previous conceptions of allies and enemies are now all but meaningless. Twentieth century icons of American power and prosperity—the Pentagon, the World Trade Center, and aviation—were proven vulnerable in ways unimaginable before that day. Our sense of security was violated, as two oceans can no longer be enough for us to feel safe. In many ways the future has never seemed so unknowable.

In addition to political changes, we have experienced economic shifts over the past few decades, such as the increased necessity for two incomes to sustain middle-class status, which has reshaped family life. Increased opportunities for women have created greater independence, making marriage less of a necessity for economic survival. Deindustrialization and the rise of an information-based economy have left the poorest and least skilled workers behind and eroded job security for the middle class. Ultimately these economic changes have made supervision of children more of a challenge for adults, who are now working longer hours.

Since the Industrial Revolution, our economy has become more complex and adults and children have increasingly spent their days separated. From a time when adults and children worked together on family farms to the development of institutions specifically for children, like age-segregated schools, daycare, and organized after-school activities, daily interaction in American society has become more separated by age. Popular culture is another experience that kids may enjoy beyond adult supervision. An increase of youth autonomy has created fear within adults, who worry that violence, promiscuity, and other forms of "adult" behavior will emerge from these shifts and that parents will have a declining level of influence on their children. Kids spend more time with friends than with their parents as they get older, and more time with popular culture too. These changes explain in large part why childhood is experienced differently now than in the past and are not only the result of changes in popular culture. Chapter 1 considers how the social and historical context of childhood today is different from the way it was in the past, and how we often overlook these historical changes within our media fears.

A Brief History of Media Fears

Fear that popular culture has a negative impact on youth is nothing new: it is a recurring theme in history. Whereas in the past fears about youth were largely confined to children of the working class, immigrants, or racial minorities, fear of young people now appears to be a more generalized fear of the future, which explains why we have brought middle-class and affluent youth into the spectrum of worry. Like our predecessors we are afraid of change, of popular culture we don't like or understand, and of a shifting world that at times feels out of control.

Throughout recorded history there have been people who have argued that children were the victims of popular culture. Fears about media and children date back at least to Plato, who was concerned about the effects the classic Greek tragedies had on children.[6] Historian John Springhall describes how penny theaters and cheap novels in early nineteenth century England were thought to create moral decay amongst working-class boys.[7] Attending the theater or reading a book would hardly raise an eyebrow today, but Springhall explains that the concern emerged following an increase in working-class youths' leisure time. As in contemporary times, youth were blamed for a rise in crime and any gathering place of working-class youth was considered threatening. Young people could only afford admission to penny theaters, which featured entertainment geared towards a working-class audience, rather than the "respectable" theaters catering to middle- or upper-class patrons. Complaints about the performances were not unlike those about contemporary culture: youngsters would learn the "wrong" values and possibly become criminals. Penny and later dime novels garnered similar reaction, accused of being tawdry in content and filled with slang that kids might imitate. Springhall concludes that the concern had less to do with actual content and more to do with the growing literacy of the working class, shifting the balance of power from elites to the masses and threatening the status quo.

Examining the social context enables us to understand what creates underlying anxieties about media. Fear of comic books in the 1940s and 1950s, for instance, took place in the McCarthy era when the control over culture was high on the national agenda. Like the dime novels before, comic books were cheap, based on adventurous tales, and appealed to the masses. Colorful and graphic depictions of violence riled critics, who lobbied Congress unsuccessfully to place restrictions on comics' sale and production.[8] Psychiatrist and author Frederic Wertham wrote in 1953 that "chronic stimulation . . . by comic books are contributing factors to many children's maladjustment."[9] Comics were believed to be a major cause of violent behavior, enabling the public to deny that violence in post-war America could be caused by anything but the reading material of choice for many young boys.

During mid-century, music routinely appeared on the public enemy list. Historian Grace Palladino recounts concerns about swing music in the early 1940s.[10] Adults feared kids wasted so much time listening to it that they could never become decent soldiers in World War II (sixty years later Tom Brokaw dubbed these same would-be delinquents "the greatest generation").[11] Palladino contends that adult anxieties stemmed from the growing separation between teenagers, a term coined in 1941, and the older generation in both leisure time and cultural tastes. Just a few years later similar concerns arose when Elvis Presley brought traditionally African-American music to white Middle America. His hips weren't really the problem; it was the threat of bringing traditionally "black" music to white middle-class teens during a time of enforced and de facto segregation. Later, concerns about subliminal messages (ever try to play an LP backwards to find a satanic message?) and panic over Prince's *1999* lyrics about masturbation in the 1980s led to the formation of Tipper Gore's Parents Music Resource Center (PMRC), Senate hearings, and parental warning labels. Both stem from parents' discomfort with their children's cultural preferences and the desire to increase their ability to control what their children know.

Concerns about popular culture are often masked attempts to condemn the tastes and cultural preferences of less powerful social groups. Popular culture has always been viewed as less valuable than "high" culture, the stuff that is supposed to make you more refined, like going to the ballet, the opera, or the symphony. Throughout history people have been ready to believe the worst about the "low" culture of the common folk, just as bowling, wrestling, and monster truck rallies often bear the brunt of put-downs today. It's more socially acceptable to make fun of something working-class people might enjoy than to appear snobby and insensitive by criticizing people for their economic status. The same is true of criticizing rap music rather than African-American youth directly. In other words, popular culture is frequently used as a proxy for hostility and so we condemn a group's cultural preferences rather than openly express hostility towards the group.

Popular culture often creates power struggles. Every new medium creates new freedom for some, more desire to control for others. For instance, although the printing press was regarded as one of the greatest inventions of the second millennium, it also destabilized the power of the church when literacy became more widespread and people could read the Bible themselves. Later, the availability of cheap newspapers and novels reduced the ability of the upper class to control popular culture created specifically for the working class. Fears of media today reflect a similar power struggle, although now the elites are adults who fear losing control of what their children know, what their children like, and who their children are.

Perhaps the biggest concern one generation can have for the next is the fear that they will be without values and lack a connection with society. Young people are routinely described in public discourse as oversexed, dangerous, self-centered fools, creating a rather convenient class of scapegoats for difficult social problems. Articles like *The Washington Post*'s "Why Johnny Can't Feel" reveal a sense that a new problem has emerged amongst the young. [12] According to a story called "It's Hard to See the Line Where Alienation Leads to Violence," being a teenage outcast today is somehow worse than ever before.[13] "It never seemed to matter as much as it does now," the authors stated, and asserted that kids today are "more sensitive than ever," which could potentially lead to violence. [14] Allegedly "the difference between alienated youths and violent youths may be little more than an inadvertent bump or whispered taunt."[15] The news media would have us believe that kids are ticking time bombs, waiting to blow. The reality is that young people are becoming *less* violent, yet they are continually maligned in public discourse. The "epidemic" of school shootings is used to support the contention that more and more young people are becoming cold-blooded killers in spite of the fact that homicides in schools *decreased* during the 1990s.[16] The facts only get in the way of creating a sensational story about the tragic downfall of the next generation.

Rather than promote an atmosphere in which we discuss the realities of children's and adolescents' lives and reconsider the pressure adults and adult-run institutions place on them by, for instance, cutting education budgets, the conversation has turned towards attempting to further restrict young people. Curfews and harsher sentences for juvenile offenders have grown in popularity despite the dearth of empirical evidence in support of these punitive policies. Calls for further media restrictions are also heard, including a group in the Senate who in spring 2001 introduced the Media Marketing Accountability Act, which would fine producers who advertise "adult-oriented" entertainment to teenagers.

Is there any wonder that many young people feel disconnected from adult authority figures? We call teens stupid and immoral, condemn them for the video games, music, and movies they like, and try to take what freedoms they have away. We wonder why, after hearing politicians blame them for many of our nation's problems, they don't rush to the polls to vote when they turn eighteen. Chapter 2 explores why we are often both afraid for and afraid of children in the United States and how this helps shape our media fears. In addition to blaming media for social problems, we all too often blame young people themselves.

Contemporary Media Fears

Today, fears of media culture stem from the decreased ability to control content and consumption. While attending the theater or reading newspapers or novels elicits little public concern today, fears have shifted to newer forms of cultural expression like television, video games, and the Internet. Throughout the twentieth century these media increasingly led to more time spent alone consuming popular culture. Before the invention of radio and television, popular culture was a more public event and controlling the information young people were exposed to was somewhat easier. Fears surrounding newer media have largely been based on the reduced ability of adults to control children's access. Personal CD players, VCRs, television sets, and computers make it nearly impossible for adults to seal off the walls of childhood from the rest of society.

The main concern critics voice about media culture is that children will imitate acts of violence and become sexually active, materialistic, or disconnected from society. There is a real fear that children cannot tell the difference between entertainment and reality. But we can ask the same question about adults, who conflate fears of real sex and violence with fears of *representations* of sex and violence. I recently attended a workshop for parents called "Television: What Every Parent Should Know" that demonstrates this point quite well. "Would you let a stranger in your home alone with your children?" the facilitator asked, and then answered. "You already do—every time you turn on the TV." A gasp echoed throughout the room as the speaker went on to list the number of violent and sexual acts their children may have already witnessed on television. No one questioned the big difference between actual intruders and entertainment.

Informal censorship such as Internet blocking software and the v-chip help willing parents become the censor. A television rating system has been implemented that is about as vague as our movie rating system, but enables Hollywood to appear responsive to our media fears without actually changing anything. An Annenberg Public Policy Center study found that only half of parents with v-chips actually used them and 90 percent of parents sampled could not correctly identify the age categories of television ratings.[17]

Parents worried about sex and violence in media have the federal government on their side. Author Cynthia Cooper analyzed nearly thirty congressional hearings held on this issue, finding them to be little more than an exercise in public relations for the elected officials, yet the investigations continue.[18] A fall 2000 report by the Federal Trade Commission concluded that movies with violence were marketed to teenagers. Action movies like the *Rambo, Die Hard,* and *Lethal Weapon* franchises have been a staple for male teenage audiences for decades, but nonetheless this report was treated like a smoking gun. The attorney general from South Carolina even said he might file a class action suit against major Hollywood studios similar to those filed against the tobacco industry.[19] Wal-Mart responded to this report by considering a ban on sales of videos containing violence. That was an ironic twist, considering a January 2001 *60 Minutes* report revealed that the chain had covered up incidents of violence within its stores, including children shot by guns on their shelves. Additionally, the California attorney general's office found that the chain had committed almost 500 violations of the state's gun laws, including skirting the ten-day waiting period and selling weapons to felons.[20] At the time, Wal-Mart did not announce a ban on gun sales.[21] As Michael Moore points out in his 2002 documentary, *Bowling for Columbine,* the American love affair with guns may be even stronger than our love of media culture.

The belief that media violence leads to increased aggression and violent behavior seems obvious to many people largely because news reports often present the results of research without much critique from social scientists who find fault with these studies' conceptualization and methods. Even when studies point to other central causal factors, media violence often enters the story. Take the Surgeon General's report on youth violence, released in January 2001. This report indicated that poverty and family violence are the best predictors of youth violence. Nonetheless, the report tosses a bone to those that fear media: "Exposure to violent media plays an important causal role," stated the surgeon general, based on research that is highly criticized by many within media studies circles.[22] Two Los Angeles area newspapers capitalized on this single statement, running stories with the headlines "Surgeon General Links TV, Real Violence" and "Media Dodges Violence Bullet."[23] This damn-the-facts, lead-with-conventional-wisdom approach helps us stay focused on the media red herring and ignore the difficult answers. Instead, we would do better to face the real issues that lead to violence, like family violence and the lingering effects of poverty in communities that society has all but abandoned. The realist in me knows that these issues don't make for easily digestible sound bites and are thus less likely to maintain our attention for very long. Nonetheless, our continued focus on the media culprit won't get us far. In Chapter 3 I consider four flawed assumptions made by those who insist media violence is a major causal factor of real violence.

Children's ability to interpret cartoons, a staple of kids' programming, has also been called into question. Can children discern fantasy from reality? Like comic books, cartoons have been criticized for containing violence that some fear children will copy, or at least fear that it will plant the seeds of aggression in young children. A Japanese animated program called *Dragon Ball Z* has come under fire for its violent content, even though it has been toned down for American audiences.[24] Concern about a Japanese cartoon creating violent American children highlights a critical point: while Japanese animation typically contains a great deal of stylized violence, Japan boasts far lower rates of violent crime than the United States; our homicide rate here is approximately *sixteen* times that of Japan.[25] We focus on violence in animation and worry about copycat behavior, but we rarely explore revisionist history or stereotypes within animated films.

Adult-approved cartoons such as Disney animation often mirror the status quo. Only a murmur of concern arises when racial stereotypes are used to connote villains in films like *Aladdin* or when history is rewritten to reinforce the viewpoint of the privileged in *Pocahontas* or *The Road to El Dorado*. Xenophobia, racism, and sexism go all but unexplored as parents take their children to see these "wholesome" forms of entertainment. Girls still see female characters existing only to be loved by a man in *Aladdin* and *The Little Mermaid*. In Chapter 4,

I argue that these are the issues we should be focusing on in children's programming. Rather than call for a ban on these movies or restrict children's access to them, we should use these films to open a dialogue about issues of race and gender and colonialism, which we often attempt to avoid in American public conversations.

While some cartoons escape adult scrutiny, others, like *South Park*, *The Simpsons*, and *Beavis and Butt-head*, have received a great deal of criticism from parents (but much support from television critics). Educator Howard Karlitz wrote in the *Los Angeles Times* that cartoons like *South Park* "impact negatively" on the "collective spirit of childhood innocence."[26] He is not alone in criticizing cartoon shows that challenge myths about childhood. Considered by many to be a corrupting influence on young people, these shows speak truths about childhood, adolescence, and family life that adults are not often willing to hear. Within both *South Park* and *The Simpsons*, for instance, children subvert parental power and often know more than their parents. Author Douglas Kellner points out that *Beavis and Butt-head* reveals the outcome of a downwardly mobile working class in which young people feel little commitment to the future.[27] The kids of *South Park* remind us that childhood is unsanitized, and it is parents who are often naïve about the realities of being a child. These cartoons reveal that childhood innocence is a fantasy, a message adults sometimes find difficult to accept. The cartoons that cause the greatest fear are those that challenge the sanctity of adult power. Chapter 4 explores why these cartoons have been the target of public scrutiny, and why others like Disney films receive very little public concern.

Video games have become a contemporary childhood pastime, which has elicited much concern. Critics argue that these games, with increasingly gory graphics, may send the message that violence is okay, rewarded by victory. News reports of studies claiming to link video games with aggression and violence are starting to emerge, again creating the belief that the fear is grounded in fact. In Chapter 5 we will see that these studies aren't nearly as convincing as the reports may suggest. Boys (and sometimes girls) have played shoot-'em-up games like cowboys and Indians and cops and robbers for generations, but the interactive format makes us concerned that video games are hands-on practice for real violence. Gerard Jones, author of *Killing Monsters: Why Children Need Fantasy, Super Heroes, and Make-Believe Violence*, argues that this type of play helps kids resolve their anxieties about violence and that it is not necessarily a precursor to the real thing. Violent play may be a way to feel powerful and work out hostilities that are the result of having relatively little power as children.

Like video games, music for young people often taps into the desire to rebel against adult authority and provides kids with the opportunity to create separate identities from adults, challenging the status quo and representing a challenge to parental control. Chapter 6 explores fears of rap and heavy metal music in particular. Behind the controversy over these musical genres lies the unwillingness of mainstream society to acknowledge the pervasiveness of sexism and racism, for instance, and thus we blame music for problems we don't know how to cope with in broader society. Music has also been accused of adding to teenagers' sense of alienation, which we would rather pin on music than explore how social institutions may make teens feel isolated.

In addition to violence, a common adult fear is that kids will be so easily swayed by advertising that they will grow up to be mindless consumers wrought with health problems and easily separated from their (or their parents') money. Susan Linn, associate director of the Media Center at the Judge Baker Children's Center in Massachusetts, wrote that advertising is linked with both obesity and eating disorders and also credited advertising with creating an environment that leads to voter apathy amongst youth and with "eroding the foundations of American life."[28] This helps us feel as if we have found the answer to several contemporary American problems all in one place, and that part of the solution to these problems is to change the nature of advertising. Linn noted that she fears advertisers undermine her authority as a mother, a fear many parents share. Advertising reveals that parents don't always have the ability to control their children's desires.

Yes, food advertised for children is often high in calories and low in nutritious value. But we need to question whether *parents* are so controlled by children that they can't say no when kids see something they want on TV. Also, childhood obesity has risen in conjunction with adult obesity. A study published in a 1999 issue of the *Journal of the American Medical Association* reported that it is *adults* eighteen to twenty-nine who showed the highest climb in obesity rates during the 1990s.[29] Yet somehow we hear only about *children* being "programmed" by advertisers. While I'm not suggesting we start thinking of adults as victims of advertisers, Chapter 7 explores why concerns about consumption tend to only focus on children.

In Chapter 7 I also explore how fear about advertising to children reflects anxiety parents feel about their reduced ability to control children's desires, identities, and growing status as consumers. Fears about advertising also reflect an unwillingness by adults to take responsibility for a culture of consumption that most of us partake in and quite often enjoy. It is easier to think of children being manipulated by amoral advertisers, rather than blaming ourselves. Chapter 7 also considers how advertisers go about selling to children; we will see that the task is not nearly as simple as many people believe. Through close examination of advertisers' words and the ads they produce for kids, we will see that advertisers understand children in a way that their parents often do not, because selling to children and teens is big business. Advertising executives consider kids far more skeptical than their parents. Teens in particular are thought to be especially cynical and ad campaigns like Sprite ("Image is nothing, obey your thirst") are very aware of this. Nonetheless they are often portrayed as incompetent victims of Madison Avenue's "invasion of the school yard and the nursery," as a *Los Angeles Times* article stated.[30] Chapter 7 examines how advertisers take the kids' side in the war parents and politicians have waged against the competency of children and teens.

Just as conventional wisdom holds that young people will imitate violence they see in media or buy things they don't need, there is fear that young people will become sexually active following exposure to sex in film and television. "Kids pick up on—and all too often act on—the messages they see and hear around them," wrote sex educator Deborah Roffman in a *Washington Post* article titled "Dangerous Games; A Sex Video Broke the Rules, But for Kids the Rules Have Changed."[31] Interesting that we don't level the same charges against adults, who are more likely to be sexually active, more likely to be rapists and sex offenders than teenagers. Roffman's article featured the story of a teenage boy from the Baltimore area who videotaped himself having sex with a classmate and then showed the tape to his friends. Certainly this story is troubling, but also troubling is the supposition that this incident is representative of all young people, whose rules of proper conduct have allegedly changed. We wouldn't dare make the same sweeping generalizations about equally appalling adult behavior.

But Roffman is not surprised: "What else do we expect in a culture where by the age of nineteen a child [*sic*] will have spent nearly 19,000 hours in front of the television . . . where nearly two-thirds of all television programming has sexual content?"[32] There are several things wrong with the assumption that sexual content from television led to this sex video. First, if our television culture is so sex-laden and causes such inappropriate behavior, we would expect even more incidents like this, but this case was enough of an anomaly that it made headlines. Clearly the story received media attention based on its shock value and its rarity. Second, the 19,000 hours is an average, and perhaps a dubious one at that. How many hours of television did you watch last week? Last night? I'm here to tell you I have no idea, and neither do lots of people who respond to surveys that statistics like these are derived from. The amount of viewing tells us nothing about the content itself. Besides, we have no idea if this kid even watches television—typically television viewing *declines* in adolescence, and adults tend to watch more television than young people do.[33] Finally, "sexual content" in such studies is often broadly defined to include flirting, hand-holding, kissing, and talk about sex so the "two-thirds of all television programming" estimate is questionable at best. Roffman compared the incident to the 1999 film *American Pie*, where the lead character broadcast a sexual encounter over the Internet. However, there is no proof the Maryland boy even saw this movie. This is a common media-blaming technique: draw a parallel with a similar scene from a movie without knowing for certain if the perpetrator actually saw it. Another tactic is to report a popular culture reference as the motive if young people even mention it when questioned by authorities. This happened in a California case in which two boys have been accused of murdering their mother and cutting off her hands, similar to a *Sopranos* episode.[34]

It is far too simplistic to blame raunchy movie scenes for changes in sexual behavior. Chapter 8 challenges this media fear by examining why sexual attitudes have changed over the past century. The way we think about sex has changed much more than the actual behavior. We will see that youth of today are not nearly as promiscuous as some might think. Rather than being blindly influenced by sex in media, teens are actively involved in trying to figure out who they are in a culture that might offer a lot of sexual imagery but little actual information about intimacy, sex, and sexuality. Chapter 9 also explores fears of sex via the Internet, where young people are feared as potential victims as well as potential sexual threats. The Internet, as a new, still-evolving medium, encapsulates our fear of the unknown and of our decreased ability to control information, as well as our anxiety about the future.

Media culture may not be the root cause of American social problems, but it is more than simply benign entertainment. The purpose of this book is not to simply exonerate media culture as inconsequential: in the book's final chapter I contend that media culture is a prime starting point for social criticism. Pointing out the real issues we should be concerned about does not absolve the entertainment industry of its excesses and mediocrity, particularly the news media, which often heightens our fears while providing little context or analysis. Chapter 10 provides suggestions for living in a media-saturated society and ideas for refocusing on the real challenges children face. Media act as a refracted social mirror, providing us with insights about major social issues such as race, gender, class, and power and patterns of inequality. The media are an intricate element of our culture, woven into the fabric of social life. We can learn a lot about American society from media culture if we stop insisting on using only cause-effect logic.

My Personal Media History

In a sense this book was born out of my personal ambivalence for the entertainment industry I wanted to be part of until I saw it close up. Like many other Americans, I have a love/hate relationship with media culture. My fascination began with old Hollywood movies, prompting me to study drama at New York University. Studying in New York was an opportunity of a lifetime, but perhaps the most important thing I learned was that I couldn't stand to be around actors. I found too many insecure and temperamental personalities in my acting classes to pursue that avenue further. Still, I knew that I wanted to do something related to the entertainment industry, but I wasn't sure what. While still at NYU I did an internship with a casting agency to see if that was my true calling (it wasn't), so I moved to Los Angeles after graduation with the hope that I'd figure things out once I got here. I thought about working at a talent agency, a record label, or an advertising agency, but nothing seemed to fit. I found myself right near the pulse of American popular culture, exactly where I always thought I'd want to be, but I was lost.

I held a few forgettable jobs to make ends meet and watched as friends went to work in "the business." I saw them begin to get sucked into the popular culture machine and I was able to watch from the sidelines as their dreams of having a fun, exciting, and rewarding career morphed into the realities of low pay, long hours, and frequent disrespect from their co-workers. My infatuation with Hollywood started to fade. A friend walked out on her public relations job after her boss threw a phone at her in a fit about getting a lunch order wrong. My then-boyfriend quit his job at a talent agency after his boss announced that even though he was putting in the requisite fourteen-hour workdays he would be getting a cut in pay. I had seen enough, heard enough stories from the trenches about how "nobodies" are treated until they become "somebodies." I decided to find a career path where it wasn't common for people to throw things or scream obscenities at me when they run out of Prozac.

As you may gather, my fascination with the entertainment industry was tempered by a good dose of reality. I still loved the security of having a familiar old movie or television show to turn on after a long day, but I grew to hate the excesses and egos that I got a small taste of in my early days living in LA. I saw briefly from the inside that celebrity is often based on smoke and mirrors, and that beneath the illusion of stardom often lie insecurity and unhappiness.

So I decided to study popular culture from a safe distance (where no one could hit me with a phone). I began to notice that just as I had mixed feelings about the entertainment industry, on a societal level we have developed a real ambivalence about Hollywood. We celebrate its excesses, make icons of actors, and include box-office tallies in our weekly news, as if we are all somehow shareholders in the business of entertainment. We have magazines like *People*, *Us*, and *Entertainment Weekly* with huge circulations, and celebrity gossip is regularly featured within mainstream news. Yet we are just as obsessed with the notion that popular culture is a major destructive force, that generations of children may be turned bad by Hollywood's misguided influence. I have to admit, when I think back to some of the jerks I met years ago, I'd like to believe all the complaints about media effects. But focusing so much energy on popular culture as the root of American social problems is like fixing a patient's x-ray and disregarding the actual tumor. All too often we choose to focus on media and ignore the major issues that are really behind today's challenges. We blame media rather than look at social changes that have altered American social life and the experience of childhood.

Ultimately, this book examines the nature of childhood and how our contemporary views of childhood have led to the fears of media culture. I know that many may be skeptical and feel that media culture *is* a major problem, that it *must* be doing something to our children because it feels like it does and we are continually told that it does. I ask you to keep an open mind and take a step back to examine the fear itself. Fear is a very powerful emotion, one that leads us to make choices we feel strongly about but in retrospect may not be the best choices.

In the next chapter, I begin by introducing the concept of childhood as a construction based on society's collective hopes and anxieties. As we will see, ideas about what childhood means and the ideals for what children should be are rooted in time, created by social contexts. We are currently in a time of flux, with an uncertain future, changes in global politics, a changing economy, a changing racial/ethnic composition, and of course changes in technology. This transition has created uncertainty about what is to come and this fear has been displaced onto children, often regarded as representatives of the future. Yet these shifts tend to be hidden by our fears of media. This book explores how fears about sex and violence, concerns about cartoons, video games, music, advertising, and the Internet, and fear for the future are rooted in anxieties we have about our rapidly changing world.

1

Why Americans Choose to Fear Media

It's Not the Media: What Really Changed Childhood

Parents have lots of fears and hopes for their children. Will they grow up to be healthy and happy? Will the kids at school like them? Will the media influence them negatively? A few years ago one of my friends had her first child, and she and her husband wanted to do everything "right." They read all the books they could find and attended parenting classes. When the baby was about a month old I volunteered to watch her one evening so my friend and her husband could have a night out together. They were relieved, but warned me that she cried practically every night from seven to nine without fail. They didn't know why she cried and gave me several suggestions of all the things they did that sometimes helped her stop.

So they went out to dinner and sure enough just after seven the baby got started. I tried all the tactics her parents told me about: feeding, changing, and rocking. But by 8:15 I had no lasting success and was growing weary. I put her in her baby seat and sat next to her on the sofa and switched on the TV. She was mesmerized by the vivid colors of a cartoon. She stopped crying.

I couldn't wait to tell my friends the simple answer to their nightly problem. When they walked in a few hours later I told them about my discovery. Their faces grew pale and they looked at each other with worry. My friend explained, "Our baby is being raised without television. We think she should be able to enjoy childhood without being corrupted by TV." Surprised, I did not question their decision. I later found out the baby was also supposed to go through childhood without sweets, soda, or anything with preservatives.

Childhood without ice cream? That doesn't sound any good. Adults have ideas about what childhood should be, and what forces "corrupt" kids; television in particular is often perceived as one of those corrupters. Even if popular culture is not tops on the list of parental concern, we're constantly told it should be. "Who's really the parent—you or the media?" Oprah asked on one of her shows. "Do you really know what your kids are watching? If not, watch out," the eleven o'clock news warns. What is it about children that we fear makes them particularly vulnerable to the influence of popular culture? Americans fear media in part because we are constantly told we should, but more importantly, because media are the most visible representation of the many economic changes that have altered the experience of childhood. In this chapter I address why media are so often considered the robber barons of childhood, the spoilers of innocence. Instead of media being the true culprit, changes in childhood, created by broader social changes over the past century have made adults uneasy about their ability to control children and the experience of childhood.

Designing Childhood

What does the word "childhood" conjure up for you? Do you think back to happy moments eating ice cream and cake at a birthday party (before you knew anything about calories or fat grams) or to the burden of homework, or do you remember ceaseless pangs of hunger? While people's experiences of childhood are quite varied, when I ask my students or seminar attendees to define the term "child," there seems to be no trouble finding common adjectives. Words like innocent, good, cute, pure, helpless, and vulnerable to mischievous, impulsive, ignorant, and selfish come up year after year. A close analysis of these terms reveals that they certainly do not apply to all children, and they actually fit the behavior of some adults. Note that these words connote either sentimental or pejorative views of young people, a caricature of a vast and diverse group.

Similar words have historically been used to describe women, people of color, and other minority groups.[1] Imagine if I were to have asked my students to come up with a list of words to describe women or members of a racial minority group; the question itself could be grounds for dismissal. Of course women are not all alike, and ethnic groups do not share any inherent personality traits. To insist that all or even most Jews, for example, could be described by a fixed set of adjectives would be considered anti-Semitic. But children are a group easily stereotyped, sentimentalized, and misrepresented. The definitions of childhood we create unwittingly contribute to their disempowered status. Qualities like innocence, for example, are both idealized and demeaned: we fight to preserve what we believe to be children's innocence and yet consider them less competent in part because of this "prized" trait. Of course children are dependent on adults for survival and support, but as they gradually become more independent we still often try to keep young people "innocent" as long as we can.

At the same time there is a danger in viewing children as a singular group. Experiences of childhood are diverse and changing, yet often our standard for the "ideal" childhood in America (and adulthood for that matter) is based on white, middle-class, and usually suburban standards. For me, childhood meant living in a Midwestern suburb and feeling safe and cared for, but also constantly struggling to make my own decisions. Childhood is rooted in social, economic, and political realities and is not a universal experience shared by all people of a certain age from the beginning of time. Certainly each one of us can think of how childhood is experienced differently now than it was in the past. In my childhood, it seems that we were allowed to spend more time playing in our neighborhoods without parental monitoring than parents would allow today. The global, national, regional, and local social settings also alter the meaning of childhood. Simply put, a girl in an economically disadvantaged urban area will likely have a different experience of childhood from her counterpart in an equally poor rural area. Further, the gender, race, and class of an individual influences one's experience. I have no doubt that growing up white, middle-class, and female influenced the experiences I had as a kid, as well as how I think about childhood now as an adult.

But we tend to define children as a unitary group and focus on their differences with adults. I know what you might be thinking; children *aren't* adults, just as women are not men. Very true, which is why we must strive to understand the full experience of each group, to understand how they define their *own* reality, rather than simply how different they are from the dominant group. Just as women's historical definition as prized yet less competent than men served to perpetuate male dominance, the social construction of childhood has served *adult* needs, and reinforced *adult* power rather than best serve the needs of young people. While young children are dependent upon adults in many ways, we tend to define them only by the qualities they lack rather than the competencies they possess.

We maintain these narrow beliefs about children because it is difficult to challenge a sentiment that seems natural. What if we were to change the way we view children? When I ask my students they often portend disaster. "Teenage pregnancy would skyrocket if adults stopped trying to control their kids," one student reasoned. "Kids wouldn't know who was boss—they'd probably be much more violent," another offered. Children running into oncoming traffic or drowning in unattended swimming pools and constant cookie-eating were other outcomes predicted, conveying the difficulty we have in challenging the current relationship between children and adults. Most of my students' comments suggested that adults would no longer care for their children, or that young children would become completely insufferable. Changing the way we think about children and childhood is different from changing individual parent-child relationships, which of course can never be completely egalitarian. The solution is not to treat children as if they were adults, which my students presumed, but to rethink what seems to be common-sense knowledge about who children as a *social group* really are.

The social construction of children as undeveloped adults needing more adult control feels appropriate because most of us have never considered an alternative, and on the surface this construction appears to be for children's own good. But the realities of childhood instruct us differently. In her analysis of child sexual abuse, sociologist Jenny Kitzinger concludes that abuse may be facilitated by our conceptualization of "good" children as deferent to adult authority.[2] We so often forget that children are most likely to be victimized by someone within their own family and that the adult power that supposedly protects children may also harm them. David Buckingham, professor of education at the University of London, further explains the danger of focusing so heavily on protecting children and suggests we instead *prepare* them to be citizens.[3] Protection is an idea difficult to let go of—it sounds so noble and above reproach. To prepare rather than protect empowers children to make their own decisions armed with the necessary information. Sounds simple enough, perhaps just a semantic difference, but rethinking what childhood means and who children are destabilizes the status quo.

Reconsidering the meaning of childhood involves a redistribution of knowledge, and a reconsideration of our fantasy of childhood innocence, which we often perceive as a natural, presocial, and ahistorical state that all children pass through.[4] Idealizing childhood as a time of innocence causes us to panic when change happens. The perceived absence or reduction of innocence leads to fear and a sense of loss. We place a great deal of blame for this "loss of innocence" on media, as if innocence were something that would stick around longer without popular culture. As we will see later in this chapter, "innocence" before the age of electronic media involved higher child mortality rates and a greater likelihood of working in factories. It is often through media that adults must face the reality that children do not necessarily embody innocence as adults expect them to. Innocence is a pawn, used in attempt to control popular culture and regulate children's knowledge.

Knowledge is the antithesis of innocence, often seen as the antithesis of childhood itself. The "knowing" child, author Joe Kincheloe points out, is routinely seen as a threat within horror movies.[5] For example, he describes the 1960s British film *Village of the Damned*, where children can read adult minds. Based on this perceived threat, the parents ultimately decide they must kill their own kids. Jenny Kitzinger notes in her study of abuse that a child who has knowledge about sex is often considered ruined and less of a victim than a more naïve counterpart.[6] Withholding knowledge is central to maintaining both the myth of innocence and power over children, which is at the heart of media fears. Media destabilize the myth of innocence and challenge adults' ability to withhold knowledge from children.

Rethinking Childhood

Childhood is a construction based on adult hopes and needs; it's something we create rather than a fixed reality. Childhood is not just a biological phase that people pass through but is an idea collectively constructed to serve adult needs and historical conditions. The idea that childhood in the past was comprised of carefree days without worry is a conveniently reconstructed version of history. This fantasy allows adults to feel nostalgia for a lost idealized past that never was. Childhood can remain a sacred shared fantasy, an illusion not unlike the Garden of Eden before eating from the tree of knowledge led to banishment. Ironically, adults mourn the expulsion from this fantasy land but also control the gates, seeking to keep people in even when they want to get out. Of course, keeping kids "in" is seen as part of what adults should be doing as good parents. The media are accused of handing over the jailer's keys, allowing children to leave this mythical garden before adults deem them ready.

For many, rethinking childhood is a very threatening prospect. If childhood does not mean what we think it does, what is adulthood? When we realize that one of our society's central organizing principles is one which we ourselves actively construct and does not just emerge from nature, our reality must shift. Childhood is of course a very real experience, but it is shaped and defined by cultural expectations and beliefs. Further, within contemporary Western society we have a tendency to understand the world in an either/or fashion. One is male or female, child or adult; we define these binaries as polar opposites rather artificially. So while the media reveal and in some ways blur the boundaries between childhood and adulthood, popular culture is not solely responsible for this ambiguity. Childhood is constantly shifting and changing and becomes defined based on the needs of society, thus transitions are inevitable.

We struggle to maintain the sense that childhood means carefree innocence and blame media culture for getting in the way. Part of the battle includes attempts to keep children away from media, away from information we regard as "adult." Sometimes this is necessary, especially when parents deem material inappropriate based on a child's age. The problem lies in confusing innocence with ignorance, when information young people need (like sex education) is withheld. Children's innocence/ignorance also serves to entertain adults, as in Art Linkletter's (and later Bill Cosby's) *Kids Say the Darndest Things.* Our conception of childhood reveals a major contradiction between the value of knowledge and the luxury of innocence.

The more closely we examine both media and the way we conceptualize childhood, the better we will understand the fear surrounding this relationship. We see how unclear the boundary between adulthood and childhood really is. Sometimes it is the media that help blur the line of demarcation, other times it is media that expose the ambiguity. We see talk shows regularly feature teens (and sometimes preteens) in adult-like situations wearing provocative clothing, and we wonder what's going on. Media content is often criticized because it challenges the sanctity and power of adulthood. Because this power seems threatened, we are now struggling to maintain control; not just of children, but the meaning of childhood itself. This loss of power fuels the fear adults have about media and childhood, particularly as the experience of childhood continues to change.

What *Really* Changed Childhood?

Drive at sixteen, vote at eighteen, and drink at twenty-one. These markers currently serve to delineate the gradual end of childhood in contemporary American society. I know I couldn't wait until these big birthdays came. Many of us can recall when these benchmark ages were different and when we reached them; we can certainly debate whether the responsibilities are in fact age-appropriate. Critics charge that we are reluctant to share the privileges of adulthood but are nonetheless quick to demand children suffer adult penalties. The age at which childhood begins and ends is not absolute now. We are particularly hazy about the privileges and responsibilities teens should have, as neither children nor adults. A brief examination of history reveals that this demarcation is constantly in flux.

Declarations of Independence: Childhood in the New World

Was there a time when childhood as we know it didn't exist? Phillipe Ariès' groundbreaking book *Centuries of Childhood: A Social History of Family Life*, published in 1962, claims that childhood did not exist as a separate social category in Western culture before the seventeenth century. Although historians have challenged Ariès on several points, his work clearly demonstrates that childhood was conceptualized very differently in the past than it is today. While Ariès' focus was on the children of French aristocrats, historian Karin Calvert describes how colonial American childhood was not regarded as an ideal time of life, as it so often is today.[7] She describes how high rates of infant mortality and childhood illness made childhood particularly risky, something to hurry up and survive rather than slow down and savor. Childhood itself became associated with illness. A colonist entering the "New World" often met with danger and growing old was a form of conquest. Unlike today, when popular culture reveres all things youthful, maturity was highly regarded and looked forward to as a time of prestige. Calvert goes on to describe that by the early nineteenth century American independence had changed the conception of childhood from a period of intense protection to one of greater freedom. She contends that coddling fell out of favor; just as over-involvement of the mother country was seen as restrictive, parents were discouraged from being overprotective of their children. The belief was that children were made strong by a tough upbringing, while coddling only weakened them.

Calvert explains that during the Victorian era, when infant mortality rates began to fall, childhood evolved into a celebration of innocence and virtue. Families of wealth attempted to keep children "pure" by separating them from adult society, even from their own parents. Governesses and boarding schools attempted to prevent "contamination" from adults as long as possible. Childhood became an idealized time of life, reflected in advertisements, which used images of children to connote purity in products like food and soap.[8]

Working in a Coal Mine: Princes and Paupers

The Victorian attempt to keep children away from the adult world was clearly only available to the affluent. For other families, childhood meant work at ages far earlier than we now are accustomed to in the United States. Children in rural areas were needed on family farms, and even if they attended school their labor was still a necessary part of the family economy. Learning a craft might have meant becoming an apprentice at age eight or nine. By twenty-first century standards, children working for wages may seem inhumane, but for many families this was economically necessary. Households required full-time labor for tasks like cooking, cleaning, and sewing, particularly in the decades before World War I when poor and rural families were unlikely to have electricity. Since an adult was needed to do the work of maintaining the family, it was necessary for nearly two million children to work for wages in 1910.[9]

Children's wages were vital sources of income around the turn of the century, particularly for immigrant families. The "useful" child was regarded as a moral child, mirroring the adage "idle hands are the devil's workshop." Work and responsibility were considered fundamental values for children, which sociologist Viviana A. Zelizer notes date back to the Puritan ethic of hard work and moral righteousness in early colonial America. Work was viewed as good preparation for a productive adult life, while higher education remained the domain of elites. The industrial-based economy did not require a great deal of academic training from its labor force. Thus, receiving only an eighth-grade education, as many did before the 1930s, was not nearly as problematic as it would be now.

Zelizer concludes that child labor "lost its good reputation" because children's labor became less necessary due to rising adult incomes and the growing need for a more educated labor force.[10] Compulsory education became more widespread in the early twentieth century not because it was necessarily more humane for children to be in school rather than factories, but because it became more *economically* necessary. With the growth of automation, the labor pool began to shrink, reducing the need for children in the labor force. The growth of public education stemmed from a desire to create a separate institution to keep children busy during the day in the interest of public safety, as the large number of immigrant children led to concerns about juvenile delinquency. Fearing that poor immigrants comprised a "criminal class," compulsory education served as a way to legally enforce social control of this group.[11] Schools provided a way to "Americanize" children, keep them out of the labor force until needed, and remove them from streets.

This is a defining moment in the history of American childhood: from this point on adults' and children's worlds became increasingly divided. Children and adults went from sharing tasks on family farms or the shop floor before the 1930s to increasingly spending more time isolated from one another and creating distinct cultures.

Separate Lives: Be True to Your School

Historian Grace Palladino argues that this separation intensified during the Great Depression, when adolescents were far more likely to attend high school than in years past due to the shrinking labor market.[12]

Whereas only about 17 percent of all seventeen-year-olds graduated from high school in 1920, by 1935 the percentage rose to 42 percent.[13] The shared space of high school led to the creation and growth of youth culture. Young people's tastes in music, for example, grew to bear more resemblance to their peers' than their parents'. Palladino cites swing music as a major cultural wedge between parents and youth in the late 1930s. Parents complained that young people wasted their time listening to the music and were not as industrious as prior generations, a reflection of children's exclusion from the labor force and increase in leisure time. This was particularly true following World War II, when economic prosperity coupled with mass marketing created even more distinction between what it meant to be a child, a teenager, and an adult.

The post-war economic boom fueled a consumption-based economy. Following strict rationing of goods during World War II, consumption and the widespread availability of goods was celebrated. The amount of consumer goods available to both adults and children exploded, and it became patriotic to spend instead of conserve. Families could also carry more debt, with home mortgages requiring much less of a down payment than in pre-war days, as well as the introduction of credit cards. Increases in wages and automation of household labor provided children with even more leisure time; this prosperity helped to create the new category called "teenager." Free from contributing to the family income, this young person had both more time and money than his or her parents likely had a generation earlier. Movies, television, and music were increasingly created with this large demographic group in mind, particularly as Baby Boom children reached spending age in the late 1950s. But perhaps most centrally, children were recognized as a distinct demographic group by market researchers. Palladino recounts that during the late 1940s market research firms emerged that focused specifically on understanding youth culture to better sell products to this increasingly important consumer group.

Controlling the Kid and the Ego

The influence of psychology both in marketing and popular culture was central in the mid-twentieth-century meaning of childhood. Rather than simply being a time of physical vulnerability, as in the colonial period or moral vulnerability as in the Victorian era, childhood was defined as a *psychologically* vulnerable time. Following the popularity of Freud in the United States, parents were not only expected to produce healthy and productive children but also charged with the responsibility of ensuring their psychological well-being. From a Freudian perspective, the adult personality is formed through childhood conflicts. If these conflicts go unresolved then neurosis or psychosis is likely to follow in adulthood, placing the burden of lifelong psychological health mainly on the mother, who, according to Freud, was central in these conflicts. This parenting approach reflected the political and economic realities of post-war America; the paranoid self-reflection of the McCarthy era is mirrored in psychoanalysis in which one's own mother cannot be completely trusted. A rigid gender ideology was also supported during mid-century, when middle-class women were herded out of the paid labor force following World War II. Children's psychological well-being was used to explain why a woman's interests should not extend beyond her family and why she should not attempt to keep the job she may have held during the war.

Mid-century also marked a change of where many people lived in America, which influenced the meaning and experience of childhood. Shifts from an agrarian to an industrial-based economy led to the growth of cities in the late nineteenth and early twentieth century, and following World War II the expansion of American suburbs altered childhood. With suburban life came the growing dependence on automobiles, often creating less mobility for young children dependent on parents for transportation, and more mobility for teens who had access to cars. The car culture symbolized American independence: advertisements boasted of the adventures a car could offer on newly constructed superhighways. Teenagers could also congregate away from parental supervision, and in many ways the widespread availability of the automobile altered teen sexuality. Movies like *American Graffiti* and *Grease* reflect the burgeoning car culture of the 1950s and the freedoms that came with it. Adolescence could be experienced with less adult control, creating adult anxiety about their children's access to the world around them.

Cultural scholar Henry Jenkins notes that families were increasingly viewed as individual "forts," or separate units striving to shield their children from the perceived harms of the larger community.[14] In this approach to understanding childhood, children are considered under siege, while individual family homes and white picket fences serve as bunkers of suburban safety. The perceived outside dangers include not only unknown neighbors, but also popular culture. This view of childhood as being in danger from the outside world and in need of parental protection continues more than fifty years later in spite of important social changes that have altered the realities of parenting and family life.

Back to the '50s?

Recently, the post-war era has been held up as ideal, a benchmark against which childhood today is often compared. But this era was itself an anomaly, the product of specific economic, political, and social realities of the time.[15] In all likelihood, this period is now viewed through rose-colored glasses because so many adults of this generation feel nostalgic longing for their own lost childhoods. This revered time of innocence is rewritten history, claims Stephanie Coontz in *The Way We Never Were: American Families and the Nostalgia Trap*. Economic prosperity was not shared by all: in 1955 African-American families earned only 55 cents for every dollar white families earned.[16] Nor was chewing gum or talking out of turn the biggest complaint adults had about children during that time, as claimed in what is now known to be a bogus list about how benign children's problems used to be in the "good old days."[17] Fears about youth violence and promiscuity were present even during this hallowed time, as they were in generations previous.

Perceptions of childhood now reflect adult anxieties about information technology, a shifting economy, a multiethnic population, and an unknown future. Not unlike the Victorian era, childhood innocence today is prized and we often attempt in vain to remove children from the adult world. Parents are viewed as the guardians of both their children and the meaning of childhood itself. Those who "permit" children to cross over into adulthood are demonized, particularly if they are poor or a member of a racial minority group. Many fear that childhood today ends too soon, with the media frequently cited as a cause of this "crisis." Innocence is seen as a birthright destroyed by popular culture or ineffective parents. Yet we often overlook the realities of childhood past and present that defy the assumption that childhood without electronic media was idyllic.

For many children, carefree play and ignorant bliss do not mark past or present experiences of childhood. Death was much more likely to be part of childhood in previous centuries, with high rates of infant mortality, childhood illness, and shorter life expectancy. Historian Miriam Formanek-Brunnell notes that nineteenth century children's doll play often involved mock funerals, reflecting anything but happy-go-lucky childhood experiences.[18] And as noted earlier, work has historically been a major part of young people's lives, and it is only relatively recently that their labor led to disposable income. It is our recent conception of childhood that insists that childhood should mean freedom from adult knowledge and responsibility.

Nostalgia for an allegedly carefree childhood of the past does not take into account the pervasive history of inequality in the United States. Those who mourn the loss of childhood innocence in the twenty-first century tend to ignore the struggles faced by many children of color. Children born into slavery, for instance, were regarded as individual units of labor and sometimes sold away from their families. We forget about inequality when we romanticize the "happy days" of the 1950s, that the prosperity of suburban life was not available for all. Fifty-five percent of African-American families, for instance, lived below the poverty line in 1959.[19] Our collective nostalgia for this mythical version of childhood calls upon memories of Cleaver-like families, when divorce and family discord were unheard of. In reality it was during the 1950s that divorce rates started to climb, and the families of old we revere were only on television.

Teens were not necessarily chaste in the 1950s either. Pregnancy was behind many marriages in the 1950s, when the median age of marriage for women dipped to its lowest point in the twentieth century, down to 20 in 1950.[20] Teenage pregnancy is seen as a relatively new social problem, believed to be exacerbated by sexual content in media, but the reality is it has been steadily decreasing. In 1950 the pregnancy rate for fifteen- to nineteen-year-olds was 80.6 per thousand, whereas by 1999 the rate had dropped to 49.6 per thousand.[21] The difference is that pregnant teenagers now are less likely to be married or to be forced into secret adoptions or abortions. Teens also have more choices, including using birth control, having abortions, or keeping their babies without getting married. The behavior has not changed nearly as much as our perception of the problem. Also changed is our idea of what it means to be a "teenager": before the mid-twentieth century people in their teen years often held adult roles and responsibilities, including holding full-time jobs and parenting. We have re-defined the teenage years as more akin to childhood than adulthood, making previously normative behavior unacceptable.

Throughout the past three centuries, childhood has gradually expanded as our economy has enabled us to delay young people's entry into the labor force.[22] We have also prolonged the time between sexual maturity and marriage, particularly as the onset of puberty happens sooner now for girls than in the past.[23] It is only within the past century that such a large group of physically mature people has had few rights and responsibilities and been considered *emotionally* immature, a luxury of prosperity. So while we mourn the early demise of childhood, the reality is that for many Americans childhood has never lasted *longer*. At the beginning of the twentieth century, a large number of young people entered the labor force and took on many adult responsibilities at fourteen and earlier, compared with eighteen, twenty-one, or even later today. Childhood has been extended chronologically and emotionally, filled with meaning it cannot sustain. Contemporary childhood is charged with providing adults with hope for the future and remembrance of an idealized past. It is a complex and contested concept that adults struggle to maintain to offset anxiety about a changing world.

Contemporary Childhood

At a conference about media and children recently, I spoke with several teachers and concerned citizens and was struck by the amount of nostalgic longing that peppered their critiques of media and childhood today. "When I was a kid we only had one TV and could only watch after dinner," one teacher said, shaking her head. "I loved nothing more than crawling into bed with a book." Another woman responded, "It seems like my kids would rather visit the dentist than read." A man recalled that as a child he spent his time outside, enjoying brooks and streams and hunting for frogs rather than playing video games.

I spent a lot of time playing outside and reading too. It seems what people are really upset about is the realization that childhood is ephemeral and changing, that the world is changing, and that experiences are rather different now than they were in the middle of the twentieth century. They are mourning the demise of the illusion that there is a single, stable, preferred version of childhood that is not bound by time or social context. Of course the idyllic memories shared by these adults reflect a somewhat selective recollection from an idealized, rather than ideal time of life that has passed. This nostalgia for the loss of a glorified experience of childhood becomes linked with media growth because changes in the media are most visible. Other economic and political factors that have led to change are harder to pinpoint.

Certainly some changes in the experiences of childhood can be attributed to media and technological changes. For example, pagers and mobile phones allow both greater freedom from and greater contact with parents. Children can use these modes of communication, as well as e-mail, to forge relationships with less parental intervention, but they can also be paged on the playground to return home. Visual literacy has also become more important in the last ten years, as video games and computer usage became staples in many homes that could afford them. Although many adults fear that playing video games or using the Internet will harm children, we forget that they also serve to prepare them to participate in a high-tech economy. The children we should be worried about are the ones that *don't* have access to these new technologies. The same adults who decry the decreased importance of the written word looked on anxiously at the success of twenty-two-year-old dot-com entrepreneurs in the late 1990s. (A little jealousy, perhaps?) For those of us who became computer literate as adults, we are hopelessly and forever behind our younger counterparts who as children were as comfortable with a computer mouse as a rattle. Our mode of communication is shifting, as it did centuries before during the transition from a spoken word culture to a written word society. I had a speech professor as an undergraduate who refused to teach her son to read until he was in school for fear he would never develop adequate oral and listening skills. That seemed a bit extreme to me, but it is not very different from completely cutting children off from television. Anxieties about current changes are partly based on adult fears of being left behind in an unknown future.

Changes in childhood may be most obvious in the uses of new mediums, but technology itself cannot single-handedly create change. It is important to consider social, economic, and political changes that made the introduction of new apparatuses possible. The same social conditions that created different perceptions of childhood were also behind the creation of these new products. The technology for television, for instance, was first developed during the 1920s, yet for political and economic reasons, television was only introduced to the public following World War II.[24] The Internet was developed some twenty-five years before its widespread availability for communication between Cold War allies, but only became public after the fall of communism in Eastern Europe and economic prosperity in the United States during the mid-1990s. Media technologies are the icons of contemporary society; they represent and reflect what scares us most about the unknown future. We tend to see the most tangible differences and credit them with creating powerful social changes without scratching beneath the surface. To understand changes in childhood we must look further to see more than media.

Childhood Lost?

Childhood has not disappeared. Instead it is constantly shifting and mutating with the fluctuations in society. The perceived crisis in childhood is derived from the gap between the fantasy of childhood and reality. We have filled the idea of childhood with our hopes and expectations as well as our fears and anxieties. We want childhood to be everything adulthood is not, but in reality adults and children live in the same social setting and have more experiences in common than adults are often comfortable admitting. Our economic realities are theirs; they suffer when parents lose their jobs, and they feel the effects of political conflicts too. Although we would like to keep the realities of terrorism and violence away from them, unfortunately we cannot.

The experience of childhood is rooted in social realities, and children are not immune to the societies in which they live. We often wish that they were, as we attempt to cordon them off from the rest of the world. We can't. We shouldn't. Children are a part of this world and need to learn about it, even some of the things we wish they didn't. The media often let some of the realities we'd like to hide into the sacred space of childhood.

In the end, the fantasy of childhood tells us far more about adults than children. It tells us about adult fears, it tells us about the sadness adults feel when they discover that childhood, like life, is fleeting and that the past is gone forever. It speaks volumes about changes in Western society, and the fear and uncertainty adults feel about living through them. But children cannot be understood outside of their own day-to-day worlds. To know about children, one must also know about the society in which they live. No matter how hard we may try to believe otherwise, children do not live in a vacuum.

If childhood has changed it is because the world has changed. Rapid change can be very frightening, even if the changes have many positive outcomes. Social life has been shifting so rapidly in the past few years that yesterday's technological breakthrough is tomorrow's dinosaur, obsolete and useless. Changes in family structure and economic realities render adult control of youth reduced. Automated households rarely require young people to perform lengthy chores to ensure the family's survival, so they are not needed at home as much as they were a few generations ago. And many young people have access to more information now than they did in the past. Yes, this is partially due to media, but it is also a reflection of changing attitudes about sexuality, for example, where open discussion of this topic is much more prevalent than in generations past.

This does not mean that adults should ignore the challenges of childhood—in fact, many of the problems children face are overshadowed by the fear of media. For instance, an up-close look at the roots of problems often blamed on media like youth violence and teen pregnancy reveals that poverty, not media, is the common denominator.[25] Poverty, not too much television, creates tangible far-reaching consequences for young people. Yet our continued response is to attempt to focus on the supposed shortcomings of parents and to see popular culture as childhood enemy number one. Politicians often help us choose to focus on popular culture instead. We as a society can feel better about spending money for v-chips instead of food stamps.

It is far easier to point the finger at media rather than point the finger back at ourselves. School levies are routinely rejected because we don't want to pay more taxes or don't trust the adults who control school budgets. Affordable, quality child care is so difficult to find because as a society we do not monetarily value people who care for children: those who do frequently earn less than minimum wage. It is not media that have changed childhood over the past century; it is our changing economy and the reluctance of the public to create programs that deal with the very real challenges children face. Ultimately, it is easier to blame media than ourselves for policies that fail to adequately support children.

It should be no wonder then that when communications scholar Ellen Seiter studied adult perceptions of media effects that the middle-class and affluent were the most likely to blame media for harming children and causing social problems.[26] Lower income people have more experience with the reality of problems like violence to know that the media are not a big part of the equation in their struggles to keep their children safe in troubled communities.

Why We Choose to Fear Media

The transformation of childhood has been evolutionary, though at times it may feel revolutionary. It's no wonder then that we focus on the most visible changes; in the last century one of the biggest transformations has been the growth of electronic media, which by their very nature command our attention. We have seen the development of movies, television, popular music, video games, and most recently the Internet, each of which has received its share of public criticism. New technologies elicit fears of the unknown, particularly because they have enabled children's consumption of popular culture to move beyond adult control. Parents may now feel helpless to control what music their kids listen to, what movies they see, or what websites they visit. Over the past hundred years, media culture has moved from the public sphere (movies) to private (television) to individual (computers), each creating less opportunity for adult monitoring.

This is not to say that media content is unimportant, nor am I suggesting that parents ignore their children's media use. These are important family decisions, but on a societal level it is problematic to view media culture as a root cause of social problems. Media *do* matter, but not in the way many of us think they do. Communications scholar John Fiske describes media as providing "a visible and material presence to deep and persistent currents of meaning by which American society and American consciousness shape themselves."[27] Media are not the central cause of social change, but they are ever-present and reflect collective hopes and anxieties, reinforcing beliefs as well as bringing social issues to our attention. Media have become an important American social institution intertwined with government, commerce, family, education, and religion. Communications scholar John Hartley asserts that media culture has replaced the traditional town square or marketplace as the center of social life.[28] He and others argue it is one of our few links in a large and increasingly segmented society, serving to connect us in times of celebration and crisis in a way nothing else quite can.[29] In a sense media have become representative of society itself. The media receive the brunt of the blame for social problems because they have become symbolic of contemporary American society.

Media culture also enables young people to develop separate interests and identities from their parents. The biggest complaints I have heard from parents is that their children like toys, music, movies, or television programs that they consider "junk," and therefore must have harmful consequences. Listen to yourselves, parents—isn't this exactly what your parents told you about the music you liked? It works both ways too. As a kid, I hated the music my parents listened to. Elvis, Neil Diamond, and Barbra Streisand were so uncool when I was a teenager—how come my parents couldn't see that? I was so tired of hearing my mother play her Willie Nelson tape that when I was about thirteen I pulled all of the brown tape out of the cassette. I caught hell for it, of course, but children's identities are frequently formed in opposition to adult culture. Telling kids we hate what they like makes it all the more appealing. Adults attempt to exercise their power by condemning tastes that differ from their own sensibilities and displace their fears of the future onto popular culture.

Rethinking the Big Bad Wolf

Popular culture often reminds us that the myth of childhood innocence cannot be maintained, and that knowledge cannot be easily withheld from children. Media threaten to expose the illusion of childhood by revealing things some adults don't want kids to know about, and in some cases by offering content that challenges the wisdom and power of adults. Fears of media power represent displaced fears about social change and changes in childhood. These changes often hamper the ability of adults to control youth.

When we continually focus on media as the Big Bad Wolf devouring childhood, we neglect to acknowledge the historical conditions that shape both the experiences and preferred meaning of childhood. It becomes all too easy to sentimentalize children and childhood rather than understand the complexity of children's thoughts and experiences. Instead, we often consider young people a potential threat that needs to be controlled, for our safety and theirs. If media can turn some children into cold-blooded killers, as some suspect, then restricting young people's behavior and access to popular culture seems reasonable. We are caught in a contradiction: children are at once viewed as potential victims in need of protection, too weak and vulnerable to make their own decisions, yet as potential victimizers in need of control, too dangerous to ignore. Fear is a central part of our social construction of childhood.

When we relentlessly pursue the idea that media damage children, we are saying that children are damaged. Adults have always believed that kids were worse than the generation before, dating back to Socrates in ancient Greece, who complained about children's materialism, manners, and general disrespect for elders. Blaming the media is much like attempting to swim full force against a powerful riptide; you end up exhausted and frustrated and get nowhere. Understanding what is really happening will allow the swimmer a better chance at success. Likewise, projecting our collective concern about both childhood and society onto media will not take us very far. It will force us to focus on only a small part of the equation and ultimately drive a wedge between generations.

2

Why Americans Choose to Fear Youth

The Politics of Youth-Bashing

During the weeks following the Columbine High School killings, one question seemed to be on every pundit's mind: What has gone wrong with kids today? Never mind that most murderers are adults and that history is filled with isolated incidents of young killers. But today's youth, especially teens, *are* different, or so you would believe listening to politicians in the days following the massacre. "We are absolutely in a culture war for the hearts and minds of our children," noted Georgia Senator Max Cleland.[1] Other lawmakers spoke of the need for "a national dialogue on youth culture and violence" and for educating parents on how to raise children with "strong morals" and the ability to "resist violent impulses."[2] The children-in-crisis theme echoed and resonated with a public that has come to believe the worst about its young. Devoid of contextual information about actual violence statistics, it would be easy to believe, from these news reports, that mainly young people commit violent crimes. During his presidency, Bill Clinton organized a conference intended to create a "national strategy to stem violent outbursts by adolescents" and to understand the triggers of "homicidal rage in young people."[3]

It is understandable that the Columbine shootings would serve as a "wake-up call" for America, as pundits often said. Unfortunately, a great deal of this energy was misdirected. The killers at Columbine and in other high-profile school shootings of the 1990s were taken as representatives of their generation, rather than frightening aberrations. Rather than treating these modern-day Billy the Kids as deviants from the norm of conformity and nonviolence, these much-publicized killers were considered examples for all that is wrong with young people today.

School killings seemed to be proof of early 1990s predictions of a "coming storm" of youth violence based simply on the rise in number of adolescent males coming of age.[4] This new breed of killer was characterized as devoid of any human qualities like empathy or a conscience. A 1991 *Washington Post* article subtitled "Police Say Disrespect for Life, Especially Among Youths, is Fueling Violence" exemplifies the "new breed" myth.[5] The story presents a police officer's account of a teen suspect who "showed no remorse and absolutely no fear of the legal system he had just entered."[6] Pop culture is charged with glorifying "thug life," which we fear will make young people more attracted to violence than ever and without awareness of the consequences.

Youth-bashing is an interesting phenomenon. We would hesitate to make the same sort of sweeping generalizations about a criminal's age if they were older (Imagine the headline: "Middle-Aged Embezzler Reveals Moral Decline of Adults"). We resist asking what's wrong with today's men or the white people of today, although we have generalized about women who commit crimes and historically have treated non-whites as part of a "criminal class."[7] Groups with the least social power are the easiest to blame for problems they are certainly not alone in causing. Even though all adults were once young, today's youth are a favorite American target.

Youth culture was immediately placed on trial for causing the alleged demise of the next generation. Was it their music? Video games? Movies? Ironically, filmmakers themselves have drawn upon the fear of youth for nearly ninety years, with movies in the dawn of filmmaking titled *Wild Youth* (1918) and *Reckless Youth* (1922), for instance, capitalizing on fears of young people no longer like their Victorian-era parents.[8] In the 1950s, movies like *The Bad Seed*, about an angelic looking blond girl who can't stop herself from killing, and *The Blackboard Jungle*, which takes place in a rough urban high school, reflect anxieties about the potential danger within the unknown next generation. The satanic child motif became popular in 1968 with *Rosemary's Baby* and continued in the 1970s with films like *The Exorcist* and *The*

Omen. In these frightening films children must be tamed or destroyed in order to save the vulnerable adults in their lives.

Historically, fears of youth have risen in times of demographic or economic flux. During the great immigration years in the late nineteenth and early twentieth centuries, fears of delinquency and promiscuity skyrocketed, in part leading to the formation of special juvenile courts. The Depression also led to an increased fear that young people would become violent, when in fact the rise in crime rates could mostly be attributed to adults. Delinquency fears during and after World War II were largely concentrated on nonwhite youths and the belief that young people of African or Mexican descent held "different values" from mainstream (read *white middle-class*) Americans. This same trend continues today, as the United States experiences a shift towards a multicultural society with the potential of no ethnic or racial majority.

In truth, the young are the conquerors of any society, eventually replacing its populace, leaders, and decisionmakers. As noted earlier, for the past seventy-five years young people have had increasingly less contact with adults, by virtue of institutionalized age segregation in schools and often in the workforce. This has led to the creation of a segmented youth culture that is often unknown, misunderstood, and dismissed by older adults.

In this chapter we will see that many pronouncements about young people today are driven by anxiety about demographic shifts and other changes in society not always readily visible. Public discourse and news reports may characterize youth as out-of-control, self-centered, shallow, and lazy, but in fact there are a lot of positive trends that don't make headlines: young people today are less likely to be violent, sexually active, smoke, or use drugs compared with their parents when they were teens. Besides criticizing the popular culture many young people enjoy, American public discourse reveals a more generalized anxiety about young people as a whole, especially teenagers. We often fear that youth culture, like music and video games, creates violence or alienation in kids. A closer look at the way both politicians and the public talk about youth reveals that we all create a hostile climate for young people and that schools and neighborhoods often contribute to feelings of alienation. With the push towards standardized testing and rigid behavioral policies, schools today emphasize conformity, while budget problems reduce the number of school counselors on staffs. Fear of media is intricately tied in with fears of youth themselves. By focusing so much negative attention on youth and youth-based media culture, we deflect our own responsibility for social problems and ultimately widen the chasm between generations.

Fear and Loathing, Present Tense

Youth-bashing is an ancient sport, one played at least since the Greeks and Romans, and is still growing strong. "Every generation thinks the kids of the next generation are both wilder and have more to contend with," stated a lobbyist for Covenant with North Carolina's Children, but concluded that "these days, it's true."[9] The belief that this generation is worse than those that came before is not new, but we now have a vast news media to fuel our fears. "They're going too far, too fast," a forty-four-year-old mother of a fourteen-year-old told a reporter for the New Orleans *Times-Picayune*.[10] A Medina, Ohio, man writes to the Cleveland *Plain Dealer* that all youths should have three years of mandatory military training to curb youth violence and promote discipline.[11] A letter to Ann Landers lamented that "Today's youth are the most stupid, impolite, self-centered people on the planet. . . . I don't know where or how this generation lost its way, but it IS lost, and I see no hope for these young people."[12] The author signed the letter "A Midwestern realist." Apparently many others share in this pessimism. According to Frame Works, a research firm based in Washington, D.C., only about one in six adults surveyed believe that the youth of today share their values.[13] A glut of youth-bashing books has hit the market in the past few years with titles like *Unglued and Tattooed, Parenting Your Out-of-Control Teenager, Now I Know Why Tigers Eat Their Young: Surviving a New Generation of Teenagers*, and *Yes, Your Teen is Crazy*.[14] Teens are often defined as unilaterally crazy, as biologists seek explanations in the frontal lobe to conclude that "temporary insanity" sets in when teens enter adolescence.[15]

Other accounts of youth suggest they just have bad personalities. A *Chicago-Sun Times* article concluded that good kids are hard to come by and that a "brat backlash . . . is building across the country."[16] The Cleveland *Plain Dealer* offered an article called "Handling Teens' Inflated Sense of Self-Importance," which provided practical tips "to make living with a self-centered adolescent easier."[17] The article began, "Welcome to early adolescence, where egocentricity runs rampant."[18]

Young teens were described as "narcissistic and inconsiderate of others." It seems we have lost any sympathy for the trials adolescents face. Insecurity has apparently given way to egocentricity, if you believe the headlines. Where has all this teen confidence come from? More importantly, where has all this adult hostility come from?

Like new forms of technology and popular culture, young people represent change, and change can be frightening. This fear of change is coupled with a news media that have grown in the last twenty years to contain multiple twenty-four hour news channels constantly in search of "news," filling much of their time with talking heads that often pontificate about the troubled state of youth. Chain ownership of newspapers has led to pooled reporting and the same stories run in multiple cities, greasing the perennial fear of the next generation. In short, lots of us fear youth because we are constantly told that we should be afraid. Very afraid.

I am close enough to my own adolescence and young adulthood to take some of these criticisms of youth personally. The 1994 film *Reality Bites* allegedly represented a growing phenomenon of twenty-something layabouts who were too self-centered and/or lazy to succeed in the world of work. Attempts to characterize an entire generation are always problematic, but I find it particularly offensive to label a group that came of age into a recession and onto the front lines of the Gulf War so derisively. I know first-hand how hard it is to enter the workforce in the middle of a recession. In 1990, when I graduated from college, my friends and I were lucky to keep the same retail or restaurant jobs we held as students, while others felt the disgrace of moving from their dorm room back to their parents' house. I was one of the fortunate ones: the retail sales job I had actually provided health benefits and I could (barely) afford my own car and apartment. Still, it stung when a slightly older acquaintance asked me why I couldn't do any better. Didn't I want a better job, or did I go to college to be a sales clerk? Of course I didn't, but since I was not a professional-level typist, I couldn't even get an interview for an office job. The slacker label implied that young adults weren't getting career-track jobs because we were self-centered, lacked ambition, and were lazy victims of our own insufferability rather than an economic downturn.

The slacker epithet was not just hurled by older adults, but by other young people, seeming to further its validity. In a 1995 *Newsweek* article, twenty-two-year-old Joshua B. Janoff, fresh from military service in the Gulf War, wrote of his culture shock upon returning to civilian life and college. He described his peers as a "lazy, apathetic group of flannel-wearing misfits," unwilling to act on their convictions or wake up on time for eight o'clock classes.[19] "Perhaps what is needed is a good swift kick in the rear," he concluded. Others agreed with this somber prognosis for youth and the future of the country. During the 1996 presidential campaign, Gary Bauer, president of the Family Research Council, complained that economics had nothing to do with the problems youth face, that it was not "lack of money as much as a value deficit" and that "There are no standards of right and wrong."[20] Bauer grimly concluded that "a lot of American children are displaying dysfunctional behavior." Young people's values thus become the cause of all of society's problems, taking adults out of the equation entirely. If we believe that youth are the problem, rather than at times *reflecting* social problems, then we absolve ourselves of examining adult-run institutions responsible for supporting youth.

The belief in the ideal-childhood myth drives the never-ending quest to attempt to preserve childhood "innocence," yet at the same time we delight in condemning kids for being ignorant of the world around them, supposedly too self-centered to focus on anything but their own pleasure. According to one poll reported in the *Los Angeles Times*, 99 percent of seventh- through twelfth-graders surveyed could identify Busch beer, but only 67 percent could identify Bush the presidential candidate during the 2000 campaign.[21] The story also noted that more young people could identify beer brands than state the purpose of the Bill of Rights. How many adults could identify Bush at the time or discuss the Bill of Rights extemporaneously? Ignorance of politicians and world affairs is certainly not limited to youth. This information, certainly important context, is not included here. We place expectations on young people to know about the world around them that we don't necessarily place on adults. Besides portraying young people as ignorant about world events, we also represent them as self-obsessed and indifferent to the rest of the world. A *Milwaukee Journal Sentinel* story reported on the local reaction to the September 11, 2001, attacks, stating that "Some high schoolers [began] thinking outside of their personal world," and included quotes from students about how much they value their families and friends.[22] But the story ends on a dour note, stating that "some have just forgotten." A teacher commented that this comes as no surprise, since so many "kids are desensitized" to violence. I'm not sure how teachers can be sure their students forgot about the horrific events just two months earlier, and blocking out such a traumatic day in order to move on is certainly an understandable coping mechanism. We were all encouraged to get back to normal as soon as possible by political leaders. But "normal" teen behavior is itself considered undesirable.

It appears that even after the start of a war and the introduction of a new threat, the young still remain high on our proverbial hit list. We evidently need youth-bashing, even in times of common struggle. The heightened fear brought about by a surprise attack created more anxiety about both the future and future generations.

The Politics of Youth-Bashing

Youth-bashing is not only widely practiced by the American public, but it is a very popular political strategy. Politicians are quick to make generalizations about all youth based on the highly publicized misdeeds of a few. For instance, Mecklenburg County, North Carolina, has a laundry list of restrictions based on youth phobia: kids can be sent to jail or fined for buying cigarettes, can have a harder time getting a driver's license, and cannot talk to county-funded counselors about sex without signed parental consent.[23] Chris Palamountain, attorney for the National Center for Youth Law in San Francisco, is critical of this trend. "People are attempting to substitute the public for parents. One way is to pass laws which are really rules you would expect parents to have in their homes."[24] Curfew laws are one example of the attempt to legislate parenting, restricting all children in the name of protection and control of troublemakers. We would all be safer if we were off the streets late at night, but to legislate common sense punishes the innocent. Nonetheless, a federal appeals court ruled in 1999 that curfews are constitutional and that teens do not have the right to be in public during restricted times.[25]

The fear of youth promotes the proliferation of such curfew laws, which are often selectively enforced and more likely to be used to punish poor and minority youths. Likewise, the perceived threat of youth has made it easier in many states to try juveniles in adult courts, even during a time when juvenile crime rates have been falling. Our fears of young people today have made us more likely to support "get tough" legislation and punish youth more harshly.

Political discussions of a "youth crisis" exacerbate existing public fears and create an apparent need for a legislated solution. This is an opportunity for candidates to claim they know what the real problems are and how to solve them. Communications scholar Susan A. Sherr analyzed over a thousand television commercials made by presidential campaigns from 1952–1996 and found that children were often used to rationalize candidates' economic agendas, to heighten the fear of crime, and to symbolize the future.[26] The 2000 presidential election was no exception, as candidates relied on the public's fear of a youth crisis in their platforms.

For candidate George W. Bush, "one of the biggest problems in our society is that our children are being freed to grow up too soon."[27] He frequently spoke of the need for "moral education" to become a national priority and expressed concern that education has not been focusing enough on making the next generation "good and kind and decent" and that "Clear instruction in right and wrong must be a priority."[28] The implication is that young people are lacking in morality and decency, the result of too much freedom. So it is not surprising that the solutions proposed include further restrictions. Both Bush and his chief rival, Vice President Al Gore, spoke of increasing penalties for juvenile offenders through either "zero tolerance in school," as Gore offered, or stricter federal sentencing laws aimed at youth crime, as Bush suggested.[29] Bush critiqued the Clinton administration for going too easy on juveniles: only eleven youth were prosecuted in federal courts for possessing handguns during the 1997–1998 school year, Bush complained, implying that this number was absurdly low.[30] Never mind that most violent crimes are state, not federal, offenses, and therefore tried elsewhere. Nor was this low figure interpreted as an indication of good news, that there were a low number of offenses. Candidate Gore also spoke about clamping down on youthful offenders, proposing to "use FBI resources to break up violent teenage gangs."[31] For both candidates, youth represented a growing menace to curb and control.

Youth-bashing can continue unabated on the political scene for one central reason: most young people cannot vote, and of those who can, few actually do. The young are in effect no one's constituents, and no powerful lobby argues on their behalf. According to the General Social Survey, a nationally representative household survey conducted nearly every year, respondents fifty and older are twice as likely to vote as those twenty-five and younger.[32] Thus, the group most likely to vote is the least likely to be directly connected with the contemporary experience of youth and the most likely to fear the next generation because of the wide age gap. Since these older voters are the politicians' real target audience, youth-bashing pays dividends.

Older voters are also unlikely to be big fans of youth culture, so along with young people, popular culture is a frequent political target. As fears of both youth and changes in media technology intensify, so does political discourse about the alleged danger media culture poses to young Americans. Media fears in American politics are often couched in the language of protection: if popular culture poses a threat, the thinking goes, then for the safety of our children we must control their exposure. The dangers of both popular culture and the vulnerability of youth are taken for granted. Children are at once portrayed as victims of media and as potential threats to society if they are not properly shielded from its influence. In 1996, presidential contender Senator Robert Dole essentially ran against popular culture (yet he has since appeared in ads for Pepsi and Viagra). In a time of peace and economic growth, perhaps Dole thought that this was his best mode of attack, especially since the incumbent, Bill Clinton, received funding from Hollywood-based resources. Dole criticized Hollywood's "moral depravity," which he argued "threatened the heart and mind of every child."[33] A *Los Angeles Times* poll conducted shortly after this speech revealed that 71 percent of Americans surveyed agreed with Dole's criticisms of the entertainment industry. Although this widespread agreement did not lead to Dole's victory in the November election, it did prove to be an issue with which politicians could connect with the electorate.

Both Bush and Gore spoke frequently about the need to "protect" kids from popular culture, or as Gore called it, "cultural pollution."[34] Perhaps trying to distance himself from Clinton's Hollywood connections, Gore blamed the entertainment industry for "making it more difficult" for parents to raise their children.[35] He and his running mate, Senator Joseph Lieberman, emphasized the need to help parents deal with "inappropriate entertainment that young children are not ready to handle."[36] Gore called on the entertainment industry for "an immediate cease-fire," invoking imagery of an actual gunfight with Hollywood attacking seemingly defenseless children.[37]

Not to be outdone on this issue, Bush also demanded that more be done to "reduce the violence that our children see on the screen," declaring popular culture "an enemy of . . . children's innocence."[38] Both candidates used the language of a battle between good and evil to appear as protectors of children's innocence and virtue. Marjorie Heins, author of *Not In Front of the Children: "Indecency," Censorship, and the Innocence of Youth*, demonstrates that the rhetoric of "protecting children's innocence" has historically been used to restrict youth. More ominously, indecency laws, allegedly in the name of children, are a surreptitious way to place restrictions on adults. Heins cites the Comstock obscenity laws, which made using the mail to circulate information about birth control a crime in the early twentieth century, as an example of how children's purity is used as a pawn to control information. A more contemporary attempt to regulate information on the Internet in the name of protecting children impacts not just youth but adults as well. With the rhetoric of protection, we unilaterally label youth as incompetent and ultimately restrict both children and adults.

Children are political pawns, used by politicians when symbolically necessary. Young people are objects rather than active subjects in American politics, rarely consulted or central in campaigns except for the age-old baby-kissing ritual or during cute fluff pieces on local news. Youth-bashing can take a subtle form; in addition to blaming youth for social problems, politicians often characterize children as helpless and in need of protection—not as much from adults as from each other and popular culture.

In early fall 2000, with the presidential campaign in its final stretch, the Federal Trade Commission (FTC) released a report revealing marketing strategies of various factions of the entertainment industry, detailing how movies, music, and video games containing violence were marketed to young audiences. The findings revealed that these companies deliberately targeted kids—not a big surprise, but treated by politicians of all stripes like a smoking gun. Representative Edward J. Markey of Massachusetts believed that these findings were analogous to marketing alcohol to children. Weeks later, a handful of studio executives were rounded up to testify before Congress for what David Crane, a Senate Commerce Committee spokesperson, called a "good old-fashioned shame."[39] Because the FTC could not legally sanction the studios, the hearing was largely cosmetic. "You have people of both parties who disagree about many other issues that join together and bash popular culture, especially teenage culture," commented Danny Goldberg, president of Artemis Records.[40] "It's practically an election-year tradition now."

Others were critical of the attempt to equate the FTC marketing report with the discovery of secret tobacco industry memos that led to billions in lawsuits. Representative Henry Waxman of California presided over the tobacco industry hearings and worried that his colleagues were "using the theater of a high-profile congressional hearing to scapegoat the entertainment industry."[41] Curiously, congressional critics of Hollywood did not question the 1996 Telecommunications Act they approved, which loosened regulations on the entertainment industry and enabled big media conglomerates to grow even larger. There was no Senate hearing on the effects of their own actions on entertainment marketing or on how it became harder for smaller media outlets to compete with the mainstream giants, the so-called sources of Gore's "cultural pollution." No, as *Los Angeles Times* columnist Brian Lowry commented, "politicians are prone to choosing safe political targets," and "the road of least political resistance."[42] Campaigning against youth culture is a win-win proposition: it draws on existing fears of youth, and political promises never have to lead to action since regulating culture is impossible in a free society.

In the process of seeking to resonate with the fears and anxieties of the older voting public, politicians have created greater divisions between themselves and the young people who are alternatively discussed as out-of-control or victims of the popular culture they enjoy. In the quest to pander to adult fears, politicians have unwittingly invited adults to indulge in both media phobia and youth-bashing. It should be no wonder that the majority of eighteen-year-olds choose not to participate in a political process that focuses on degrading them in so much of its rhetoric.

Alienation Creation

Following the 2000 election, Dee Anna S. Behle, a senior at a California university, complained that the candidates completely ignored issues important to young voters.[43] Behle wrote in a *Los Angeles Times* op-ed that issues such as the rising cost of education, the lack of affordable housing, and the environment are central to her age group, but were absent from the campaigns. The lack of relevance to their concerns, combined with a tendency to heighten fears of youth, leaves many young people critical of politics as usual. When Representative Johnny Isakson of Georgia held a feedback session with teens, a student told the Atlanta *Journal and Constitution*, "It's about time. I've always felt like kids understand a lot more about what's going on than people think."[44] John Halpern, a Long Island, New York, high school senior, told New York's *Newsday*, "I really do care. I just get fed up with all the creeps in politics today."[45]

Similarly, during my dissertation research in several Los Angeles area high schools, many students communicated that they knew a lot about politics and that, like many adults, they felt a real disdain for politicians. Students at one school in a working-class area described presidential candidates as greedy hypocrites who "kiss anybody to win" and believed that "the vote of the people doesn't really count."[46] A tenth-grade boy told me, "They always say they are going to do this or they are going to do that, but when they are president they don't do nothing." A student at another school expressed disgust that political news was, in his words, "condescending . . . as though we couldn't think for ourselves." Ironically, politicians who argue against "big government" communicate that government is the problem, not the source of solutions, yet when young people voice the same ideas we worry that they are alienated or apathetic.[47]

So when we talk about young people not caring about politics, not knowing about anything beyond their own lives, we are often wrong. Low voter-turnout rates are often taken as indicators of apathy, as proof that young people care only about themselves, but perhaps it is politics that fails young people and creates distance. Alienation, or the feeling of disconnection from others and from society, is a central adult fear, but is a condition that the youth-bashing discourse itself often serves to create. There is no evidence that young people today are any more alienated than previous generations were, nor that they are more prone to turn alienation into violence. Still, the Columbine shootings raised new questions about the threat of alienation and the potential for violence made people start asking what led youths to feel so disconnected that they would methodically murder those around them. Youth culture does not create alienation. On the contrary, it frequently creates connections for those who feel outside of the mainstream. It is adult-run institutions, like politics, that exclude and caricature youth and fail to meet the needs of many young people.

Following the 1990s school-shooting tragedies, a bit more attention has been paid to the role that clique structures play in both middle and high schools, as well as to the problem of bullying. Long-term qualitative studies in school settings have found that teachers and administrators often favor those at the top of the social-clique hierarchies, further distancing outcasts from others.[48] Traditionally, adult response has been to shrug and say "kids will be kids," which prevents us from considering that the institution itself may need to change.

Nineteenth-century high schools (which only a small proportion of teens attended) sought to provide youths with practical skills for professional success and presumed most students would not be attending college, as most did not.[49] In contrast, we now view college admission as the central purpose of high school, yet nearly half of high school graduates do not attend college, so a college prep curriculum does not meet the needs of a large proportion of students. For these students, school may hold no real purpose. Donna Gaines, sociologist and author of *Teenage Wasteland: Suburbia's Dead End Kids*, found that students labeled "burnouts" appeared more committed to vocational training because it offered practical instruction, and more importantly, they no longer had to experience the constant failure and social rejection of the college prep world. There is, of course, the danger of tracking kids into vocational training based on socioeconomic status or race and not offering college prep opportunities to all who should have it. But it is clear that college prep is not for everyone. As schools experience cuts in funding for things that won't show up in standardized test results, the non-college-prep student will likely have even less opportunity to find a meaningful connection within educational institutions.

It is easy to understand how those in impoverished urban communities may feel both fear and alienation: such settings fail to instill a sense of hope for the future and may create feelings of hostility towards mainstream society. But suburbs and rural areas can also create alienation. Young people may be geographically separated from adults and each other and have little access to public spaces, as some communities attempt to restrict young people from malls and other shopping areas. The presence of youth in public is often considered problematic, leading to increased curfew enforcement. Public schools in lower middle-class communities are often forced to cut funding for extra-curricular activities or classes that won't directly lead to higher test scores. Even affluent kids in well-funded schools can fall through the cracks. We take for granted that the promise of economic achievement should motivate everyone, but for some people it is an empty goal. Suburbia often offers few other models of purpose and success.

The labor market also bears a relationship to alienation. When we are told national unemployment figures, we rarely hear that for young adults employment is often far more tenuous. For instance, while the nation's unemployment rate in May 2002 was a relatively low 5.8 percent, for those sixteen to twenty-four it was exactly double at 11.6 percent. For sixteen- and seventeen-year-olds, the rate of those unable to find work was 20.7 percent, or more than one in five teens seeking employment.[50] But even once employed, non-college-bound workers tend to hold jobs that have little stability, contrary to the manufacturing jobs of a generation ago that offered a living wage and often union benefits. What promise does the future hold for working-class youth who can't afford college? As our economy increasingly becomes two-tiered, those in service-sector jobs like customer service or retail often earn low wages, have few growth opportunities, and receive little respect. How can we expect young people to buy into mainstream society when it offers little to them? But somehow most do, in spite of a tenuous future.

The Kids Are All Right

In the face of a steady diet of doom-and-gloom reports about young people, on the whole the news is good. Youth violence dropped considerably during the 1990s. The teen birthrate fell 22 percent in the 1990s and is now at an all-time low.[51] According to the Centers for Disease Control and Prevention, fewer teens reported being sexually active in 1999 than in 1991, and those who are used condoms more often.[52] Fewer were involved in fistfights or reported carrying guns compared with the early '90s, and young people were more likely to wear seat belts and avoid riding in a car driven by a drunk driver. The percentage committing or contemplating suicide decreased steadily as well.

Teens aged twelve to seventeen were far less likely to drink alcohol at the end of the '90s, down to 19 percent compared with 33 percent in 1990 (and 50 percent in 1979 when their parents were likely teens).[53] Binge drinking, defined as five or more drinks on one occasion, also declined for this age group, to 8 percent in 1999 compared with 15 percent in 1990 and 22 percent in 1985. While marijuana use was higher than in 1990, at 7 percent it was still low and half the 1979 rate of 14 percent.

So in spite of the public perception and the fears that the new media technologies are breeding a violent, sex-obsessed, hedonistic, and self-indulgent young generation, young people seem to be more sober, chaste, and well-behaved than their parents were or than my generation was in the 1980s. They are more likely to finish high school than any generation before and are also more likely to earn bachelor's degrees than their parents' generation.

Although headlines like "Teens at 14 Are Still Living a Self-Centered Life" would have us believe otherwise, nearly 60 percent of teens volunteer, averaging three and a half hours of service each week.[54] While stories of youth volunteers don't make front-page news, their quiet contributions are many. For instance, a Baltimore area camp is so popular it has to turn away dozens of teen volunteers each year.[55] An eighteen-year-old volunteer told the *Baltimore Sun* that she "likes to help out," and is not volunteering only for the community service requirement that her school, like many others, now mandates. A Denver teen mobilized his classmates to volunteer weekends, summers, and holidays to work at a local food bank. The teen, Christopher Teel, 18, said he worked hard to organize classmates because his family struggled financially and were themselves often short of food.[56] At nineteen, Danny Seo published *Generation React: Activism for Beginners* after successfully founding Earth 2000, an animal rights and environmentalist group when he was just twelve. The book provides advice for young people on organizing fundraisers, getting publicity, and lobbying on behalf of causes they believe in.

Youths are often thought to be ignorant and apathetic about politics, but this is often because teens' political action cannot be measured in voting behavior and is typically local in nature. A large degree of political action by teens focuses on their schools. A group of Los Angeles teens brought disposable cameras into their schools to document the terrible state of disrepair of bathrooms, some of which had only one functioning toilet to be used by thousands of students. A Palmdale, California, student was suspended for distributing flyers on campus that criticized the school's dirty bathrooms, the yearbook's emphasis on the popular students, the principal, and campus security.[57] Youths are derided with the apathy label, but when young people do question or challenge the status quo they are frequently punished. Youth activism often challenges adult authority—perhaps apathy is more of a wish than reality.

While youths are typically part of political discourse as objects of concern or as a way to create emotional support for new policies, a University of Michigan professor, Barry Checkoway, argues we need to recognize young people as potential resources. Checkoway suggests that we acknowledge kids' "right to participate in the decisions that affect their lives and a responsibility to serve their communities."[58]

For instance, anti-smoking campaigns have been particularly success-ful using young people to create messages. Ad execs recognize that youths possess a unique viewpoint, which is more effective for reach-ing other teens than preachy-sounding adult messages.

By continually characterizing young people as a problem rather than a resource, adults, politicians, and the news media create further gaps between generations. This group of young people is no worse and in some cases better than those who came before them, yet youth-bashing continues to strike a resonant chord in adults. So if kids today aren't more violent, more out of control, why do we try so hard to fur-ther restrict them and to "scientifically" scrutinize their popular cul-ture, looking for the origins of a crisis that does not exist? What do we gain from this exercise in futility?

The Threat of Generation Next

As we move into a new century and a new millennium, the future has perhaps never seemed so unknowable. Changes in the American eco-nomic structure, new technologies, and a new war with an unconven-tional enemy have created anxieties about the world we live in and our future. These fears are deflected onto youth and youth culture, repre-sentatives of the future. What will become of them, of us, we wonder? In a time when so much seems beyond our control we are attempting to clamp down on the one thing we think we can control: our children. We ask entertainment producers to help us by crafting ratings and we attempt to restrict youth from the media porthole to the adult world. In short, the world feels like a scary, dangerous place, so exposing children to these realities via media culture may make for a dangerous and scary next generation, or so we fear.

Extreme fears or phobias are often based on a kernel of a real threat that is mistakenly applied to more situations than necessary. Fear is rarely wholly irrational—the high-profile school shootings are held up as real possibilities of what can happen, even in Middle Amer-ica. Within these modern morality tales the innocent can either be-come killers or killed, and we fear it impossible to predict whom this fate may visit. The presumed message is, if it can happen here, in the heart of the so-called American Dream, then it can happen anywhere. Any child becomes a potential victim or threat. No longer are the children of immigrants, the poor, or racial ethnic minorities the only ones feared. We now fear and fear for an entire generation.

In reality, the probability of any child being killed (or killing, for that matter) at school is exponentially low: children are far more likely to be victims of violence in their own homes. School shootings are also not just phenomena of the 1990s; while rare, violent rampages have dotted the American landscape. For instance, in 1979 a sixteen-year-old female fired into an elementary school, killing two and wounding nine, because she didn't like Mondays.[59] The most deadly school shooting rampage took place in 1967 at the University of Texas in Austin, when a twenty-four-year-old student shot forty-six people from a clock tower, killing sixteen of them. He had killed his wife and mother earlier that day. In context we see that such acts of extreme violence are rare, but not new, and certainly not limited to youth. Workplace rampages by adults are in fact far more common. The school-shooting motif helps manufacture generalized fears of youth, and our anxieties set the stage for twenty-four-hour news coverage of any incident, as well as for national news wires carrying stories about suspected shootings nationwide. We are caught in a vicious cycle: these tragedies did not create our youth anxiety, but built on and mushroomed existing fears.

People tend to fear the unknown, and ironically our fears of youth have heightened the sense that kids today are different, a new breed, not like we were. This fear echoes through the news and through political platforms and creates yet more distance and disconnection between youth and their elders.

The concerns that swirl around media culture and youth draw on fears for the future as well. We fear that media violence will create violence, or at least make a generation unable to feel sympathy or remorse for those who are victims. We fear that the different forms of media violence today, for instance, graphic movies or video games, are more powerful than the comic books or cowboys-and-Indians variety of violent entertainment in the 1950s. This fear contains two assumptions: first, that young people are in fact more violent and less caring, and second, that this is caused by media violence. As this chapter has detailed and the next will explore in depth, youth today are actually less violent than in the past and there is absolutely no evidence to suggest that they are less caring.

In truth, it is *adults* who appear less caring, slashing funding for the millions of children living in poverty and providing overcrowded schools that sometimes even lack adequate bathroom facilities. Adults have forgotten about the heavy education subsidies during the Cold War era, which made it possible to obtain a college degree without graduating with six figures of student loan debt. More than just a misunderstanding, portraying youth as out of control and dangerous attempts to justify the creation of punitive policies and to excuse ourselves from responsibility for failing today's youth. If we can convince ourselves that young people are to blame for their own supposed failings, then there is nothing we need to do but shake our heads and lock them away.

The other central media-related fear draws on the belief that young people are excessively hedonistic, prone to hypersexuality and hyperconsumption. As we have seen, teens today are less sexually active and less likely to become pregnant than their predecessors. Yes, sex is much more visible today than a generation ago, and cable television, movies, and the Internet make it more difficult to control what young people know about sex, a symbolic dividing line between childhood and adulthood. And as we have transitioned into a consumer-based economy following World War II, political leaders define being a consumer as part of being a good citizen. As we will see, marketers are willing to invest in making children consumers, but we are seriously falling short in our investment to create citizens. By blaming media culture for stepping into the vacuum we have created, we can deflect responsibility from ourselves.

Fearing youth and media culture may be a popular pastime, but it is a dangerous one. First, we consistently underestimate young people. Second, we create a hostile environment in which control and punishment replace patience and support. The popular culture so many adults decry resonates with young people in ways that adults often cannot. By rethinking both media and youth, we will see that each are far more complex than the simple cause-and-effect thinking that dominates our understanding of media would have us believe. By failing to explore youth and media more deeply we do both a major disservice.

Part Two

3

Fear of Media Violence

Four Fallacies
of Media-Violence Effects

In June 1999, just two months after the Columbine shootings, I attended the National Media Education Conference in Saint Paul, Minnesota. Although scheduled far in advance of the tragedy, the conference seemed to hold a great deal of urgency for the attendees and attracted more reporters than the meeting the year before. I rode in a shuttle from the airport with a reporter, who asked me what I thought should be done about the media-violence problem. I replied that while media violence may seem to explain otherwise "unexplainable" youth violence, and may be a small part of what makes someone become violent, there were other critical factors we often overlook. This is partly because news reports of Columbine and other dramatic events paid so much attention to the media explanation. Once I arrived at the conference, media violence was the hot topic. A special session was held to discuss the Columbine–media violence connection and was standing room only. The session was extremely emotional, and like other public forums I have attended that discuss media and violence, quite heated at times. Talking about media violence creates a war of words—ironically far more than discussions about actual violence do.

Discussing the fear of media violence is like jumping into an argument where most people are no longer listening, just shouting louder and louder at each other. This is not just an intellectual issue for many people but one that is deeply personal. In fairness, the social science research isn't readily available (nor particularly interesting) for the public. So most of us don't realize that the research is not nearly as conclusive as we are so often told or that results suggest only a weak connection between violent programming and aggressive behavior.[1] It is fear that fuels the impassioned pleas to sanction Hollywood for "poisoning young minds" with media violence, as a woman wrote in a letter to the *San Francisco Chronicle*.[2] Everyday citizens fear "what this country is coming to" at the hands of "demented" writers and producers.[3] The fear and anger are very real. And unfortunately, often misplaced.

This chapter offers a critical view of the fear and assumptions contained within the contours of the panic surrounding media violence. I hope to press the pause button and stop the voices of impending doom for a moment in order to examine *why* the fear persists and why it is so misdirected. The news media often guide us to think of media violence as the creator of real violence rather than the more complex causes, like poverty and the availability of guns. As Michael Moore's 2002 documentary *Bowling for Columbine* demonstrates, we are a society that is ambivalent about gun control, so it becomes easier for the news media in particular to focus on media culture than to question our gun culture. While on the surface our fear seems to be about violence, we will see that actual violence has little to do with media violence. As I hope to demonstrate, the host of assumptions about media violence stem from anxiety about a changing world and an unknown future and serves to justify control of (usually other people's) children.

When I began graduate work in psychology, the studies of effects of violent media on behavior seemed overwhelming. The argument made sense to me at the time, especially since I hate violent movies. I had seen a movie called *Predator 2*, which I reluctantly agreed to watch with a very persistent boyfriend. I really can't tell you what the movie was about since I found it so offensive that I kept my eyes closed through most of it. I was really angry with him for taking me to see a movie in which people appeared to be skinned alive and vowed intellectual revenge by showing him that these movies were not just stupid and repulsive, but harmful too. Students of psychology are taught that the individual is the primary unit of analysis, and that something that may be bad for the individual can be multiplied many times over and thus become a social problem. This perspective is complementary to the American focus on individualism, where we often believe that our success or failure stems directly from our personal characteristics and actions rather than social forces.

But as I began to review the research, I saw that the results were not as compelling as I had hoped or had heard on the news. I eventually realized that my feelings about violent movies were driven more by my personal taste than social science. Other scholars, like psychologist Jonathan L. Freedman, challenge the conclusions of this research too. Freedman evaluated every study exploring the media violence connection published in English and concluded that "the evidence . . . is weak and inconsistent, with more non-supportive results than supportive results."[4] Later, when I began work in sociology, I saw that sociological explanations were needed in addition to focusing on individual behavior. Both media and violence are sociological as well as psychological phenomena.

Yet historically, psychologists have focused the bulk of the research about media and violence on individual "effects" that have been used to draw conclusions on a sociological level. Adding sociological analysis gives us information about the larger context. We will see that from a sociological perspective media violence is important, but not in the way we tend to think it is. It cannot help us explain real violence well, but it can help us understand American culture and why stories of conflict and violent resolution so often reoccur.

Media violence has become a scapegoat, onto which we lay blame for a host of social problems. Sociologist Todd Gitlin describes how "the indiscriminate fear of television in particular displaces justifiable fears of actual dangers—dangers of which television . . . provides some disturbing glimpses."[5] Concerns about media and violence rest on several flawed, yet taken-for-granted assumptions about both media and violence. These beliefs appear to be obvious in emotional arguments about "protecting" children. So while these are not the only problems with blaming media, this chapter will address four central assumptions:

1. As media culture has expanded, children have become more violent.
2. Children are prone to imitate media violence with deadly results.
3. Real violence and media violence have the same meaning.
4. Research proves media violence is a major contributor to social problems.

As someone who has been accused of only challenging the media–violence connection because I am secretly funded by the entertainment industry (which I can assure you I am not), I can attest we are entering hostile and emotional territory.[6] This chapter demonstrates where these assumptions come from and why they are misplaced.

Assumption #1:
As Media Culture Has Expanded,
Children Have Become More Violent

You won't get an argument from me on the first part of this assumption—media culture has expanded exponentially over the last few decades. The low cost of production of the microchip has made a wide variety of new media technologies like video games and computers available to a large number of consumers, and we have been buying billions of dollars worth of these products. Traditional media like television have expanded from a handful of channels to hundreds. Our involvement with media culture has grown to the degree that media use has become an integral part of everyday life. There is so much content out there that we cannot know about or control, so we can never be fully sure what children may come in contact with. This fear of the unknown underscores the anxiety about harmful effects. Is violent media imagery, a small portion of a vast media culture, poisoning the minds and affecting the behavior of countless children, as an August 2001 *Kansas City Star* article warns?[7] The fear seems real and echoes in newsprint across the country.

Perhaps an article in the *Pittsburgh Post-Gazette* comes closest to mirroring popular sentiment and exposing three fears that are indicative of anxiety about change. Titled "Media, Single Parents Blamed for Spurt in Teen Violence," the article combines anxieties about shifts in family structure and the expansion of media culture with adults' fear of youth by falsely stating that kids are now more violent at earlier and earlier ages.[8] This certainly reflects a common perception, but its premise is fundamentally flawed: as media culture has expanded, young people have become *less* violent. During the 1990s arrest rates for violent offenses (like murder, rape, and aggravated assault) among fifteen- to seventeen-year-olds fell steadily, just as they did for people fourteen and under.[9] Those with the highest arrest rates now and in the past are adults. Fifteen- to seventeen-year-olds only outdo adults in burglary and theft, but these rates have been falling for the past twenty-five years. In fact, theft arrest rates for fifteen- to seventeen-year-olds have declined by 27 percent since 1976 and the rates for those fourteen and under have declined 41 percent, while the arrest rate for adults has increased.[10] Yet we seldom hear public outcry about the declining morals of adults—this complaint is reserved for youth.

Let's consider for a moment the fear that media violence is creating a new breed of young killers. True, we did see a rise in homicides committed by teens in the 1980s, but we also saw a rise in homicides committed by adults during that period.[11] Eighteen- to twenty-four-year-old adults have been and are now the age group most likely to commit homicide. After reaching their peak in 1993, homicide rates steadily declined in the late 1990s, perhaps in part due to improved economic conditions. Those who blame media violence for an alleged wave of youth violence ignore these facts.

An even bigger misconception is the belief that very young children are now becoming killers in epidemic proportions. If we look at homicide arrest rates for children six to twelve we see they are miniscule: in 1999 there were seventeen arrests out of a population of 27.7 million children.[12] Still, seventeen kids is seventeen too many, until we consider that this was the *fewest* number of arrests since the FBI began keeping separate numbers for young children in 1964. Overall, the period between 1968 and 1976 featured the highest arrest rates, with the numbers generally plummeting since; the 1999 arrest rate was 75 percent *less* than the 1970 rate. Bottom line: kids are less likely to be killers now than in the past.

So why do we seem to think that kids are now more violent than ever? A Berkeley Media Studies Group report found that half of news stories about youth were about violence and that more than two-thirds of violence stories focused on youth.[13] We think kids are committing the lion's share of violence because they comprise a large proportion of crime news. The reality is that adults commit most crime, but a much smaller percentage of these stories make news. The voices of reason that remind the public that youth crime decreased in the 1990s are often met with emotional anecdotes that draw attention away from dry statistics. A 2000 Discovery Channel "town meeting" called "Why Are We Violent" demonstrates this well. The program, described as a "wake-up call" for parents, warned that violence is everywhere, and their kids could be the next victims. Host Forrest Sawyer presented statistics indicating crime had dropped but downplayed them as only "part of the story." The bulk of the program relied on emotional accounts of experiences participants had with violence. There was no mention of violence committed by adults, the most likely perpetrators of violence against children. Kids serve as our scapegoat, blamed for threatening the rest of us, when, if anything, kids are more likely to be the victims of adult violence.

But how do we explain the young people who do commit violence? Can violent media help us here? Broad patterns of violence do not match media use as much as they mirror poverty rates. Take the city of Los Angeles, where I live, as an example. We see violent crime rates are higher in lower-income areas relative to the population. The most dramatic example is demonstrated by homicide patterns. For example, the Seventy-Seventh Street division (near the flashpoint of the 1992 civil unrest) reported 12 percent of the city's homicides in 1999, yet comprised less than 5 percent of the city's total population. Conversely, the West Los Angeles area (which includes affluent neighborhoods such as Brentwood and Bel-Air) reported less than 1 percent of the city's homicides but accounted for nearly 6 percent of the total population. If media culture were a major indicator, wouldn't the children of the wealthy, who have greater access to the Internet, video games, and other visual media be at greater risk for becoming violent? The numbers don't bear out because violence patterns do not match media use.

Violence can be linked with a variety of issues, the most important one being poverty. Criminologist E. Britt Patterson examined dozens of studies of crime and poverty and found that communities with extreme poverty, a sense of bleakness, and neighborhood disorganization and disintegration were most likely to support higher levels of violence.[14] Violence may be an act committed by an individual, but violence is also a sociological, not just an individual, phenomenon. To fear media violence we would have to believe that violence has its origins mostly in individual psychological functioning and thus that any kid could snap from playing too many video games. Ongoing sociological research has identified other risk factors that are based on environment: poverty, substance use, overly authoritarian or lax parenting, delinquent peers, neighborhood violence, and weak ties to one's family or community.[15] If we are really interested in confronting youth violence, these are the issues that must be addressed first. Media violence is something worth looking at, but not the primary cause of actual violence.

What about the kids who aren't from poor neighborhoods and who come from supportive environments? When middle-class white youths commit acts of violence, we seem to be at a loss for explanations beyond media violence. These young people often live in safe communities, enjoy many material privileges, and attend well-funded schools. Opportunities are plentiful. What else could it be, if not media?

For starters, incidents in these communities are rare but extremely well publicized. These stories are dramatic and emotional and thus great ratings-boosters. School shootings or mere threats of school shootings are often not just local stories but make national news. Public concern about violence swells when suburban white kids are involved. Violence is not "supposed" to happen there. Central-city violence doesn't raise nearly the same attention or public outcry to ban violent media. We seem to come up empty when looking for explanations of why affluent young white boys, for example, would plot to blow up their school. We rarely look beyond the media for our explanations, but the social contexts are important here too. Even well-funded suburban schools can become overgrown, impersonal institutions where young people easily fall through the cracks and feel alienated. Sociologists Wayne Wooden and Randy Blazak suggest that the banality and boredom of suburban life can create overarching feelings of meaninglessness within young people, that perhaps they find their parents' struggles to obtain material wealth empty and are not motivated by the desire for money enough to conform.[16] It is too risky to criticize the American Dream—the house in the suburbs, homogeneity, a Starbucks at every corner—because ultimately that requires many of us to look in the mirror. It is easier to look at the TV for the answer.

The truth is there is no epidemic of white suburban violence, but isolated and tragic examples have gained a lot of attention. Between 1980 and 1999 the homicide arrest rate for whites aged ten to seventeen fell 41 percent.[17] In 1999 there was 1.1 arrest for every 100,000 white kids—hardly an epidemic. Fearing media enables adults to condemn youth culture and erroneously blame young people for crimes they don't commit.

Assumption #2:
Children Are Prone to Imitate
Media Violence with Deadly Results

Blaming a perceived crime wave on media seems reasonable when we read examples in the news about eerie parallels between a real-life crime and entertainment. *Natural Born Killers, The Basketball Diaries, South Park,* and *Jerry Springer* have all been blamed for inspiring violence.[18] Reporting on similarities from these movies does make for a dramatic story and good ratings, but too often journalists do not dig deep enough to tell us the context of the incident. By leaving out the non-media details, news reports make it is easy for us to believe that the movies made them do it.

Albert Bandura's classic 1963 "Bobo doll" experiment initiated the belief that children will copy what they see in media. Bandura and colleagues studied ninety-six children approximately three to six years old (details about community or economic backgrounds not mentioned). The children were divided into groups and watched various acts of "aggression" against a five-foot inflated "Bobo" doll. Surprise: when they had their chance, the kids who watched adults hit the doll pummeled it too, especially those who watched the cartoon version of the doll-beating. Although taken as proof that children will imitate aggressive models from film and television, this study is riddled with leaps in logic.

Parents are often concerned when they see their kids play fighting in the same style as the characters in cartoons. But as author Gerard Jones points out in *Killing Monsters: Why Children Need Fantasy, Super Heroes, and Make-Believe Violence,* imitative behavior in play is a way young people may work out pent-up hostility and aggression and feel powerful. The main problem with the Bobo doll study is fairly obvious: hitting an inanimate object is not necessarily an act of violence, nor is real life something that can be adequately recreated in a laboratory. In fairness, contemporary experiments have been a bit more complex than this one, using physiological measures like blinking and heart rate to measure effects. The only way to assess a cause-effect relationship with certainty is to conduct an experiment, but violence is too complex of an issue to isolate into independent and dependent variables in a lab. What happens in a laboratory is by nature out of context, and real world application is highly questionable. We do learn about children's play from this study, but by focusing only on how they might become violent we lose a valuable part of the data.

So while this study is limited because it took place in a controlled laboratory and did not involve actual violence, let's consider cases that did, which on the surface seem to be proof that some kids are copycat killers. In the summer of 1999, a twelve-year-old boy named Lionel Tate beat and killed six-year-old Tiffany Eunick, the daughter of a family friend in Pembroke Pines, Florida. Claiming he was imitating wrestling moves he had seen on television, Lionel's defense attorney attempted to prove that Lionel did not know what he was doing would hurt Tiffany. He argued that Lionel should not be held criminally responsible for what he called a tragic accident. The jury didn't buy this defense, finding that the severity of the girl's injuries was inconsistent with the wrestling claim. Nonetheless, the news media ran with the wrestling alibi. Headlines shouted "Wrestle Slay Boy Faces Life," "Boy, 14, Gets Life in TV Wrestling Death," and "Young Killer Wrestles Again in Broward Jail."[19] This case served to reawaken fears that media violence, particularly as seen in wrestling, is dangerous because kids allegedly don't understand that real violence can cause real injuries. Cases like this one are used to justify claims that kids may imitate media violence without recognizing the real consequences.

Lionel's defense attorney capitalized on this fear by stating that "Lionel had fallen into the trap so many youngsters fall into."[20] But many youngsters don't fall into this "trap" and neither did Lionel. Lionel Tate was not an average twelve-year-old boy; the warning signs were certainly present before that fateful summer evening. Most news reports focused on the alleged wrestling connection without exploring Lionel's troubled background. He was described by a former teacher as "almost out of control," prone to acting out, disruptive, and seeking attention.[21]

Evidence from the case also belies the claim that Lionel and Tiffany were just playing, particularly the more than thirty-five serious injuries that Tiffany sustained, including a fractured skull and massive internal damage. These injuries were not found to be consistent with play wrestling as the defense claimed. The prosecutor pointed out that Lionel did not tell investigators he was imitating wrestling moves initially; instead he said they were playing tag but changed his story to wrestling weeks later. Although his defense attorney claimed Lionel didn't realize someone could really get hurt while wrestling, Lionel admitted that he knew television wrestling was "fake."[22]

This story would probably not have made national news if Lionel's lawyers had not invoked the wrestling defense, but the publicity surrounding the case ultimately reveals a double tragedy: Tiffany's death and Lionel's trial as an "adult" and subsequent sentence of life in prison. We as a society promote the idea that children are too naïve to know the difference between media violence and real violence, but we are also quick to apply adult punishment. Completely lost in the discussion surrounding this case is our repeated failure as a society to treat children like Lionel *before* violent behavior escalates, to recognize the warning signs before it is too late.

The imitation hypothesis suggests that violence in media puts kids like Lionel over the edge, the proverbial straw that breaks the camel's back, but this enables us to divert our attention from the seriousness of other risk factors. Another murder case demonstrates this point. In February 2001 an argument between two eleven-year-old boys at a Springfield, Massachusetts, movie theater resulted in the death of Nestor Herrera. In spite of the fact that the investigation concentrated on a dispute between the two boys, a *Boston Herald* story focused almost exclusively on the slasher movie, *Valentine*, which the accused stabber had just watched.[23] The article implied that the similarities between the stabbing and the movie could partly explain why Nestor was killed. Rather than explore why Nestor's killer was carrying a knife or investigate the family or community background, the *Herald* warned parents to limit their children's media use, or "the effects could be devastating."[24]

Two days after the initial report, the *Herald* ran another story, which revisited the gory details of the movie and noted almost as an aside that the suspect's home was plagued with violence. The suspect also had a history of discipline problems, which caused him to change schools.[25] The nature of the boys' argument (the *motive*) was apparently not as important as the movie in the *Herald*'s initial reports. As it turned out, the suspect was jealous—the victim was at the movie with a girl he liked. Although the district attorney prosecuting the case stated to the press that the movie clearly did not provoke the stabbing, a February 7 editorial in the *Herald* focused on media violence as the central problem, stating that "Hollywood's product is often as toxic as that of the tobacco industry."[26]

There is a problem here, but it's not the slasher film. The problem lies in how easy it is for news reports and subsequent public concern to overlook the central facts of a case like this: a troubled boy is shuffled around and does not receive appropriate intervention until he brings a knife to a movie and kills someone. The movie is not what we should be focusing on: clearly family violence, a history of discipline problems, and the fact that the boy carried a weapon merit further examination.

The biggest problem with the imitation hypothesis is that it suggests that we focus on media instead of the other 99 percent of the pieces of the violence puzzle. When a lack of other evidence is provided in news accounts it appears as though media violence is the most compelling explanatory factor. It is certainly likely that young people who are prone to become violent are also drawn towards violent entertainment, just as funny kids may be drawn to comedies. But children whose actions parallel media violence come with a host of other more important risk factors. We blame media violence to deflect blame away from adult failings—not simply the failure of parents but our society's failure to create effective programs and solutions to help troubled young people.

Assumption #3:
Real Violence and Media Violence
Have the Same Meaning

Nestor Herrara's accused killer watched a violent film; on that much we can agree. But what the film actually *meant* to the boy we cannot presume. Yet somehow press accounts would have us believe that we could read his mind based on his actions. It is a mistake to presume media representations of violence and real violence have the same meaning for audiences. Consider the following three scenarios:

1. Wile E. Coyote drops an anvil on Road Runner's head, who keeps on running;
2. A body is found on *Law and Order* (or your favorite police show);
3. A shooting at a party leaves one person dead and another near death after waiting thirty minutes for an ambulance.

Are all three situations examples of violence? Unlike the first two incidents, the third was real. All three incidents have vastly different contexts, and thus different meanings. The first two are fantasies in which no real injuries occurred, yet are more likely to be the subject of public concerns about violence. Ironically, because the third incident received no media attention, its details, and those of incidents like it, are all but ignored in discussions of violence. Also ignored is the context in which the real shooting occurred; it was sparked by gang rivalries which stem from neighborhood tensions, poverty, lack of opportunity, and racial inequality. The fear of media violence is founded on the assumption that young people do not recognize a difference between media violence and real violence. Ironically, adults themselves seem to have problems distinguishing between the two.

Media violence is frequently conflated with actual violence in public discourse, as one is used to explain the other. It is adults who seem to confuse the two. For instance, the *Milwaukee Journal Sentinel* reported on a local school district that created a program to deal with bullying.[27] Yet media violence was a prominent part of the article, which failed to take into account the factors that create bullying situations in schools. Adults seem to have difficulty separating media representations from actual physical harm. Media violence is described as analogous to tobacco, a "smoking gun" endangering children.[28] This is probably because many middle-class white adults who fear media have had little exposure to violence other than through media representations.

I discovered the difference a few years ago as a researcher studying juvenile homicides. We combed through police investigation files looking for details about the incidents while carefully avoiding crime scene and coroner's photographs to avoid becoming emotionally overwhelmed. One morning while looking through a case file the book accidentally fell open to the page with the crime scene photos. I saw a young man slumped over the steering wheel of his car. He had a gunshot wound to his forehead, a small red circle. His eyes were open. I felt a wrenching feeling in my stomach, a feeling I have never felt before and have fortunately never felt since. At that point I realized that regardless of the hundreds, if not thousands, of violent acts I had seen in movies and television, none could come close to this. I had never seen the horrific simplicity of a wound like that one, never seen the true absence of expression in a person's face. No actor has ever been able to truly "do death" right, I realized. It became clear that I knew nothing about violence, thankfully. Yes, I have read the research, but that knowledge was just academic; this was real.

This is not to say that violent media do not create real emotional responses. Good storytelling can create sadness and fear, and depending on the context violence can even be humorous (as in *The Three Stooges*). Media violence may elicit no emotional response—but this does not necessarily mean someone is "desensitized" or uncaring. It may mean that a script was mediocre and that the audience doesn't care about its characters. But it could be because media violence is not real and most of us, even children, know it. Sociologist Todd Gitlin calls media violence a way of getting "safe thrills."[29] Viewing media violence is a way of dealing with the most frightening aspect of life in a safe setting, like riding a roller-coaster while knowing that you will get out and walk away in a few minutes.

Nonetheless, many people, fueled by media reports of studies that seem to be very compelling, fear that kids can't really distinguish between real violence and media violence. An unpublished study of eight children made news across the United States and Canada. "Kids may say they know the difference between real violence and the kind they see on television and video, but new research shows their brains don't," announced Montreal's *Gazette*.[30] This research, conducted by John Murray, a developmental psychologist at Kansas State University, involved MRIs of eight children, aged eight to thirteen. As the kids watched an eighteen-minute fight scene from *Rocky IV* their brains showed activity in areas that are commonly activated in response to threats and emotional arousal. This should come as no surprise, since entertainment often elicits emotional response; if film and television had no emotional payoff, why would people watch?

But the press took this small study as proof of what we already think we know: that kids can't tell the difference between fantasy and reality. A *Kansas City Star* reporter described this as "a frightening new insight," and the study's author stated the children "were treating *Rocky IV* violence as real violence."[31] And while Yale psychologist Dorothy Singer warned that the size of the study was too small to draw any solid conclusions, she also said that the study is "very important."[32]

If a small study challenged the conventional media violence wisdom, you can bet that it would have been roundly dismissed as anecdotal. But instead, this study was treated as another piece to the puzzle, and clearly made the news because of its dramatic elements: a popular movie, medical technology, and children viewing violence. In any case, there are big problems with the interpretation offered by the study's author. First, this study actually discredits the idea of desensiti-

zation. The children's brains clearly showed some sort of emotional reaction to the violence they saw. They were not "emotionally dead-
ened," as we are often told to fear. But kids can't win either way within
the media-violence fear, since feeling "too little" or "too much" are
both interpreted as proof that media violence is harmful to children.

Second, by insisting that children are completely different from
adults we ignore the likelihood that adult brains would likely react in
much the same way. Yet somehow by virtue of children being children,
their *brains* can know things that *they* don't. Do an MRI on adults
while they watch pornography and their brains will probably show
arousal. Does that mean the person would think that he or she just had
actual sex? The neurological reaction would probably be extremely
similar, if not identical, but we can't read brainwaves and infer meaning. That's what makes humans human: the ability to create meaning
from our experiences. And adults are not the only ones capable of
making sense of their lives.

Professor Murray's comments imply that researchers can "read"
children's minds and find things that the kids themselves cannot, a
rather troubling presumption. Violence has meanings that cannot simply be measured in brainwaves, MRIs, or CAT scans. No matter what
these high-tech tools may tell researchers, experiencing real violence
is fundamentally different from experiencing media violence. It is
adults, not kids, who seem to have trouble grasping this idea. Somehow lost in the fear of media violence is an understanding of how actual violence is experienced.

If we want to learn about actual youth violence and what causes
kids to commit acts of violence, depictions of media violence won't
help us much—talking with people who have experienced both will.
For several years in the mid-1990s, I worked with criminologists on a
broad study of juvenile violence to understand the causes and corre-
lates of youth violence in Los Angeles.[33] We wanted to understand the
full context of violence in order to help develop conflict management
programs with community members. Usually when we talk about violence and media, it is common to defer to the traditional experts. These
well-intentioned, often rather distinguished individuals have most
likely spent many years studying about media, and perhaps about violence too.[34] However, truly knowing both violence and media comes
from experiencing them both first hand, something I fortunately have
not. But we knew there were many young people in Los Angeles who
had and that they were real violence experts whom we could interview.

To do so, we went to the areas with the highest violent arrest rates (not to those with the most video gamers). Initially, we conducted a survey to ascertain the level of violence in each neighborhood. We then did follow-up in-depth interviews with fifty-six males, aged twelve to eighteen, who had experienced violence as victims or offenders (or both) to understand how they made sense of both real and media violence.[35] Our interviewees clearly described the differences between media violence and actually experiencing violence first-hand.

Above all, their stories tell us that the meaning of violence is made within particular social contexts. For most of those interviewed, poverty and neighborhood violence were overwhelming influences in their lives, shaping their interactions and their understanding of their futures. More than three-quarters of respondents (77 percent) noted that gang activity was prominent in their neighborhoods. Slightly less than half (48 percent) reported feeling tremendous pressure to join gangs, but less than one in ten (9 percent) claimed gang membership. Eighty-eight percent heard guns being fired on a regular basis, and nearly one-third (30 percent) had seen someone get shot. More than one-quarter (27 percent) had seen a dead body, and 14 percent had been threatened with a gun themselves. Almost one-quarter (23 percent) had been attacked with some sort of weapon.

Through interviewing these young people, we found that the line between victim and offender is hard to draw and that violent incidents occur within murky contexts. The people we call violent offenders are not necessarily predators, looking to swoop down on the weak and innocent. Instead, we see that violent incidents often happen within a larger context of fear, intimidation, despair, and hopelessness. These kids were trying to survive in destroyed communities as best they could. Unfortunately, violence was often a part of their survival.

Public discussions about violence often ignore these violence experts, who clarified several key differences between their actual experiences with violence and media violence. For one, many described media violence as gorier, with over-the-top special effects. Over and over the boys described how fear in their lives comes not from seeing blood on or off screen but from the uncertainty about when violence will next occur. In post–September 11 America, with threats of terrorism and ongoing military conflicts, this makes a great deal of sense. One seventeen-year-old stated that because violence in his neighborhood was so pervasive, media violence was strangely comforting: he said at least when it occurred on television, he knew he was safe.

Another key difference in meaning is the clear distinction between good and evil in media depictions of violence. "It's more pumped-up like, (a) heroic thing," an eighteen-year-old informant told us. "Like most of violence on TV is like a heroic thing. Like a cop does something amazing. Like somebody like a bad guy, the violence is usually like pinpointed toward a bad person." Other boys described the lack of punishment in their experiences compared with media violence; law enforcement to them was not as effective as it may appear on police dramas. A seventeen-year-old compared his experiences with the *Jerry Springer* show, saying "They have security that break it up if something happens. (Nobody) is really going to get hurt that much because there probably will be two or three blows and security will hop on stage and grab the people." He went on to describe how, in his experience, the police were not concerned with who the "good guy" was, that there is no discussion and often no real resolution. Ironically, one of the central complaints about media violence is that often there are no consequences, but our informants told us that in reality things are even worse.

A major concern about media violence is that it creates unfounded fear that the world is a dangerous place. Communications scholar George Gerbner describes this as the "mean-world" syndrome: by watching so much television violence people mistakenly believe that the world is a violent place. But what about people who *do* live in dangerous communities? With the boys we interviewed, poverty and hopelessness gnaw away at them on a daily basis. "It's just poverty," an eighteen-year-old told us. "I wouldn't recommend nobody comin' here. . . . I just wouldn't recommend it." Not surprisingly, the majority of boys we interviewed did not find media violence to be a big source of fear. In fact, some boys said they enjoyed watching violence to point out how producers got it wrong. As experts, they can detect the artificiality of media violence.

There is also resentment when their neighborhoods are used in stereotypical portrayals. "The people that make the movies, I'm pretty sure they never lived where we live at, you know, went to the schools we went to," explained a seventeen-year-old we interviewed. "They were, most of 'em were born in you know, the upper-class whatever, you know? I don't think they really have experienced how we live so that's why I don't think they really know how it is out here." Others explained how movies, violent or otherwise, were a luxury they could rarely afford. Besides, impoverished communities often have no movie theaters. One boy told us he never went to movies because it wasn't safe to be out at night or to go to other neighborhoods and possibly be mistaken for a rival gang member.

Some of the boys did say that media violence made them more afraid, based on the violent realities of their communities. "If you watch a gangster movie and you live in a neighborhood with gangsters you think you'll be killed," an informant said. Another respondent, who said he had to carry a knife for protection, told us, "It makes you fear going outside. It makes you think twice about going outside. I mean, how can you go outside after watching someone get shot on TV? You know, (my friend) was just walking outside of his house and got shot. And you think to yourself, damn, what if I walked out of my house and got shot?" In both cases the fear that stemmed from media violence was rooted in their real-life experiences.

Violence exists within specific social contexts; people make meaning of both real violence and media violence in the context of their lives. It is clear from these examples that neighborhood violence and poverty are important factors necessary to understand the meanings these young people give to media violence. Other contexts would certainly be different, but focusing on media violence means real-life circumstances are often overlooked.

Watching media violence is obviously different from experiencing actual violence, yet public discourse has somehow melded the two together. Clearly media violence can be interpreted in many ways: as frightening, as cathartic, as funny, or absurd. We can't make assumptions about meaning no matter what the age of the audience.

We also need to acknowledge the meaning of violence in American media and American culture. It's too easy to say that media only reflect society or that producers are just giving the public what it wants, but certainly to some extent this is true. Violence is dramatic, a simple cinematic tool and easy to sell to domestic and overseas markets, since action-adventure movies present few translation problems for overseas distributors. But in truth, violence and aggression are very central facets of American society. Aggressive personalities tend to thrive in capitalism: risk-takers, people who are not afraid to "go for it," are highly prized within business culture. We celebrate sports heroes for being aggressive, not passive. The best hits of the day make the football highlights on ESPN, and winning means "decimating" and "destroying" in broadcast lingo.

We also value violence, or its softer-sounding equivalent, "the use of force," to resolve conflict. On local, national, and international

levels violence is largely considered acceptable. Whether this is right
or wrong is the subject for a different book, but the truth is that in the
United States the social order has traditionally been created and maintained through violence. We can't honestly address media violence
until we recognize that in part our media culture is violent because as
a society we are.

Assumption #4:
Research Conclusively Demonstrates
the Link Between Media and Violent Behavior

We engage in collective denial when we continually focus on the
media as main sources of American violence. The frequency of news
reports of research that allegedly demonstrates this connection helps
us ignore the real social problems in the United States. Headlines
imply that researchers have indeed found a preponderance of evidence to legitimate focus on media violence. Consider these headlines:

> "Survey Connects Graphic TV Fare, Child Behavior" (*Boston
> Globe*)
> "Cutting Back on Kids' TV Use May Reduce Aggressive Acts"
> (*Denver Post*)
> "Doctors Link Kids' Violence to Media" (*Arizona Republic*)
> "Study Ties Aggression to Violence in Games" (*USA Today*)

The media-violence connection seems very real, with studies and
experts to verify the alleged danger in story after story. Too often studies reported in the popular press provide no critical scrutiny and fail to
challenge conceptual problems. In our sound-bite society, news tends
to contain very little analysis or criticism of any kind.

The *Los Angeles Times* ran a story called "In a Wired World, TV
Still Has Grip on Kids."[36] The article provided the reader the impression that research provided overwhelming evidence of negative media
effects: only three sentences out of a thousand-plus words offered any
refuting information. Just two quoted experts argued against the conventional wisdom, while six offered favorable comments. Several
studies' claims drew no challenge, in spite of serious shortcomings.

For example, researchers considered responses to a "hostility questionnaire" or children's "aggressive" play as evidence that media violence can lead to real-life violence. But aggression is not the same as violence, although in some cases it may be a precursor to violence. Nor is it clear that these "effects" are anything but immediate. We know that aggression in itself is not necessarily a pathological condition; in fact we all have aggression that we need to learn to deal with. Second, several of the studies use correlation statistics as proof of causation. Correlation indicates the existence of relationships, but cannot measure cause and effect. Reporters may not recognize this, but have the responsibility to present the ideas of those who question such claims.

This pattern repeats in story after story. A *Denver Post* article described a 1999 study that claimed that limiting TV and video use reduced children's aggression.[37] The story prefaced the report by stating that "numerous studies have indicated a connection between exposure to violence and aggressive behavior in children," thus making this new report appear part of a large body of convincing evidence. The only "challenge" to this study came from psychologist James Garbarino, who noted that the real causes of violence are complex, although his list of factors began with "television, video games, and movies." He did cite guns, child abuse, and economic inequality as important factors, but the story failed to address any of these other problems.

The reporter doesn't mention the study's other shortcomings. First is the assumption that the television and videos kids watch contain violence at all. The statement we hear all the time in various forms—"the typical American child will be exposed to 200,000 acts of violence on television by age eighteen"—is based on the estimated time kids spend watching television, but tells us nothing about what they have actually watched.[38] Second, in these studies, aggression in play serves as a proxy for violence. But there is a big difference between playing "aggressively" and committing acts of violence. Author Gerard Jones points out that play is a powerful way by which kids can deal with feelings of fear.[39] Thus, watching the Power Rangers and then play-fighting is not necessarily an indicator of violence, it is part of how children fantasize about being powerful without ever intending to harm anyone. Finally, the researchers presumed that reducing television and video use explained changes in behavior, when in fact aggression and violence are complex responses to specific circumstances created by a variety of environmental factors. Nonetheless, the study's author stated that "if you . . . reduce their exposure to media you'll see a reduction in aggressive behavior."

A spring 2003 study claiming to have long-term evidence that children who watch television violence become violent adults even made news the week that American troops entered Iraq. This study is unique in that it tracked 329 respondents for fifteen years, but it contains several serious shortcomings that prevent us from concluding that television creates violence later in life.[40] First, the study measures aggression, not violence. Aggression is broadly defined by researchers, who constructed an "aggression composite" that includes such antisocial behavior as having angry thoughts, talking rudely to or about others, and having moving violations on one's driving record. Violence is a big jump from getting lots of speeding tickets. But beyond this composite, the connection between television viewing and physical aggression for males, perhaps the most interesting measure, is relatively weak. Television viewing explains only 3 percent of what led to physical aggression in the men studied.[41] Although some subjects did report getting into physical altercations, fewer than 10 of the 329 participants had ever been convicted of a crime, too small of a sample to make any predictions about serious violent offenders.

By focusing so heavily on media violence, both researchers and news accounts divert attention from the factors we know to be associated with violence. Both also downplay the serious limitations of traditional media-effects research. A *Boston Globe* article conceded that a great deal of "evidence" is anecdotal, stating that "the real link between televised sex and violence and actual behavior has been difficult to prove," but only after seven paragraphs about the "growing concern of mental health specialists."[42] In spite of news reports about the "tremendous problem" of media violence allegedly demonstrated by "classic studies" and "sweeping new" research, as the *Boston Globe* and *Los Angeles Times* reported, this body of research contains leaps in logic, questionable methods, and exaggerated findings.[43]

There is a preponderance of evidence, but not the result of "thirty years of research and more than 1000 studies," as the St. Louis *Post-Dispatch* described, but the fact that Americans spend so much time, energy, and money researching this loaded question instead of researching violence itself.[44] If youth violence is really the issue of importance here, we should start by studying violence, before studying media. But media culture is on trial, not violence. These studies are smoke screens that enable us to continue along the media trail while disregarding actual violence patterns.

Interestingly, the media blamers seem to feel that they are against a great deal of media resistance to their cause. But there seems to be no shortage of newspaper editors willing and eager to play upon this fear in print. A St. Louis *Post-Dispatch* editorial called "Poisonous Pleasures," railed against "our caustic culture and pervasive appetite for violent and obscene entertainment." [45] The paper plainly stated that "Media violence is hazardous to our health," but we are allegedly "a nation desperate to ignore it."

Media-violence detractors fear those of us who don't buy it, and lots of people are not willing to accept such hyperbolic threats about the dangers of media culture. A May 2001 Gallup Poll asked respondents to name the single most important preventative measure we could take to avoid another school shooting; 31 percent named more parental involvement, while only 5 percent said reduce media violence. [46] We are ignoring something, but it's not the "danger" of media, it is the origin of real violence, like problems in families and communities, poverty, and substance abuse. I am willing to offer that media violence may be a small link in a long chain, but certainly it's not the central link. The problem with both this body of research and the lack of critical coverage it gets is that it diverts attention away from the very real contexts of violence. Individuals might commit violence, but social contexts create violent individuals.

The public hears little about research that challenges the conventional wisdom or the studies that seek to understand how young people make sense of media violence. The American news media is rarely interested in covering media-violence research without a cause-effect result. British scholar David Buckingham writes that Americans "persist in asking simplistic questions about complex social issues" to avoid talking about controversial issues such as gun control. [47] We have been held hostage by denial, while European and Australian media scholars in particular study media in a much more complex fashion.

For example, a British study found that children's definitions of violent television differed by gender, telling us that masculinity claims are made by boys "tough enough" to not be scared by media violence. [48] The genre and context of the story contribute to whether or not kids consider a program violent. [49] Like adults, children tend to think media violence is harmful, just not for them—kids younger than them may be affected, they tell researchers.[50] A study of children's emotional responses to horror films found that they did sometimes have nightmares (parents' biggest concern for their children), but chose to watch scary films so they could conquer their fears and toughen up.[51] Horror films helped the children experience fear and deal with anxiety in a safe setting. The study's author concluded that watching media violence might be a way for children to prepare themselves to face their fears more directly.

As a child, I used to watch movies like *The Wizard of Oz* to conquer my fear of the wicked witch and her evil monkeys and I would see if I could get through more than I did the last time it aired. I also loved *Willie Wonka and the Chocolate Factory* but was terrified of the Oompa-Loompas and challenged myself each year not to run away screaming when the little orange creatures appeared. While parents may hope to prevent their children from ever being scared or having a bad dream, nightmares are a normal way for children (and adults) to deal with fear and anxiety.

Studies like the ones described above are absent from American news reports about media and violence, so we are encouraged to keep thinking about children as potential victims of popular culture. American researchers are quick to discount children's abilities as media audience members, as is evident in traditional media-effects research in which children's ideas are missing.

While the most frequent tactic is to ignore research that challenges conventional wisdom, media-violence critics occasionally attack more directly. Making statements that "almost all academic researchers" support the media-violence connection and that those who disagree are "an extreme minority" makes it appear as though research is in fact conclusive.[52] Sometimes their tactics are even more direct and personal.[53]

Whenever critics challenge the results of media effects research, authors tend to respond with arrogance, hostility, and occasionally personal insults. The spirit of debate is all but absent. Within the scientific method, researchers are supposed to continually consider the possibility that they are wrong. But within this field dissenters are not just researchers with different findings, they are regarded as heretics. If this is indeed an open-and-shut question, as its proponents argue, why do media-effects researchers get so nasty with their critics?

Perhaps science itself is in question—good science is supposed to encourage, not suppress, debate. Ideally the scientific community shares ideas not to intimidate dissent or boost egos, but to improve scholarship. Instead, media-violence research has created a sort of intellectual totalitarianism, where researchers only listen to people who agree with them.

The media-violence story, the research, and its emotional baggage make open debate next to impossible. Those who fear media violence police the boundaries of this dogma to avoid challenging their intuitive belief that popular culture is dangerous. But taste and influence are two very different things: media researchers are often media critics in disguise. There's nothing wrong with media criticism—we could probably use more of it—but when media criticism takes the place of understanding the roots of violence we have a problem. Dissent is dismissed as Hollywood propaganda, reinforced when the press quotes a studio executive to "balance" a story on media's alleged danger.

Media violence enables American discussion about violence to avoid the tough questions about actual violence: Why is it so closely associated with poverty? How can we provide families with resources to cope in violent communities? By focusing so much energy on media violence, we avoid our responsibility to pressure politicians to create policies that address these difficult issues. To hear that "Washington (is) again taking on Hollywood" may feel good to the public and make it appear as though lawmakers are onto something, but real violence remains off the agenda.[54] This tactic appeals to many middle-class constituents whose experience with violence is often limited. Economically disadvantaged people are most likely to experience real violence, but least likely to appear on politicians' radar. A national focus on media rather than real violence draws on existing fears and reinforces the view that popular culture, not public policy, leads to violence.

Violence in media reminds us that we cannot control what children know about. But unfortunately many children are exposed to real violence, not only in their communities, but sometimes in their own homes. We should not deny this and use the illusion of childhood (as always carefree until the media gets to them) to shield ourselves from this reality. The concern about media and violence is not just a fear for children, but a fear *of* children. We often deal with this fear by calling for stricter controls of other people's children, both by the state and by parents. These "solutions" fail to address the real problems. In the next chapters I explore specific forms of media culture that elicit fears of violence. Chapter 4 looks at cartoons, often the first place children see violence in the media.

4

Fear of Cartoons

Role Models for Bad Behavior?

To my knowledge, cartoons were not part of the post-Columbine blame game. But cartoons elicit the fear that such staples of early childhood will "plant seeds" of violence in the youngest viewers. Critics complain that cartoons are violence-filled, exposing young children to more violence than other forms of media. News stories warn about the potential dangers of cartoons. An ominous *Kansas City Star* op-ed piece warned, "Cartoon Violence Is No Laughing Matter," as the author argued that cartoons provide kids the first dose of dangerous media violence.[1] A *Wall Street Journal* headline declared "Kids Are Glued to a Violent Japanese Cartoon Show—'Dragon Ball Z' is Bringing Impalement, Strangulation to the After-School Crowd."[2] In response to reading this article, a reader (who admitted he had never seen the program) wrote the *Wall Street Journal* a letter titled "Violent Cartoon Show Can Destroy Childhood."[3] A front-page *Pittsburgh Post-Gazette* article called "Children See Most Violence in Cartoons, Study Says" begins with the warning "Parents, beware: many cartoons can be harmful to the mental health of children under seven."[4] It would be hard for any parent to keep up with all of the new animated options. The biggest change in cartoons now, compared to when I was growing up, is that there are a lot more of them: there is even a cable network devoted only to cartoons. Should today's parents be concerned about the cartoons that kids are watching?

My answer is yes and no—but all too often we are steered towards focusing only on violence, adding another layer of blame for parents

85

who allow kids to indulge in Bugs Bunny unsupervised. By taking that Acme anvil as the biggest problem, we ignore stereotypical portrayals of race and gender that often pervade children's programming. I can understand concerns about why cartoons predominately created for children contain violence, especially karate-style violence. But we also need to consider that cartoon violence is often slapstick in nature, more comic relief than an anger management tool.

For instance, a study conducted by the Harvard School of Public Health made media waves in the spring of 2000. Initially published in the *Journal of the American Medical Association*, the study analyzed the amount of violence in Disney-animated features from 1937–1999 and concluded that the cartoons were becoming more violent, up from an average of six minutes per film in 1940 to just over nine in 1999.[5] Researchers warned parents that a "G" rating does not mean the cartoons are violence-free. In an attempt to remain objective, the study included things like Dumbo spraying peanuts as an act of violence and *Winnie the Pooh*'s romping Tigger is classified as violent when he bounces into other characters. The shooting of Bambi's mother has been the source of many a toddler's tears, and it too is included in this study.

These examples point to the broad scope of how violence is defined and to the broad-brush interpretation of violence as universally damaging. The researchers, however, were very clear that their study could not determine whether any type of causal relationship exists between Disney films and the behavior of viewers. Nonetheless, the study was widely reported on in *Time*, the *Washington Post*, the *Los Angeles Times*, and the New York *Daily News*, though not every story was in favor of a new campaign against cartoons.[6] The *Daily News* article began by asking facetiously, "Will *Bambi* turn your kids into serial killers?" and calls the study a "Sleeping Beauty" which "The public has no patience for."[7] Responding to a 1998 study on cartoon violence, an editorial in the *Pittsburgh Post-Gazette* argued that "demonizing Saturday morning TV" is itself a "cartoon" explanation for real-life violence and presumed that children under seven cannot distinguish between fantasy and reality.[8]

Cartoons do indeed flout the conventions of reality. The sky may be green and the grass blue, Wile E. Coyote gets an extra second to realize in horror that he has stepped off the cliff before he falls, and the ghosts in Scooby-Doo do seem real until those "meddling kids" solve the mystery. Perhaps the biggest problem with fears of cartoon violence is that they seem to discount the role of this sort of slapstick and the ability of young viewers to appreciate it.

Cartoons by nature are freer, less constrained by the confines of reality and convention. There are fewer rules to abide by; thus cartoons in many ways mirror the creativity of childhood, before the cans and can'ts and shoulds and musts of adult reality are firmly entrenched. Animation allows us to see the world in a more "child-like" way, one less constrained by convention. Cartoons enable adults to reconnect with some of the creativity we lose when we learn to become logical and rational, which is likely why we feel particularly anxious about cartoons, even when they are intended for adults.

Cartoons mock the rules of the adult world: animals sometimes talk; people may have only four fingers and neon yellow skin and die over and over in every episode. As adults struggle to get children to conform to the rational world, animators co-conspire with children's imaginations and challenge adult reality. Not only can animals talk in cartoons, but sometimes cartoon parents don't know everything. Cartoons challenge the adult conception of reality and tamper with the rules adults try so hard to impose on children. Are we really afraid that children will get confused and never learn the rules, like if you step off a cliff or an anvil drops on your head you will get hurt? If children were so malleable, parents wouldn't have nearly the struggle they do to get kids to comply with their authority.

We have to recognize the fundamental differences between cartoon "violence" and real-life violence. Sure, I admit it: I am completely desensitized to cartoon "violence." I cringe but laugh when Kenny inevitably finds a way to be killed on *South Park*. That's because no violence has taken place—no one is hurt and I know it, and so do kids at very early ages.[9] It is absurd to believe that Wile E. Coyote's head injuries can be compared in any way to real-life violence, and condescending to think children can't distinguish between the two. Since media culture is virtually everywhere, children learn very early on the difference between animation and reality.

We could ask why cartoons do contain so much violence, and why violence is presented as funny. These are deep cultural questions that could merit a book apiece, but the short version is that themes of violence run through Western culture. Cartoons provide comic relief, a way of reducing tension and fear by laughing at what scares us most.[10] We tend to underestimate the ability of even very young children to read the codes that tell them the difference between animation and regular programming, and especially the difference between animation and reality. In short, our cartoons are violent because we are; we were violent before animation and if we got rid of cartoon violence I am sure we will still be violent. As a society we solve conflicts through use of force, both locally and internationally. We glorify war if the cause is perceived as just, yet somehow we think children only learn about violence through entertainment, and not through families or communities. It is no surprise that our myths and stories also contain violence.

Although not animated, professional wrestling has garnered a great deal of public concern recently. A Kentucky psychologist calls wrestling "all the ills of society wrapped into one."[11] Concerns about wrestling draw on similar fears of cartoon violence, although the majority of wrestling's fans are between eighteen and thirty-four.[12] The presentation of wrestling is itself very cartoonish. Its characters are highly colorful, exaggerated caricatures and its story lines are very melodramatic. Jeffrey Brown, an expert in popular culture at Bowling Green State University, calls wrestling "a comic book come to life" with "very clear cut heroes and villains."[13] Personally I don't understand its appeal, but many of the young adults I have spoken with tell me they have been lifelong fans and describe wrestling as something one graduates into from cartoons. The pleasure, my informants tell me, comes from the fact that they know it's fake but it looks real, in contrast with cartoons which are fake and *look* fake. It's not just about the violence, but how the line between fantasy and reality is blurred.

So while adults often fear that young people don't know the difference between what's real and what's not, the struggle to delineate between the two is part of where the enjoyment lies within cartoons. Thinking like an adult and caring about the difference between fantasy and reality is a process and it is possible that stories that blur the boundary are particularly appealing for this reason. Rather than worry that young children cannot tell the difference between fact and fiction, we need to recognize that popular culture can be used to help negotiate the boundaries between the two.

When parents fail to fear cartoon violence, some researchers argue that the parents themselves must be "desensitized" to violence.[14] I'd rather think that parents and the public are better able to recognize the capabilities of their children and that unlike kids, some researchers take cartoons too literally and ignore their unique contexts.

Dangerous Cartoons?

While violence is often central to adult fears concerning cartoons, adults are also concerned about the way some cartoons challenge their omnipotence. Some fear cartoons that challenge adult authority will serve as bad role models for kids. In many cartoons, children are often central characters who know more than their elders do, which challenges the sanctity of the adult world. We will see that it is not the lack of reality that often bothers many adults, but the fact that shows like *The Simpsons* and *South Park* speak many plain truths about family life and life from a child's perspective. Episodes regularly focus on Homer Simpson's lack of parenting skills and inability to meet children's needs. These programs reveal that adult power and childhood innocence can be illusory.

Animated programs such as *The Simpsons, Beavis and Butt-head,* and *South Park* have raised ire because they are rife with social criticism and challenge the adult view of the world. But rather than address the provocative critiques of childhood, adolescence, and family life these programs offer, we prefer to complain about how children may imitate the characters. The truth is these cartoons challenge the complacent way we think about children and society.

In contrast to these three cartoons are the animated programs that present an idealized version of both childhood and American society. The Disney genre, although at this point certainly not limited to films produced only by Disney, presents life from a traditional perspective where "other" is always the villain and femininity is best achieved through the love of a man.[15] Aside from concerns about violent content, such films have received only a murmur of public protest, and the public brings children en masse to see them. I'm not suggesting that parents add Disney films to their taboo list, but instead we need to critically address how xenophobia, racism, and sexism are reflected in many films of this genre. Lest you think I'm advocating forming a brigade of the politically correct police, I think that it is important to watch these films and begin to talk about the nature of power and inequality in contemporary America. Set in the past and in "a land far, far away," these modern-day fairy tales are begging for critical attention. Rather than assuming that these issues "just go over their heads," it is also crucial to discuss these issues with young people. In the last part of this chapter I discuss how films like *Aladdin, Beauty and the Beast,* and *Tarzan* naturalize power in terms of race, nationality, and gender.

Role Models for Bad Behavior?

Maybe it's because cartoons are so associated with childhood that they are frequent targets of criticism. *The Simpsons* was initially met with a great deal of concern largely because Bart talked back to his parents and teachers and bullied his sister. *Beavis and Butt-head* was even more iconoclastic and the program was accused of inciting kids to put animals in microwaves and light things on fire. Most recently, *South Park*'s foul-mouthed elementary school boys have yielded complaints based on the fear that kids will imitate the characters' creative use of obscenities.

A closer look at the fear of these shows reveals more than just a concern about copycat behavior. These programs are not necessarily intended for children, but they engage issues of childhood that challenge the myths and ideas of what children are and should be. Cartoons like *South Park, Beavis and Butt-head,* and *The Simpsons* have elicited both praise and criticism. While many observers note the strong elements of social satire present within each, concern has swirled around the fear that children who watch will imitate the central characters. It should be no wonder that parents would be worried, since characters on these shows question and challenge authority, especially the authority of adults over children. While it may seem on the surface that critics are really upset about smart-mouthed kids, it is the subversive nature of these programs that make some adults nervous. Just as business owners often seek to discredit union organizers, adults may subconsciously want Bart, Beavis, and the boys of South Park far away from their children lest they question adult power.

South Park

We like to believe that children are pure, innocent, and without guile until corrupted by adults (or the media). Ideally, we'd often like to keep elementary school children untainted by the adult world. *South Park* explodes this fallacy by showing a version of childhood that is raw and uncensored. These kids are sexually curious, although not necessarily clear on the facts. Episodes where the boys try to become lesbians or eagerly await their first periods demonstrate that their awareness of adult life is sometimes murky.

The program debuted on Comedy Central in 1997 and the usual suspects complained about the characters' bad language and disregard for authority. Detractors called the show "vile trash" and claimed that the program is evidence of "the collapse of standards."[16] But other critics recognized that this show often contains well-crafted cultural satire.[17] "Its creators are not simply out to offend people but are exploring the surreal terrors of childhood," wrote James Collins in *Time* magazine.[18] Rick Marin of *Newsweek* argued that the show is firmly grounded in reality and that hoping to maintain childhood innocence "is like squeezing toothpaste back into the tube."[19] Cultural critics within academia have taken notice as well. Helen Nixon, of the University of South Australia, asserts that the program "requires serious consideration for the significant questions it raises about the relations between childhood and adulthood."[20]

Although the program is intended for adult audiences and airs on cable at night, parents seem to fear that young children would be drawn to this cartoon and repeat the bad language. However, 77 percent of the audience is estimated to be over eighteen, and less than 5 percent is believed to be younger than eleven, in contrast to the belief stated in *The American Enterprise* that *South Park* is "The most popular comedy show among kids today."[21] The real danger here goes beyond language: perhaps adults really fear that children will learn that adult authority is often arbitrary. The show serves as a powerful critique of childhood, particularly addressing the struggle children face with adults. Helen Nixon notes that "Adults' patronizing attitude towards children, as well as their blatant hypocrisy is . . . glaringly exposed by *South Park*."[22] *South Park* reminds us that simply increasing adult control over children is tempting but impractical; that in many cases adults are well-intentioned but clueless about the realities of childhood.

For instance, one episode deals with a common childhood experience: getting the chicken pox. The boys' parents decide it would be best for the kids to catch the disease at once and get it over with. The parents go out of their way to expose their respective children, and one by one they get sick. When the boys learn their parents conspired to make them ill they band together to get their parents sick—with herpes. The episode challenges conventional wisdom that parents always know best.

From a child's perspective, adults just don't always get it, which is revealed in episode after episode as the boys deal with their parents and teachers. They do not set out to embarrass authority figures; it is the adults who make themselves look foolish. An episode featuring a

disabled boy clearly demonstrates how adults, no matter how well in-
tentioned, misunderstand him and children in general. Timmy, the new
boy in a wheelchair, is apparently mentally challenged and only able to
say his name. He is sent to the principal's office for "acting out" when
the school counselor realizes there is probably something wrong with
Timmy. He is sent to a psychologist to be tested—for attention deficit
disorder (which they diagnose by reading an entire novel and then ask
ultra-specific questions about what a character said in any given chapter). When Timmy fails the test, it is confirmed: he has ADD and is ex-
cused from homework assignments. Of course, when the other kids
hear about it they all insist they have ADD, are tested in similar fashion, and are all ultimately prescribed Ritalin.

The irony here runs deep: not only did the adults fail to see
Timmy's obvious mental and physical impairments, but the definition
of normative children's behavior (sitting and listening to an entire
novel and remembering specific details) is completely unrealistic. The
Ritalin did the trick: the children began behaving just like adults.

This is indeed a powerful critique of adult-child relations, where
adult behavior is considered ideal, and child behavior pathological.
Critics have charged ADD is an over-diagnosed disorder, the result of
over-crowded classrooms and the failure of our educational system to
provide adequate channels for youthful energy.[23] Funding for physical
education, music, and the arts have been cut while diagnoses for behavior disorders like ADD have risen. One has not necessarily caused
the other, but we have shifted responsibility away from the problems
within our social institutions to children themselves. I am not denying
that the disorder is real, only that it is a label all too easily applied to
children when they don't conform to adult expectations.

Honesty is a major issue between adults and children, but usually
we think only in terms of kids learning to tell adult authority figures
the truth. But how many lies do parents tell children? An episode
about the tooth fairy confronts the reality of adults' dishonesty and the
impact this has on children. The show begins with one of the boys losing a tooth and getting money from the "tooth fairy." He then reports to
his friends that if they can come up with a bunch of teeth they can finally buy the video game console they have all wanted. They go about
stealing teeth until the boy's mother runs out of money. One by one,
each boy learns that his parents have been lying about the tooth fairy,
which makes them question everything their parents told them, including what they have learned about religion. Cultural anthropologist

Cindy Dell Clark writes of the contradictions surrounding myths adults encourage children to believe during childhood.[24] For example, believing in the tooth fairy connotes innocence and gullibility, traits that kids are encouraged to have yet are degraded for possessing. Adults believe that these falsehoods will enrich the experience of childhood, but it is often adults who benefit most by using their power to define reality, and it is adults who are often saddened when their children no longer believe. Clark also notes that religious faith is based on similar principles, but adults who have faith are not necessarily considered naïve or immature.

South Park demonstrates truths about childhood and adult power. It reveals that adults may be doing what they truly think is best for children, but ultimately their actions serve *adult* needs just as much as (if not more than) as children's. And *South Park* reminds us that although adults may wish that children spoke no obscenities, the reality is they sometimes do. Nor is the world of childhood devoid of sexual curiosity; it is not the pure, sanitized world that adults would rather it be. *South Park* challenges the illusion of childhood innocence and adult competence. This is what bothers its critics: the real fear is that children will see this critique of childhood and recognize themselves and their own struggles with adults.

South Park creators take a sardonic approach to the show's criticism. The "warning label" at the start of each show suggests it is not appropriate "for anyone." Their 1999 feature film highlights this issue as well, as the boys sneak into an R-rated movie and continually repeat the bad language they hear in the film. A 2001 episode also parodied the criticism that kids will mimic language from television. In this episode a "must see" television program promises to feature a four-letter word typically censored from the airwaves. Both children and adults eagerly anticipate this "event," as kids gather around living room TV sets together while adults pile into the local bar to watch. One boy complains that his father wants to watch the show with him to "explain what it all means" to him. But the joke is on dad; we as audience members know that this is clearly not a new word for the boy or his peers. By including this word over and over (even including a counter to tally the number of times the word was used) the show's creators taunt their critics. Towards the end of the episode overuse of the word has unleashed evil spirits and the world nearly ends, which the boys are central in saving. Producers lampoon their critics while the kids are portrayed as the voice of reason.

Beavis and Butt-head

While the boys from *South Park* are foul-mouthed but well-intentioned, Beavis and Butt-head are every parent's nightmare. They are vulgar, rude, and don't believe in anything, including each other. They spend their days insulting and often brutalizing each other and everyone else. They have a deep disrespect for all authority, be it their reactionary neighbor or their ultra-sensitive liberal teacher—to the boys they are all ridiculous. Beavis and Butt-head's only interest is in watching music videos (except the ones that "suck"), trying to "score" with "chicks," and in early episodes, hurting animals and lighting things on fire.

Beavis and Butt-head embody our deepest fears for the next generation: they are slackers who have no respect for living things, property, or any form of authority. They have no future and are proud of it.[25] School is a big joke, as is their fast food job. Any responsibility they are given, whether it is to mind the store or do yard work for their neighbor, ultimately leads to disaster with no real consequences. Unlike *South Park*, which reveals unspoken truths about childhood, *Beavis and Butt-head* portrays adolescence at its worst, a caricature of adult fears that kids are amoral loafers with no direction.

So why was this show so popular with young people during its MTV run from 1993–1997 and so hated by many adults? Beavis and Butt-head's disdain for authority serves as a powerful critique of adult-run institutions such as school and low-wage work, where young people are often challenged to find meaning and relevance. Parental authority doesn't exist for Beavis or Butt-head; their parents are all but absent, with the exception of an occasional misogynist remark about the other's mother. The boys are free to do whatever they want, including sit in front of the TV all day or wreak havoc in their neighborhood. While certainly most young people would not consider either boy to be a role model, their bold contempt for and freedom from adult authority strike a powerful chord.

The anti-establishment themes are exactly what trouble the show's critics. Beavis and Butt-head display disdain for the institutions adults want young people to buy into and fear will collapse without the next generation's support. In the show's early days, much attention was paid to every kid who played with matches or hurt an animal. Of course I do not want to downplay the seriousness of either of these things, but direct causal links to this show were often made with little investigation. These connections serve to discredit the show and to negate the cultural criticism embedded within the lead characters' antics.

For one, Beavis and Butt-head's working-class world is one of downward mobility, featuring declines in real wages and job security. The future they are supposed to be committing themselves to holds no such commitment to them. The boys are all but abandoned, first by their parents and then by the social institutions that fail to engage them or offer a future worth striving for.

As a society we'd rather not critically engage these ideas and explore the effects of deindustrialization and the globalization of the labor force on the working class. We are instead consumed by the fear that kids will adopt Beavis and Butt-head's language (assuming they don't use it already) and bad attitudes or commit acts of violence. It is far easier to blame a cartoon than it is to explore the underlying conditions that explain *why* young people may feel alienated. Doing the hard work of examining society's structural problems is unappealing; criticizing economic conditions and power arrangements is sometimes considered un-American, especially in the post–September 11 era. Beavis and Butt-head present adults' worst fears about adolescents and invite us to address the structural factors that may lead to youth apathy. Nonetheless, it is our tendency to blame the messenger and demand the message go away rather than to examine where it *really* comes from.

The Simpsons

The Simpsons has become a widely celebrated series, but when the show first became popular in the early 1990s there were lots of criticisms. During a 1992 speech, former President George H. W. Bush proclaimed, "We need a nation closer to the Waltons than the Simpsons."[26] Parents and educators expressed their disapproval of Bart, fearing that children would revere him as a role model. A school in South Carolina was to be named "Springfield Elementary" until it was discovered that Springfield was the name of Bart Simpson's school.[27] In short, the Simpson family was considered the prime example of everything wrong with American families at the century's end. The kids talked back to their parents and teachers and challenged authority during a time when politicians spoke profusely about the need to reaffirm "family values," which *The Simpsons* allegedly betrayed. Critic Frank McConnell noted that *The Simpsons* "deconstruct the myth of the happy family wisely and miraculously leave what is real and valuable about the myth unscathed."[28] If we take a closer look at the Simpsons, we see a two-parent family where the mother stays home with the kids while the father works in the paid labor force. Wasn't this Newt and company's dream? Well, not exactly. *The Simpsons* serve as a powerful critique of every American social institution, including commerce, government, religion, education, and the beloved family. What the critics didn't get when they worried that kids would become smart-asses like Bart was that we are *all* Simpsons. Springfield is Anywhere, USA, and as much as we hate to admit it, real families resemble the Simpsons much more than the Waltons.

The Simpsons contains elements of family life usually left hidden from the public eye. Homer is often portrayed as an overweight slob who rejoices in his own laziness. In a first-season episode, the Simpson family is about to go to the company picnic at the boss's house. Homer is apprehensive about his family, fearing that they will embarrass him in front of his boss and co-workers. Of course he is right. When told to make themselves at home, Bart comments, "Did you hear that, Dad? You can lay around in your underwear and scratch yourself." This is not your father's television family—the Simpsons display the secret unmentionable truths about family life.

Disappointed in their "performance" as a family, Homer decides that they need to attend family therapy. Within the therapy session, the Simpsons have no problem expressing their hostility towards each other. The therapist coaches them to act out on their anger, saying that instead of hurting each other emotionally, they should learn to hurt each other physically. Family violence, often an unspeakable facet of American life, is ironically encouraged on *The Simpsons*. During the Cosby era, television families might have expressed hostility towards each other through witty repartee and an occasional put-down, but here anger is right in the open. The Simpsons' hostility reveals the hidden hostility within many families. As daughter Lisa says in this episode, "the sad truth is all families are like us."

The Simpsons demonstrates the irony inherent in American family life. Within the Simpson family, the parents are not portrayed as role models for their children. In fact, it is often unclear whether it is Homer who imitates Bart's actions or vice versa. In a 1995 episode, both father and son end up getting arrested by security guards while visiting a theme park (a Disney parody called "Itchy and Scratchy Land") for kicking the mascots. We see Bart doing this first and Homer then copies him. When Bart finds Homer in the detention area, Bart assumes an understanding but parental tone with his father, saying, "There's just no way to resist, is there?" Later, during the theme park parade, the programmed robots begin to attack. When Homer mistakenly thinks an aggressive robot is "coming on to him," daughter Lisa is the voice of reason. As he avoids the robot's swinging ax, Homer yells, "Don't contradict your elders!"

This is a bold statement about the American family, where we assume that the parents "parent" the children and impart their values and wisdom. However, *The Simpsons* expose the reality that sometimes children hold wisdom that their parents do not. It is clear why parents would be uneasy with this instability, which exposes how tenuous parental power over children really is.

Within the travel brochure of Itchy and Scratchy Land, such wholesome activities as bowling and dancing on "Parents' Island" are contrasted with "over 100 bars and saloons" and "a world-class chemical dependency center." This description is reminiscent of the contradictions that exist within "family" entertainment (like Las Vegas or Anheuser-Busch theme parks). Marge is unsure about not only Itchy and Scratchy Land, but about a family vacation in general, where she is often embarrassed and returns "more miserable than when (we) left." All promise that this vacation will be different, or, as Homer says, "we'll all agree to disband and join other families," to which they all joyfully agree.

Within the Simpson family parents don't always know best; they are fallible and not all-knowing by any means. In fact, the children often know more than their parents. This is the real problem detractors probably had with *The Simpsons*: through satire they reveal that the differences between adults and children are not as absolute as we adults often insist. Adults appear incompetent in all aspects of social life. The mayor is a corrupt womanizer, and the police force is comprised of lazy donut eaters, but the electorate doesn't seem to mind and is easily manipulated into supporting leaders' whims, such as a town monorail. Religion is not immune to the scathing criticism of the show's creators, as the faithful are portrayed as daffy or hypocritical. Industry is also a central target, embodied by the callous and greedy Mr. Burns. His nuclear power plant pollutes the environment and his safety inspector (Homer Simpson) is totally inept. Mr. Burns fires employees for sport—job security is a joke, and there is no union to speak of. *The Simpsons* also cast a critical eye on education. Along with families, the institutions created to serve children's needs are clearly far from ideal. Burned-out, incompetent administrators and teachers who seem to dislike children run the local school. The "educational" system provides adults with jobs and a place to send children to keep them out of sight. Brainy Lisa Simpson highlights this problem: her intelligence does not elicit praise from teachers but instead annoyance.

The Simpsons provide social criticism at its most subversive: the program is enjoyable yet challenges us to rethink core social institutions like education, business, government, religion, and the family. Perhaps most dangerous, *The Simpsons* reveals that adult power is sometimes arbitrary and misguided. Father (or mother or any other adult) doesn't always know best. Who wants their kids to find that out? The truth is that eventually we all learn that parents and other adults are not demigods.

In recent years *The Simpsons'* critics have either been won over or have simply faded away. Both critical and entertaining, *The Simpsons* takes on the absurdities of contemporary American life. The program has become the longest-running animated series and is also shown in syndication, triumphing over the "family values" movement that demanded that families resemble a very narrow model that most of us can't (or don't want to) live up to.

Dangerous Cartoons? The Disney Curriculum

In contrast to the three cartoons that have garnered public criticism and concern, the Disney genre is widely considered acceptable fare for children and has generated little public concern. There certainly have been groups critical of the portrayal of Native Americans in *Pocahontas* and of Middle Easterners in *Aladdin*, but by and large the Disney-style animated feature is seen as child-friendly material.[29] In direct contrast to the cartoons discussed in the previous section, Disney-style animation tends to support the dominant view of the world. In the wonderful world of Disney, Euro-whites are the civilized heroes and men the protectors and defenders of women. Disney-style films are often set in another time and place, which decontextualizes their troubling representations of race, gender, and nationality. These movies are considered acceptable for children because they don't rock the boat or threaten the ideology prevalent in middle-class America that power is distributed fairly.

Thinking back to classic Disney films like *Snow White* (1937) and *Cinderella* (1950), we might argue that the traditional messages about gender clearly mirrored the times in which they were produced. In each, the love of a powerful, handsome (and almost always white) man saves the beautiful heroine, who is often of a lower social status than he is. Now we might look back and say, boy, we have come a long way. Women don't need to wait for men to provide them with a new life. We can look at pre–civil rights America and might conclude that the white-washed world of the classic films reflected old ways of thinking, that we are more enlightened now, that the colonialism reflected in *The Jungle Book*, for instance, is a thing of the past.

But a closer look at contemporary Disney-style films reveals that things have not changed as much as we would like to think. These stories are still told through the lenses of Euro-whites; the presumptions about gender and nationality are more complex but still intact. Why is it we cry foul when programs for children challenge the status quo but bring children in droves to the films that have racist and sexist undertones?

Some of you are probably thinking that people like me read too much into these films, that we should just relax and enjoy them. The irony here is that the very same people who choose to overlook issues of inequality are often the same ones who fear that children are strongly affected by language and violence and that kids are prone to copying what they see.

Before we go on, let me make one thing clear: I don't hate Disney-style films nor am I advocating a boycott or censorship in any way. I like some of these films (and by coincidence happen to be wearing a Mickey Mouse T-shirt as I write this) and feel a sense of nostalgia when I watch them. They are a journey into another world, or so it seems. So having put that out there, I think we have a responsibility to critically analyze traces of racism or sexism when we see them. Sometimes people believe that to both criticize something and at the same time enjoy it makes one a hypocrite. I disagree. It is dangerous to only criticize what we dislike and let things we enjoy slip away without scrutiny. So the next section is not a way to bash the films I discuss, but is instead intended to reveal how contemporary films contain some problematic content that goes largely unchallenged by the public. Instead of worrying what popular culture may do to us, we can use it as a guide to look at our society more critically.

When I teach about issues of race, gender, and nationality in my sociology courses, people who have never critically explored such topics are often resistant. Americans are taught that we just don't talk about these things, that to criticize is to wholly denounce. I mention this because some of you may react the same way to the next section as I discuss troubling representations. Keep in mind I am not suggesting that children or adults blindly absorb the content and adopt racist or sexist views. Instead, my goal is to point out that the children's entertainment many adults support serves to uphold ideologies of inequality.

Race and nationality are often a big part of these films set in "faraway" lands. How are different ethnic groups portrayed in contemporary Disney-style films? Within these films there is a consistent pattern of privileging a white, European perspective of history, and Disney's "new" heroines tend to reflect a rather traditional understanding of gender.

Consuming Innocence

Whereas *The Simpsons* and company challenge conventional thinking about childhood, the Disney-style films embrace sentimental beliefs about childhood and innocence. In fact *this* is what Disney is selling; innocence and nostalgia for an idealized past are the real products we are consuming when we visit Disneyland or see a Disney-style film.[30] The stories may change and the settings may differ, but the common thread that invites us to this familiar world is the ideal version of our "small world." Nostalgia is big business; I confess that I am just as likely to be lured into this fantasy world as the next person. Good and evil are crystal clear and happiness is all but guaranteed upon admission. I have fond childhood memories of visiting Disneyland and watching the old Disney classics on Saturday afternoons in the school gym during the winter (no doubt to give parents the afternoon off). As an adult I have visited Disneyland several times, and once even attended a bachelorette party there for a friend giving childhood a final sendoff. The Disney appeal includes the opportunity to visit a lost childhood as well as the comfort of knowing that all will work out in the end.

So while I'm critical of the sanitized reality Disney presents, I certainly acknowledge that this fantasy world is highly alluring. Innocence is a powerful hook, and innocence is largely why these films seem to be "good" for kids, in contrast to media content that appears to challenge innocence. Part of Disney's phenomenal success is based on its reliance on our desire to maintain the myth of childhood innocence and cling to illusions about the past, frequently by revising it. In the Disney version of history, good always beats evil, and every story contains an adventure. While there may be a few bad apples, Euro-whites are presented as mostly benevolent visitors to the "exotic" lands they encounter. Love conquers all in Disney's history, proving that people from different backgrounds can peacefully coexist so long as there is romance between a beautiful heroine and a strong hero. Historical truth is incidental, as films like *Pocahontas* and *The Road to El Dorado* have been criticized for rearranging facts to create an Anglo view of the past.[31] However incorrect, representations such as this serve a powerful purpose: they justify European colonialism and dominance, specifically male dominance. Explorers refine savages, so European power appears natural and for the greater good. Many Disney films are set in the past to add to the element of fantasy. But if a utopian world is what producers hope to portray, why not set the films in the future instead of rewriting the past? The answer is these films are by their very nature political and reactionary, implying that we should use the past to guide our fantasies of the future. By setting films in the past or using animals instead of humans, difference is romanticized and male dominance appears natural. Although we think Disney films are set anywhere but here, Disney films tell us a lot about the fantasies about American society we hope to pass on to children. Difference either creates romantic tension between lead characters, is completely ignored, or, in the worst instances, power inequities are portrayed as natural.

Recasting Race

Race remains a difficult topic in contemporary American public discourse. When racial minorities point out their experiences of inequality, they are often accused of being overly sensitive or of being stuck in the past.[32] The Disney genre likewise treads lightly on the issues of race and nationality, using subtle markers to connote difference. The use of European voices, for instance, are used to imply high status in films like *The Aristocats*, *Tarzan*, and *Beauty and the Beast*. *Aladdin* may be set in the Middle East and its characters similar in skin tone, but heroes speak with American accents, while villains have Middle Eastern accents and stereotypical facial features, like heavy beards and large noses.[33]

The spirit of adventure within Disney films is often drawn from the European history of colonialism without any mention of the genocide or slavery that often came with "exploration." The 1999 remake of *Tarzan* is a great example. Historian John Newsinger argues that the film is a powerful metaphor of the Disney corporation's (and the American) goal to colonize world markets.[34] Within the film, Africa is portrayed as an animal kingdom without humans until Europeans arrive. Tarzan is called a wild man by the friendly and curious British researchers who want nothing more than to see gorillas (which they alternately refer to as monkeys and apes—for researchers, they don't seem to know much about their subject). They observe Tarzan's family, yet it is ultimately the British who "civilize" Tarzan by teaching him about Western culture and how to speak English. For Disney, becoming human means becoming European.

In the end, Tarzan's world welcomes the European visitors when they unite against the evil Clayton, who hopes to cage and sell the animals to Europeans. This allusion to the enslavement and transport of Africans is portrayed as something perpetrated by a few rogue explorers rather than a state-sanctioned policy. Jane and her father decide to stay in Africa, because she and Tarzan are in love. Since love conquers all in Disney's reality, they swing happily together off into the sunset.

Stories like this, which sanitize the history of European and North American brutality to the African continent, are more than benign fairy tales. Like *Pocahontas* in 1995, these stories justify European domination of native peoples. Sure, documentaries of slavery or genocide don't make for great fantasy entertainment. But we have to question why we prefer to lie about history in the stories we tell children. Wrapped up in childhood innocence is an attempt to create the illusion that the past was innocent as well. Again, if fantasy is really the goal, why not tell stories based on the future rather than the past? We use history in this way to convince ourselves that the past, like childhood, was a time of innocence. Of course we are wrong on both counts.

You've Come a Long Way, Baby?

Disney heroines of old like Snow White and Cinderella need men on white horses to rescue them and present them with the ultimate triumph: marriage. But that was then, right? Before the second wave of feminism, before women's numbers in the paid labor force rose, we might have expected this sort of resolution. A closer look at Disney's contemporary heroines reveals that little has really changed in the way that girls and women are portrayed. For instance, *The Little Mermaid*'s Ariel must surrender her voice for the love of a man. Clearly it is not necessary for a woman to have ideas of her own here, as the prince falls in love with her appearance. *The Aristocats* features a rough and tumble tomcat that must save the demure damsel cat in distress. Sound familiar?

The troubling aspect of these "new" heroines is that on the surface they appear to be independent women, but they are equally as dependent on male characters as their predecessors—a confusing message to kids whose own moms likely work outside the home. Take *Beauty and the Beast*'s Belle. She appears to be different: she loves to read and rejects the handsome yet pompous Gaston's marriage proposals and proclaims she wants more from life. So far so good. But even in her rebuffs of Gaston she remains polite, even as his propositions grow more and more threatening. She tries to let him down easy by saying she doesn't deserve him and she never directly rejects him, remaining a "nice" girl. But the most problematic element of the film begins when she becomes the Beast's prisoner and somehow is charmed by her captor. During the time she is in captivity she manages to tame the Beast, implying that the love of a good woman can turn a man from abusive and violent into a big teddy bear that just needs to be understood. This tale looks like an allegory of how any abusive man can change if a woman just loves him enough. His behavior is *her* responsibility; the whole plot turns around her saying "I love you" to transform the Beast into a handsome prince.

This film may as well be subtitled "Smart Women, Foolish Choices." But in the wonderful world of Disney this is par for the course: be nice, loving, and above all beautiful (in a European sort of way), and you will be rewarded with a man and riches. One way these films explain the reactionary view of gender is that they are set in the past. In this past older women are mostly absent (as in *Beauty and the Beast*, *Aladdin*, and *Pocahontas*) or they serve as the nemesis to the young and beautiful (*Snow White*, *The Little Mermaid*, and *Cinderella*). Sure, there are men who are demeaning to women, but there are plenty of kind gentlemen and handsome princes to save women from these scoundrels. Of course the realities of women's disenfranchisement are absent: no scarlet letters, no legal beatings, rapes, or murders, as was often the case when women challenged patriarchy throughout history. In this past women knew their place and if they played their cards right could end up in the lap of luxury. Beauty is bestowed on the good, ugliness on the evil. Male dominance seems natural and without negative consequences for "good" women.

Using animals is another way to present patriarchy as natural.[35] In *Tarzan*, the mother ape is terrified of her domineering mate, the king of the apes. His rule is justified throughout the film, even his dominance over Tarzan, who inherits his position of power when the king is slain. *The Lion King* features a similar power structure. Women with power, if you can find them, are portrayed as evil and must be destroyed to protect the young heroine. Even Jasmine, the princess in *Aladdin*, has little power. Her only freedom is that she gets to choose who she marries, but she cannot choose a commoner or simply opt not to marry at all.

Aladdin, a Disney-animated film released in 1992, was widely successful, becoming the most profitable animated film of its time. The brief synopsis of the film on the back cover of the video case describes Princess Jasmine, Aladdin's love interest, as a heroine of the Nineties. She is described as strong-willed and almost given feminist qualities within this description, yet in the film she resembles heroines of old, waiting for her "prince" to come and rescue her and using traditional feminine wiles to get her out of trouble.

Aladdin takes place in a Middle Eastern locale, and its characters are constructed to fit within the American stereotype of life in the "barbaric" Middle East. Images of sword swallowing, snake charming, beds of nails, and walking atop hot coals are introduced within the opening minutes of the film. Perhaps by bracketing this setting as foreign and "barbaric" (*Aladdin*'s 1992 release date coincides with the end of the Gulf War) there is an implication that images of gender within this film are foreign and somehow different from the Western world.

The narrative focuses on the adventures of Aladdin, a young man who must fend for himself on the streets of Agraba. He meets Princess Jasmine, the only main female character in the film, when she finds herself in trouble after naively stealing a piece of fruit for a poor child.

Jasmine is in the marketplace because she has sought freedom from her life within the castle, where she has been forced to choose a husband. Her choice, however, is highly constrained by the fact that she *must* marry a prince. Jasmine's need for a husband is the most pressing matter of business for her father, the Sultan. After discussing the urgency of this matter with Jasmine, the Sultan jokingly tells Raja, Jasmine's pet tiger, "Allah forbid you should have any daughters," lest they give him the same trouble Jasmine has been giving the Sultan.

When Aladdin and Jasmine finally meet in the marketplace, he is immediately struck by her beauty and is quick to come to her rescue. He saves Jasmine from having her hand cut off by an angry merchant by insisting that she is his crazy sister. He remains her protector, lecturing that Agraba is a dangerous place, cautioning her to watch her head and helping her walk. Both proclaim that what they really want is freedom, for Aladdin the freedom from poverty, and for Jasmine, the freedom to marry for love (as if this is the only freedom women really need).

When Jasmine returns to the castle, the necessity of marriage intensifies. The Sultan consults with the villainous Jafar to solve the problem of Jasmine's necessary marriage. Jafar puts a spell on the Sultan, who agrees that Jasmine will marry Jafar if a suitable prince does not appear soon. Aladdin then shows up as Prince Ali to claim her, but Jasmine exclaims, "I am not a prize to be won!" Yet she is clearly impressed by his charm, magic carpet, and his ability to "show her the world."

Jasmine is later used by Jafar to lure Aladdin to his destruction. Jafar turns Jasmine into a harem girl and threatens to hit her when she disobeys him. Once again, Jasmine relies on old-fashioned feminine wiles (speaking seductively, touching suggestively) to distract Jafar so that Aladdin may come to her rescue. As a reward for his loyalty, the Sultan allows Aladdin to marry the princess.

This is most certainly not a new brand of fairy tale. Female characters are visibly absent from the narrative and appear only incidentally as harem girls or lusty overweight women who pose yet another threat to Aladdin. Jasmine claims to be fighting for her freedom, but her only challenge to the status quo is that her husband need not be a prince. The fact that she must marry by a certain age or at all is never questioned. Her defense mechanisms, feigning insanity and sexuality, are successful in saving Jasmine and more importantly, Aladdin.

In the end of nearly every Disney film love conquers all. The happy resolution of the conflict is heightened by the promise of living happily every after. *Pocahontas*, a notable exception, ends with the heroine letting her love John Smith leave for England alone, but she does this out of her devotion to her people, not herself. She is deeply saddened by this decision, and not necessarily emancipated.[36] Female characters in the Disney genre basically exist to fall in love; once it works out, the story ends. I admit this is an extremely satisfying experience, to enjoy the resolve of tension and the promise of never-ending love. So while everyone loves a happy ending, we can certainly see that Disney's heroines are not new at all, and don't reflect the reality (or necessarily the fantasies) of most contemporary women.

My point here is not that children shouldn't watch these fairy tales or that Disney films should adopt a *cinema verité* style and show life's ugly side. We embrace these films for children (and ourselves) precisely because they are fantasies. The question is, *whose* fantasies are these? The Disney genre tells stories about a glorious past with no problems that couldn't be solved by a valiant hero with a heart of gold. Poverty is just one's lot in life. Besides, a crafty hero like Aladdin can overcome anything with wit and determination. There are no problems that love and hard work can't solve.

Disney films serve as cheerleaders for the American Dream, that personal struggles can be overcome with love and determination, and that leaders who are unkind will be overthrown by the benevolent. Relations of power in regards to race, nationality, and gender in this version of reality are considered inevitable, occasionally humorous, and in the end for the best. The heroes always rise and villains always fall. This is the fantasy of social stagnation, where things remain as they always have been and the past is always better than the present. The films don't criticize or satirize the present, don't threaten to shake things up. Not a surprise, considering the multibillion-dollar Disney empire has much to lose by any such challenge. Unlike the cartoons we love to hate, the Disney version of the world is embraced for children because it tells us everything is fine the way it is. These cartoons reinforce our fantasy of childhood innocence.

Rethinking Cartoon Danger: That's Not All, Folks

Films like *Aladdin* and *Beauty and the Beast* don't create gender inequality, but do help to reinforce traditional beliefs about gender and relationships. Yet animation that critically challenges the status quo, particularly relations of power between adults and children, is viewed as inappropriate if it threatens dominant ways of thinking. Childhood innocence is exposed as a myth in *South Park*, and teen alienation in *Beavis and Butt-head* reveals the disconnection between young people, adults, and adult-run social institutions. *The Simpsons* details how parents and adults are flawed, even if well-intentioned.

These snapshots of social criticism threaten the way we think about ourselves and American society, challenging what we take for granted about children, teens, and families. Yet the stories that sentimentalize childhood and power inequities are largely considered unproblematic, if not preferred entertainment for kids. We need to take a closer look at both of these categories. There is danger in whitewashing the past and glorifying a history that was neither pure nor innocent. When we choose to see both the past and childhood as an innocent fantasy, we ignore the struggles of children past and present. Cartoons are fantasies, but feeding on illusions of the past and present provide the biggest threat: they enable us to engage in collective delusion. Cartoons are an important part of children's media culture. Typically, though, we tend to stop at violence when thinking about cartoon content, worrying about behavioral effects rather than the meanings that kids make of this childhood staple.

5

Fear of Video Games

The Blamed Games

Perhaps more than any other medium, video games were singled out as the most important media connection to the Columbine killings. The shooters were allegedly aficionados of "Doom," a game where the heavily armed protagonist stops demons from taking over the earth, and had used their classmates' images during their play target practice. John Leo of *U.S. News & World Report* even described the murder scene as staged like a video game. According to Leo, their "cool and casual cruelty" pointed to "sensibilities created by the modern video kill games."[1] Leo concluded that "If we want to avoid more Littleton-style massacres, we will begin taking the social effects of the killing games more seriously."[2]

Others also found the connection between video-game playing and the shooting compelling. After all, the shooters loved video games and on close-circuit video they looked as if they were dispassionately playing a game, methodically taking out anyone in their scope. It was easy to jump to conclusions, especially since concern about video games had been brewing since the early 1980s when gaming meant Frogger leaping in and out of traffic or Pac-man devouring innocent little dots in his way. Adult concern had grown as graphics became even more realistic and the video game industry grew to its multibillion-dollar status during the 1990s. Fears emerged that the time some young people spent playing and the frustration felt when losing was indicative of a new phenomenon: video game addiction.[3] The Columbine killings seemed to prove what many had feared: video games were training a new generation of obsessed and desensitized psychopaths.

Many of the Columbine victims' families, robbed of their day in court when the killers committed suicide, filed lawsuits against those who seemed like the next in line of responsibility, the video game manufacturers. Claiming that the games led to the shootings by "making violence pleasurable and disconnected from reality," a five-billion-dollar lawsuit was filed against Eidos, maker of games like "Sword of Berserk" and "Urban Chaos."[4] Another suit alleged that the creators were responsible because they knew that violence would result from playing the games. Both suits were thrown out and never went to trial, but the belief that video games can be "dress rehearsals" for the real thing lingers.[5] Curiously, the same fervor was never directed against gun manufacturers, whose products will clearly kill or maim when used correctly. On the contrary, a bill breezed through Congress in early 2000 that made it more difficult to sue gun manufacturers, a victory for the powerful gun lobby.

The belief that video games create real-life killers exists in part due to a book that made the media rounds in 1999 called *Stop Teaching Our Kids to Kill*, by retired Army Lieutenant Colonel David Grossman. In his book, Grossman argued that video games serve as training for killing, similar to military-style preparation. Grossman's take-no-prisoners speaking style made for good sound bites and fed the video game fear. "There's a generation growing up that the media has cocked and primed for draconian action and a degree of bloodlust that we haven't seen since the Roman children sat in the Colosseum and cheered as the Christians were killed," he warned.[6] While I agree with Grossman that video games are skill-building simulations that strengthen hand-eye coordination and build quick reflexes that could make them better shooters, the claim that video games create the *desire* to actually kill a live human is not supported by evidence. If this were the case we would see far more of the millions of video game users become violent instead of an extreme minority. Grossman's argument is compelling because we have been primed to believe that the media made the Columbine killers and other school shooters do what they did.

Video game players tend to be young males (many of whom are adults), and many games do simulate violence. Whereas television and movies have traditionally been criticized as "passive" mediums, video games are instead interactive, and this interactivity is perceived as a threat to create both violent players and violent people once the console is turned off. I have to say, the violent content of many of these games is shocking, and we ought to take a step back and ask why simulated killing is frequently a young male pastime.

But even though many people are disgusted by game content, scientific proof of a causal relationship between video games and violence has not been clearly demonstrated. Reviews of research appear regularly in scholarly journals, and even researchers can't agree that video games can be linked with actual violence. Although a 1998 review in the journal *Aggressive and Violent Behavior* declared that a "preponderance of evidence" suggests video games lead to aggression, a review the next year in the same journal argued that methodological problems and a lack of conclusive evidence *do not* enable us to conclude that video games lead to aggression. A 2001 review in *Psychological Science* concluded that video games "will increase aggressive behavior," while another 2001 analysis in *Journal of Adolescent Health* declared that it is "not possible to determine whether video game violence affects aggressive behavior."[7]

So why do we fear the effects of video games if no definitive legal or scientific proof exists to suggest they can cause real violence? Cops and robbers, cowboys and Indians are all modes of play where children, often boys, have acted out violent scenarios without widespread public condemnation. These games are reality-based, often involving costumes and toy guns. But video games receive public concern because they alter the nature of play. Video games are very visually alluring and can be played in isolation. Although kids may play with each other, their play is mediated by the game, bounded by the logic of the game makers. Fantasy violence in video games is mediated by an adult creator, rather than what we may think is a more "natural" use of violence in children's play. Adults scrutinize play and often label what kids do for fun as "good" or "bad." In the case of video games we seem focused on the possible negative aspects instead of the positive ones, because of the isolated incidents of school shootings in which perpetrators apparently played regularly. For instance, video games provide training in quick thinking, in learning to operate within a set of external rules, and in learning to operate effectively within such parameters. I'm not trying to argue that video games are intrinsically good or bad; I raise these points to demonstrate that we have chosen to focus on the negative to increase fears of video games.

In this chapter I explore why we fear that video games are behind acts of violence. Video games are representative of the digital age, where play and much of our daily routine is mediated by a microchip. Like fears of other media, as entertainment enjoyed mostly by the young, video games are often misunderstood by older adults and easy to blame for creating violence, alienation, and disconnection. The fear builds on the mistaken perception that youth today are in fact more alienated and more violent. As we will see, no conclusive study demonstrates a causal link between video games and violence. We want research to support our fear so badly that even a minor study filled with flaws will be published and circulate throughout the news media. The dangerous content that grabs headlines presumes players are blank slates, easily influenced with no clear distinction between right and wrong, although most players are in their teens or older.

Rather than implanting violent images, video games enable players to indulge in dark virtual fantasies, to act out electronically in ways that the vast majority of them would never do in reality. Sometimes these fantasies themselves are rather frightening, and for those of us who grew up without virtual reality, the fact that video games can help players explore their dark side is scary in itself. Did video games give the Columbine shooters "the will to kill"? I doubt it. I do think that they probably used the games to practice acting out their rage onto others, but where the will came from is much more complex. As Henry Jenkins, director of comparative media studies at MIT, explained, the boys "drew into their world the darkest, most alienated, most brutal images available to them and they turned those images into the vehicle of their personal demons."[8]

Following the massacre, many parents and politicians called for stricter video game regulations. Video game fears create a seemingly rational reason to further restrict young people and to divert attention away from the main sources of violence and social problems. We can once again blame media culture and its consumers rather than ask hard questions about where violence really comes from and why young people who seem to have every material advantage could become so alienated in the suburbs where so many aspire to live.

Dangerous Games

Many video games contain violence—not much room for debate there. Although some studies have been quite liberal in defining violence and include low-tech classics like Pac-man in this category, it is clear that video games are derivative of the action-adventure movie genre, but, due to their interactive nature, include a semblance of player control. Like action-adventure films, video games thrill users with special effects and appeal to mostly male audiences. As in many action films, most protagonists in video games are white males, with people of color overrepresented in villain roles. Female representations have been limited as well. A 1998 study found that 41 percent of that year's most popular games contained no female characters, and when they did, the women were often highly sexualized and/or the target of the virtual violence.[9] Often the content is troubling, and it raises more complex questions about why violence-oriented games are so appealing, especially to boys, questions that we miss when we only consider what it may do to young players. We could also ask where the hostility towards women comes from.

Because we know that the vast majority of players never become school shooters and no evidence proves that we can predict even lesser forms of violence caused by video games, it is more useful to consider what may draw players to these increasingly more realistic virtual violence experiences. Although some may use games to fuel their existing anger and alienation, for most players video game violence enables them to break rules in a safe setting, to engage in antisocial behavior they would never actually commit in real life. This simulated interactive experience scares critics of video games. Players are not just observing staged violence, as in television and movies, but "inflict" it with joysticks. Once players become accustomed to causing video game "violence," fear may lead us to ask what is stopping young people from feeling that *actual* violence is okay?

The big problem with this line of thinking is that it doesn't bear out in reality. As noted in Chapter 3, during the 1990s video game explosion, violent crime amongst youth plummeted. But fears grow in the dark, not in the light of day where they can be put in context and called to task. The fears and assumptions about the frailty of youth and the power of games are presented as real threats because it is the supposed experts, social scientists and politicians, who repeat them. Video games are an easy target for older adults who are not likely to be video game aficionados themselves. From the outside, many of the newest games do seem outrageous. Grand Theft Auto III made news upon its 2001 release for featuring the ability of players to steal cars and kill pedestrians, including old ladies, cops, and hookers. Even those in the video game industry concur that this game, although restricted for adult sales only, is shocking. *USA Today* described it as "a virtual apprenticeship in crime," so I decided that in the spirit of research I would give the game a try.[10] But just nine months after the controversial game's release, several major retailers told me that they didn't even carry it. My local Blockbuster clerk looked surprised when I asked for the game and told me they had taken it off the shelves permanently.

Of the games available, most were rated "T" for teen, and the majority contained sports-oriented content, including golf, baseball, football, and wrestling. Most of the "M" (mature) games were fantasy-oriented adventures where you fight to stave off alien invasions and nuclear disasters or you can "picture yourself in King Arthur's court." The ratings make it clear what kind of restricted content the "M" games contain, which I suspect works as effective advertising for a product if one is specifically into "coarse language" or "blood and gore." But a true thrill-seeker wouldn't have been too excited by the selection, which I found quite tame in comparison with the hype. None of the video games that Senators Joseph Lieberman and Herbert Kohl warned about in a 2001 holiday watch list was available to rent.[11]

Because video games are a young person's medium, older critics frequently fail to understand the games well enough to consider their meaning. To know about video games from the inside out you must do more than play them and look to be disgusted—you need to be able to understand that the pleasure players take from these games is not necessarily a sign of early serial-killerdom. I can attest to the addictive quality of the games when I made my own foray into this alien world. As a novice, you constantly fail as you learn the rules and strategies of the game. Video games challenge the imagination by immersing the player in a different world. And I have to admit, game killing *is* seductive, particularly because it is something most of us would never really do.

There is pleasure in breaking the rules without really breaking the rules. As philosophy professor Crispin Sartwell observes, violent video games enable users to play "with the idea of doing harmful things in a harmless context."[12] The player can act out antisocial fantasies without harm to self or others. Violent video games are a lot like dreams where we work out fears or anxieties without actually engaging in them. A twenty-three-year-old player told the *Los Angeles Times* that rather than being seduced by the violence, his ample time spent playing has taught him about the dangers of war without actually facing danger himself. "You get to see what combat's like without risking your life, satisfying this inherent curiosity. In an intense game, your heart is racing, you're sweating, but you're never scared. Honestly, I don't want to know any more information about what it's like to be under fire."[13]

While it is certainly possible that angry, dispossessed players may use video games to prepare for real battle, the evidence does not support our widespread fear that video games inspire real murder. But the fear pervades. Communications scholar Stephen Kline says that ironically, fear may be behind the popularity of video games. He cites parents' anxiety about the danger of the outside world as a major factor in home entertainment spending.[14] Parents don't want kids out of their sight so video game playing is seen as an acceptable alternative.

Fears of video games also draw on anxieties about change. Graphic video game technology is somewhat new, and its codes and conventions are not well understood by non-players. For parents who came of age playing Pong or Space Invaders, the attempts at realism in today's games may seem shocking and disturbing. In fact, this approximation of reality heightens fears that young people will not be able to distinguish between the game and reality, particularly heavy users who immerse themselves in video game worlds at length. But video games, especially violent ones, are more likely to be played by teens and young adults than young children. There really isn't solid evidence that video games impair young people's ability to recognize the difference between fantasy and reality, but our continued fear of youth violence makes us continually ask this question.

The fear of video games reflects both fear of youth and fear of change. Although some worry that a generation is being raised on simulated murder, a more realistic concern we could raise is about who *doesn't* play video games. Girls, for instance, make up a small proportion of players, and at $200 for a console and about $25–$50 per game, low-income kids are also often left out. Girls and low-income kids will therefore have less opportunity to gain technological competencies that may translate into valuable knowledge and skills in our high-tech age.

Fears of video games rest on the belief that they are creating changes in children and childhood itself. Physician Michael Brody's comments to the Senate in July 2000 exemplify this anxiety. Brody described video games as "Darwinian, paranoid and controlled," as well as devoid of empathy.[15] He declared that they are "not toys or even games in the traditional sense," arguing that they "do little to act as catalysts for the telling of a child's own stories, as real toys do." He also charged they do nothing to "promote imagination" or "develop strategies for problem solving." Of course, the same might be said of coloring books, and reading a book doesn't necessarily help children tell their own story either.

Brody's comments reflect a perceived distinction between traditional child's play as good and video games as new and in his estimation not even play at all. Video games are representative of technological changes many older adults don't understand. For them, virtual reality poses a threat, but it's not the kids who are having trouble distinguishing fact from fiction. Violent video games are a way to deal with age-old anxieties about violence in real life, to experience a forbidden thrill in a safe setting. At no time would this type of play feel more relevant than in the present, when we have experienced such large-scale violence that we were psychologically unprepared for. Violence itself is never simply a benign fact of life, but rather than seeing video games as a main source, we would do better to look at the world around us to understand why violence is such a pervasive theme now (and in the past) in young people's play.

The Theory of Interactivity

In theory, video games are even more influential than movies, television, or music because the player is actively participating in the game. This, of course, is what makes video games fun and exciting and sets them apart from other media where consumers take on more of a spectator role. Critics fear that players of violent games are rewarded for their virtual violence, which they believe may translate into learning that violence is acceptable. Straight out of B. F. Skinner, the fear stems from the idea that we learn from rewards, even vicarious rewards—behaviorism pure and simple. The prevalence of violent video game playing amongst young boys troubles many for this reason. The theory of interactivity is also based on the belief that young people cannot discern between fantasy and reality, and that this failure will condition players to regard violence as a rewarding experience. It's important to note that the inability to distinguish fantasy from reality is a key indicator of psychosis in adults, but we seem to accept this as a natural condition of childhood. While very young children may be learning the differences between what's real and what isn't, violent video game players tend to be older teens and young adults.

The theory of interactivity also leads us to think that even if kids themselves argue they know they are just playing games and that real violence is wrong, we adults often believe that they really *don't* know better. Let's briefly revisit the John Murray study from Chapter 3, where physiological changes in brain activity were taken as "proof" that kids' brains can't distinguish between media violence and the real thing.[16] Physiological reactions to video games are conflated with psychological and cognitive changes. In an *ABC World News Tonight* broadcast, a thirteen-year-old boy described how his "palms get sweaty," he gets nervous, and he feels "an adrenaline rush" while playing video games.[17] Reporter Michele Norris interprets this reaction as an admission "that the line between fantasy and reality is not always clear." But physiological changes are not indicators of a shift from reality. As sports fans will tell you, the Hail Mary pass, the bottom of the ninth inning, and so forth can lead to very real changes in heart rate and blood pressure without the fan believing that they are really playing.

Speaking of sports and interactivity, if anything teaches young boys that violence and force are acceptable it is contact sports where the hits are real. But we generally think of participation in sports as character building and an opportunity to learn about teamwork, similar to military training. Video games are certainly not the only arena in which violence is rewarded. In addition to sports, political conflicts settled through violence also serve as vicarious teachers. News coverage of both Gulf Wars has at times resembled a video game. We know the stakes are real, but for many of us watching on television the suffering is something we only see on TV. We *should* ask questions about why violence pervades entertainment for both adults and children, but we need to do so while looking at violence in its context, not just on the video screen.

Following the Research Trail

Government funding and public interest in finding out what video games may "do" to young people make us perk up our ears when the news media report a study that seems to confirm what we fear. Many social scientists hang their professional hats on the notion that media culture can be dangerous. So it is no surprise that this assumption, this expectation really, has led to a preponderance of research that focuses on one central "effect" of video game usage: aggression. Articles like "Video Games and Real-Life Aggression" (2001), "Video Games: Benign or Malignant" (1992), and "Is Mr. Pac-Man Eating Our Children?" (1997) are just a few examples of a flurry of studies that have appeared in professional journals since the 1980s, all assessing that one outcome.[18] The reason that so many studies focus on the same issue is because none are as conclusive as the authors sometimes suggest. The main problem, as noted in Chapter 3, is the way that aggression is tested and defined. For instance, a 1987 study had subjects impose fake money fines on opponents as an indicator of aggression.[19] A pretty big stretch, but equally questionable measures are often used to imply that not only will video game users become aggressive, they will become violent too. As much as social scientists claim they can be completely objective, in truth even scholars have preconceived beliefs and agendas that color the research questions they ask, the way their studies are designed, and the interpretations that follow.

In fairness, nearly all professional researchers are up front about the shortcomings of their findings and point out that their results are preliminary or that they cannot truly state that video game playing *causes* violence. But when a journal article hits the news wires, cautious science tends to fly out the window. Serious problems in conception or method rarely make it into press reports because they complicate the story. This is not entirely the researcher's fault, but ultimately the public is led to believe that a preponderance of evidence against video games exists, when instead it is a preponderance of *studies* that have been done to try and prove our fear of video games is rational.

A 2000 study by psychologists Craig Anderson and Karen Dill is a case in point. "Video Games and Aggressive Thoughts, Feelings and Behavior in the Laboratory and Life" was published in the prestigious *Journal of Personality and Social Psychology* and quickly made international news.[20] Not coincidentally, the two were the authors of the two reviews cited earlier that assert that video games do lead to aggression. This study was reported on in newspapers, magazines, and even other professional journals as definitive evidence that video games can increase aggressive behavior. There's just one problem: upon close inspection, the studies the article based its conclusions on are riddled with both conceptual and methodological problems. Based on their research we cannot conclude that "playing violent video games can contribute to aggressive and violent behavior in real life," as *Time* reported in May 2000.[21]

The Anderson and Dill results are based on two studies done with their introductory psychology students, so the sample is not representative. Part of their study looks at whether past video game use is associated with delinquency, but the most serious delinquent youth rarely make it to college, let alone show up for an appointment to participate in a study. Further, their first study used nearly twice as many female students as males in spite of the fact that most video gamers are male. In the first study, the students completed a questionnaire that asked about their favorite video games as teens, how violent they thought the games were, how much time they spent playing, and then their history of aggression and delinquency. Students were asked to think back and recall information from four to ten years prior, depending on their age. From this survey, researchers claimed they found a correlation between time spent playing video games and their aggressive and/or delinquent behavior. But this study was not designed to assess causality, just the existence of a relationship between time spent playing games and rating higher on irritability and aggression questionnaires.[22] Nonetheless, the authors claim that video games "contribute to (the) creation of aggressive personality," a conclusion that is a clear leap in logic.[23] Because correlation measures association, not cause and effect, it is equally possible that those with "aggressive personalities" are more likely to enjoy aggressive video game playing.

The second study Anderson and Dill reported on is based on a laboratory experiment in which students played a video game for fifteen minutes; some played a violent game and others played a non-violent educational game. When they finished, the students were asked to read "aggressive words" (like "murder") on a computer screen and were timed to see how fast they spoke the words. Because the violent game players repeated the words faster, they were deemed to have "aggressive thoughts" and perhaps be more prone to violence. Another leap in logic and questionable interpretation, as the words they read on the screen were not indeed their own thoughts, nor are aggressive *thoughts* necessarily dangerous. It is what we do with our hostility that is important. I would argue that the researchers have stumbled onto something interesting: even a short time spent playing computer-generated games appears to quicken visual reflexes. But the fact that the study chose to focus instead on a flimsy aggression claim tells us more about the fear of video games than about the video games themselves. It seems we're less interested in learning more about actual effects of video games than in trying to justify our anxieties.

The study also included a follow-up one week later. Students returned to the lab and played another game for fifteen minutes. If they won, they were allowed to blast their opponent with noise (unbeknownst to the subjects, they played against a computer and their opponent wasn't real). The violent-game players blasted their perceived opponents slightly louder and longer, and this was taken as the indicator of increased aggression caused by video games. We have to seriously question whether making noise is a good proxy for aggression, and if this form of "aggression" is in any way linked with violence. Making loud noises one day, murder the next?

The authors admit in their report that "the existence of a violent video game effect cannot be unequivocally established" from their research.[24] Nonetheless, this study was widely reported on in the news media as proof that "even small doses of violent video games are harmful to children," even though children were not the subjects of the study.[25] One article skillfully used preexisting fears to prime readers before presenting the "findings" of this study. An *Alberta Report* article titled "Mortal Konsequences" begins by introducing Jane Baker, a regular "Calgary mom" who doesn't like video games. The story goes on to proclaim that this study "discover(ed) what some parents have always suspected" and then presents the dubious results of the Anderson and Dill study. Studies like this get published and reported on because they serve as justifications of our fears, which attracts readers and viewers, plus the results seem even more compelling because they are presented in tandem with other weak studies. As it turns out, Mrs. Baker will now never allow video games in her house; the message here is no other parent should either. *Time* concurred: "None of this should be surprising," the author stated, listing the violent nature of games like Doom and Mortal Kombat.[26] Even the venerable British medical journal *The Lancet* reported on this story without critical scrutiny.[27]

So it doesn't matter how weak a study may be; it can still gather international attention as long as it tells us what we want to hear. Other results that are less dramatic fail to make headlines, such as the conclusion of a 1993 study by psychologist Guy Cumberbatch. He found that children may become frustrated by their failure to win at video games, as most games are designed to be increasingly difficult, but this anger will not necessarily translate to the outside world. Cumberbatch concluded, "We may be appalled by something and think it's disgusting, but they know its conventions and see humor in things that others wouldn't."[28] We also don't hear the results of studies that fail to demonstrate a link between violent video games and aggression. After his study found no evidence that violent video games led to more aggression, psychologist Derek Scott concluded in 1995 that "one should not overgeneralize the negative side of computer games playing."[29] But apparently stories like these are not as newsworthy as those that justify our need to fear media.

Governing Games

Video game fears are not just reinforced by news reports, but by the involvement of elected officials. In 1993, the Senate Judiciary and Government Affairs Committee met to discuss video games, which resulted in the industry's agreement for more self-regulation in the form of ratings. In an attempt to avoid further government intervention, the Interactive Digital Software Association created a rating system in 1994, using categories like "E" for everyone, "EC" for early childhood, "T" for teens, "M" for mature, and "AO" for adults only. The results of implementing a rating system were questionable at best. As with television and in some cases movie ratings, game ratings may be confusing to parents.[30] Like music warning labels, ratings may also serve to draw even more attention to violent products than if no labeling existed. Critics also point out that many games rated "E" contain some type of violence.[31] Calls for self-regulation through things like ratings are just about all the government can do, since the First Amendment generally prohibits intervention.

But that hasn't stopped politicians from claims of taking on the video game industry. Explicit censorship of entertainment is impossible in a free society, as government officials are constitutionally prohibited from regulating culture. So for the most part politicians are limited to meetings with industry leaders and making speeches expressing their disdain for video games, which resonates with their constituents. They cite vague notions that the video game violence/real violence connection has been scientifically proven and can lead to tragedies like the Columbine massacre.

"This is one of the vehicles by which politicians try to be famous," complained a video game distributor in Tampa, Florida.[32] A few of his state's members of Congress proposed new legal restrictions that would prevent minors from purchasing or renting "M" rated games. Representative Doug Wiles spoke in late 2001 of making violent video games "on par with . . . the rental or purchase of adult movies."[33] "M" rated video games would be displayed in a separate room like pornography according to this plan, which Representative Joe Barca introduced as the "Protect Children from Video Sex and Violence Act of 2002" in May 2002. If this bill passes, selling or renting violent video games to minors would become a federal crime. First time offenders would be fined $1,000, and repeat offenders could be fined up to $5,000 and serve a possible ninety-day jail term.

Criminalizing video rental clerks may seem like a solution (can you imagine them in the slammer with tax evaders?), but *Forbes* estimates that 90 percent of video game purchases are made by *adults*, not "two year-old(s) with a bunch of money," as the *Tampa Tribune* ominously warned.[34] It's likely that parents make many of these purchases and rentals; *Forbes* reported that of the adult game buyers, nearly two-thirds have children in their households. In spite of congressional attempts to regulate retailers, it appears that many parents have not bought into the video game menace and are the main purchasers of video games. So when Senators Joseph Lieberman and Herbert Kohl sent letters to retailers during the holiday shopping days of December 2001 to ask them "to stop peddling so much gore and sex to children," it appears they didn't realize that the retailers were mainly peddling the "gore and sex" to adults.[35]

If retailers aren't constructed as the problem, then parents are. When politicians run out of ways to try to restrict game makers and distributors, the next tack is to blame parents for not policing their children as much as the government may wish it legally could. A *Chicago Sun-Times* headline, "Parents Cautioned to Heed Ratings," is an example of calls for parents to restrict their kids' video game use.[36] An *ABC World News Tonight* report on video games in July 2002 featured a parent who felt her son was mature enough to play Grand Theft Auto III. Her decision was described as "giving in" to her son, to which an expert responded that decisions like these were "irresponsible."[37] It seems we're all experts on what is best for other people's children.

What policymakers fail to realize is that digitized information is increasingly easy to duplicate and distribute underground. "Illegal" games are likely to add even more to the outlaw mystique that playing violent games often provides. Adults-only regulations create an arbitrary dividing line between maturity and immaturity, drawn not by those who know a young person best, but by a government acting like a punitive parent. Politicians who try to micromanage childhood and adolescence will fail on several counts: they miss the big picture issues that could explain why some young people may spend so much time playing video games and what else could be done instead (like funding more extra-curricular activities or job training programs). Of course there is nothing wrong with kids having leisure time and fun too. Politicians who fail to understand the pleasure in popular culture alienate young people, who may feel more like pawns of the political system rather than true constituents. Government attempts to regulate what video games kids play simply won't work in a digitized era.

We should be asking bigger questions, like whether we want politicians dictating parenting choices and deciding what is best for young people to do with their free time. While we fear the content of video games may be harmful, we also need to consider the harm of diversion, or the issues that politicians could be exploring instead of leading the video-game fear brigade. We might ask why we are so afraid for kids to play outside in their communities, and why many neighborhoods have few spaces for teens in particular to congregate. We could also consider using video gaming to build other skills and interests. The army has created a game to promote enlistment (ironically this is a nonviolent game).[38] Rather than fighting the tide we could ride it creatively, using the technology, style, and fast-paced action of video games for other purposes. We can also recognize some of the positive skills that video gaming provides, instead of only bemoaning the perceived negative effects. We should see through the games politicians play too, and avoid falling into the culture-blaming trap we are so often led into.

Violence elicits fear because it sometimes defies prediction, as the Columbine shootings and September 11 exemplify. We look to find predictors so we can know better for the future. In the face of something so horrific we are open to lots of explanations, including the role that video games may have played. There is little doubt that the shooters' rage was exercised through video game play. But in truth, the Columbine case is noted for both its magnitude and, thankfully, its rarity. Unlike the Columbine shooters, the majority of young people who turn to violence have a number of other risk factors that we should turn our energy towards: violence in the home and/or neighborhood, a personal and/or family history of substance abuse, and a sense of hopelessness due to extreme poverty. The vast majority of homicides in Los Angeles involving young offenders, for instance, are gang-related, drawing on the aforementioned problems, not video games. If kids in impoverished communities actually had video games there may even be a *reduction* in violence, not simply due to a cathartic effect, but because they would have something else to do other than congregate in dangerous places. I say this semi-seriously, but to understand why people become violent we need to start by looking at garden-variety violence rather than the headline-grabbing exception.

The bulk of youth violence is mundane, less exciting than video games. The school shootings act as the evidence we have been hoping to find to convict youth culture for allegedly creating the downfall of the next generation and the future we fear. We choose to fear video games because that allows us to focus our attention away from problems we'd rather not think about, and are therefore unlikely to solve.

6

Fear of Music

Musical Murder and Misogyny?

Along with interest in video games, news reports detailed the Columbine shooters' musical preferences, looking for clues as to whether music could be held partially responsible for their violent rampage. "Can music cause murder?" reporter Larry Katz of the *Boston Herald* asked while calling his fellow journalists to task for focusing so heavily on the alleged music-murder connection.[1] Stories suggested there were few other plausible explanations: "the inquiry . . . has yielded no clear answers, leaving a bewildered nation to focus on reports that the killers reveled in playing the video games Quake and Doom and listened to the grisly music of Marilyn Manson," the *Los Angeles Times* reported.[2]

The fear that music incites violence is not new. In the 1970s music supposedly contained satanic messages, audible when played backwards, its proponents argued. In the 1980s lawsuits alleged that the music of Ozzy Osbourne and Judas Priest was responsible for suicides, but ultimately the musicians were not considered legally liable. As in other forms of popular culture, musical audiences have become increasingly segmented, so blaming music for creating violence and alienation is particularly easy for adults who find the musical tastes of young people questionable. The fear of music also draws on beliefs that media culture is toxic to the young, but what kind of music did the Oklahoma City bombers enjoy, or parents who kill their children? We don't know because music is only considered an explanation for *young people's* bad behavior. We place blame on the effects of music on kids in the same way we blame movies, cartoons, and video games.

I'm not attempting to excuse the bad language some music contains or to change anyone's musical preference, but instead to look critically at the worry that music makes listeners violent, suicidal, or misogynist. We also need to consider the positive role that music plays in people's lives—the way it helps us to construct identities and claim group allegiances, especially among young people. Music speaks to our emotions and brings enjoyment to our lives, and certainly preferences vary by generation. We will see that beyond the four-letter words often lay anti-authority themes (as has been the case for decades) that do more than simply offend sensibilities, but challenge the nature of power and authority. In particular, rap music directly questions the traditional social order, while other genres that may contain equally violent and sexist imagery escape the same level of public outcry. Additionally, heavy metal and "shock rock," a genre of music associated with the macabre that pushes the limits of conventional sensibilities, both often challenge authority and mainstream religion while addressing alienated youth. But rather than seek to understand why anti-authority themes or images of violence and misogyny resonate so well with some young people, we tend to focus only on the alleged danger of the music and what it might "do" to them.

Questions continue about the responsibility of musicians: Aren't pop stars role models for millions of young people? Do recording artists justify and reinforce antisocial beliefs in their listeners? Typically we listen to music because it strikes an emotional chord with us on some level. Could a depressed, suicidal person listen to music that seems to affirm suicide and feel more strongly about going through with it? Perhaps—but the danger is in focusing on music as the *only* cause. Likewise, depressed young people might spend more time alone playing video games, watching cartoons, and listening to music. But music alone certainly does not create depression, alienation, violence, or misogyny, and focusing only on music enables us to ignore, for instance, how our society may breed alienation.

That said, just like video games, the content of music is occasionally pretty shocking. I have sometimes asked students to bring in lyrics to songs about relationships to analyze messages about sex and love in music. I have to admit that some of the lyrics were so obscene I felt rather embarrassed when students read them aloud. So I am not claiming that lyrics people find objectionable are without meaning and should just "lighten up," but instead suggest that we dig deeper to uncover the roots of such sentiments. A look beneath the surface reveals how economic shifts better explain why people may become alienated and gravitate towards music that reflects their anger. We begin by considering how people use music not merely to create divisions, but to establish group and individual identity.

Come Together: Music and Identity

When I was in my teens, music served many different purposes for me both personally and socially in ways it no longer does. Some music was for private consumption, sometimes amongst only my closest friends. I listened to songs with themes that drew on intensely private emotions alone. My friends and I might have shared with each other that the lyrics to Wham's *Careless Whisper*, for instance, were *exactly* how we felt about the boy who seemed to be interested one week only to ignore us the next. My female friends and I would use music to drive our fantasies about boys and dating by dividing up members of a band into who we would want for boyfriends. We negotiated our imaginary relationships with males by having total control over choosing them, not waiting to be chosen in our fantasy life. The only obstacle was making sure the man wasn't already "called" by a friend; for some reason we couldn't all have crushes on the same unattainable rock star.

This was the semi-private but still social use of music that we didn't share with our male peers. When they found out someone had a crush on a rock star, that person would be in for ribbing and the rock star was endlessly made fun of. Wearing a concert T-shirt from a Rick Springfield (my personal choice), Duran Duran, or Wham! concert to school would create more trouble than it was worth. Those shirts were reserved for weekends or for sleeping. But wearing a T-shirt revealing you had recently been to a Genesis or Bruce Springsteen concert would be a social advantage. In my Midwestern school heavy metal T-shirts worn too frequently could be a one-way ticket to unpopularity. School trips were times when music was shared, albeit with occasional bickering. Genesis, Elvis Costello, Squeeze, and occasional classics by the Beatles or Simon and Garfunkel kept us company on long bus rides. Arguments did erupt when one person's choice seemed to take up too much time or too many decibels for those who were listening to a Walkman. Nearly every ride was punctuated with an ongoing feud between two classmates, who vigorously debated whether Bruce Springsteen or John Mellencamp was more true to his working class roots. Music meant everything at that time in our lives; as maligned as '80s pop is now, I can't help feeling nostalgic when I hear one of those songs.

But somewhere during my freshman year of college I started to lose touch with pop music. When I returned home for the summer and got into a friend's car and she tuned to a top 40 radio station, I felt ignorant about youth culture for the first time in my young life. Not drastically disconnected, but enough to realize that my taste was starting to shift. Now that I'm a thirty-something adult, music still holds value but not nearly the same personal and social meaning it held in my teens. I left the last concert I attended, six years ago, early in spite of having excellent fifth-row seats. Why? Because it was too loud—and I'm not ashamed to admit that either. I find myself settling into the musical tastes of my youth, just as my parents did before me with the music of their generation. Transitioning into adulthood, music no longer serves the purpose it did in my adolescence, linking me to my peers and separating me from my parents.

I admit that I am not living on the musical cutting edge, nor am I a fan of music so often criticized for content. I don't like aggressive-sounding lyrics and music and am appalled by some of the language, particularly when it degrades women. But at the same time I realize this music is largely misunderstood and underestimated by my fellow non-fans. It's very easy to criticize music we find offensive to the ear as noise and still recognize that one person's noise is another's melody.

That's why even though my personal tastes are very different from many of today's teens, I try to refrain from putting their musical preferences down; I realize that music is central in creating both independent and social identities. Jeffrey Jensen Arnett, an expert in adolescent development, notes that music and other forms of popular culture are used by young people in the identity formation process, as a way of developing a private self and also as a coping mechanism.[3] Music ties teens with youth culture and helps them deal with the emotional challenges of growing up. For instance, Arnett found that heavy metal fans often listen when they feel angry. They report that the music provides a powerful purging function that helps calm them down.[4] Rather than creating anger, as the cause-effect thinking about youth and music would suggest, it is preexisting anger that instead draws them to the music. Adolescents are active music listeners who specifically choose their music just as I did; we miss an important facet of the listening experience by simply focusing on music's allegedly bad influence. When we condemn the music enjoyed by young people, we are inadvertently condemning them and their emotional realities.

Music, like sporting events, helps to create group identity, to define us as part of some groups and apart from others. After September 11, 2001, national anthems in ballparks were special celebrations included in both the television broadcasts and the highlight reels. Anthems are played in honor of Olympians for the same reason, to create a sense of nationalism and unity.

Music can be a vehicle for creating national, regional, ethnic, and age-based identities. Historian Grace Palladino describes how American teenagers' musical tastes were usually identical to their parents' before the 1930s, when few adolescents attended high school. During the Depression, high school enrollment climbed sharply and young people spent more time with each other and less with adults, creating a new youth culture. So although we take youth culture for granted now, before this time musical taste was much more likely to be divided along regional or ethnic lines than by age.

Jazz and swing music were perhaps the first musical genres that created real generational divisions in the United States. Even language began to separate generations, as slang words such as "daddy-o" and "square" created both a distinct youth identity and riled adult concern. Music and youth rebellion thus has its roots at least as far back as the 1920s and became especially pronounced after World War II, when many young people had more leisure time and more money to spend on music thanks to economic good times. Not accidentally, the beginning of rock and roll coincided with a surge in concerns about juvenile delinquency. Rock and roll was co-opted from African-American rhythm and blues, and (mainly white middle-class) adult concerns centered on the fear that this rhythmic, historically black music would tempt young people to become sexually active. Later, the folk and psychedelic music of the 1960s reflected a rejection of the status quo and challenged dominant norms and values. Although not all listeners necessarily politicized their musical consumption, musical taste created a shared generational culture, perhaps no better exemplified than with '60s protest musicians such as Bob Dylan and Joan Baez. Rebellion is a natural part of growing up, which is frequently reflected in young people's music regardless of the generation. While certainly not all youth culture is subversive, the twentieth century shift towards the creation of a separate youth culture has periodically been constructed in direct opposition to adult sensibilities.

Marilyn Manson: Satanic Verses?

After the shooting rampage at Columbine High School in 1999, music was not only blamed for inciting violence, but for creating a sense of alienation in its listeners. Even though it is unclear whether the Columbine shooters were actually fans, the "shock rock" band Marilyn Manson garnered a lot of criticism. Marilyn Manson relentlessly challenges a traditional facet of mainstream America: Christianity. The front man (also referred to as Marilyn Manson) has shredded Bibles on stage and is a vocal critic of what he sees as hypocrisy within organized religion. Born Brian Warner, Manson is a product of a Christian school that he insists "turned its back" on him.[5] He explains that he is not "opposed to the values set forth in the Bible," but argues that mainstream religion is rife with hypocrisy. [6] "I think you'll find most hate groups use God as their backbone," he told a reporter from the *Pittsburgh Post-Gazette*.[7] In response to claims that his music was partially responsible for inspiring the Columbine killers, Manson wrote the following in a 1999 *Rolling Stone* article:

> I'm a controversial artist, one who dares to have an opinion and bothers to create music and videos that challenge people's ideas in a world that is watered-down and hollow. In my work I examine the America we live in, and I've always tried to show people that the devil we blame our atrocities on is really just each one of us.[8]

Marilyn Manson's appeal lies in part within their critique of mainstream values and rejection of the social institutions so many of their fans feel have already rejected them.

I will admit that I am not a fan of Marilyn Manson. Yet the rage the band incites in adults (allegedly for inciting rage and alienation in listeners) is a great example of how fears of music enable worried adults, parents, and politicians to blame music for a grab bag of social problems. Dick Armey, then the House majority leader, alleged that the band's lyrics "tout suicide, torture, and murder."[9] Protesters repeatedly followed them to concert venues.[10] In 1998, state legislation was proposed in Michigan and South Carolina that would impose a ratings system on live concerts, targeted at acts like Marilyn Manson. The law would restrict minors from shows deemed to promote "sex, drugs, suicide or Satanism."[11]

There is a real problem with focusing so much effort on stopping acts like Marilyn Manson, especially when opponents don't understand what the performers are really saying or why listeners are drawn to the music. Is simply discussing violence in music a form of promoting violence? Music that is admittedly angry and rage-filled speaks to the experiences of some of its listeners. Contrary to the belief that it is music like Manson's that "brings our children into darkness," as a detractor told the Milwaukee *Journal Sentinel,* music like this finds many young people already in darkness.[12]

Fans like a fourteen-year-old girl tell reporters that they have been picked on and teased by their peers and that Manson's lyrics often refer to similar experiences, which makes them feel less alone.[13] Kids who feel rejected can relate to songs like *The Lunch Box,* which is about standing up to school bullies. Beyond the shock of his appearance (lingerie, pale makeup, and opaque contact lenses), Manson attempts to speak to kids who feel like outcasts growing up, as he did. "Sometimes music, movies and books are the only things that let us feel like someone else feels like we do," he wrote in *Rolling Stone.*[14] Instead of understanding why some people find solace in Marilyn Manson and considering the very real problem of bullying, we often choose to blame the music and to fear acts like Manson and their fans. Ultimately the fear of bands like Marilyn Manson promotes ostracizing and further alienating many young outcasts rather than reaching out to those rejected by their peers.

In addition to lyrics that challenge mainstream norms and values, this music challenges traditional musical structure of harmony and melody. The sound itself is often aggressive and not necessarily pleasing to the ear. In part, critics who may argue that this isn't even "music" at all are responding to this violation of convention. But opponents of these musical genres are protesting more than taste. This music gives voice to those outside the mainstream and provides a challenge to the status quo. Rather than address the real sense of disdain felt by some young people or the social criticism that bands like Manson touch on, our response has typically been to condemn only the music.

Instead of endlessly looking for music's "effects" on people, we would be better served by understanding that many young people who are rejected by their peers are also rejected by the adults around them. The alienated are feared—particularly the white middle-class alienated—because their rejection of mainstream norms most threatens the continuation of the status quo. Fears of Marilyn Manson stem from the rejection of mainstream culture by those who theoretically have the opportunity to benefit most from it. And if they aren't buying it we are forced to ask some real unsettling questions about the middle-class American Dream, the same questions we are reluctant to address in the case of the Columbine High School shootings.

Pearl Jam Triggered Rampage?

The Columbine murders were not the first time that music was blamed for inspiring a school shooting. The alternative band Pearl Jam's *Jeremy*, a song about a bullied boy who strikes back, was blamed for a February 1996 shooting rampage. Fourteen-year-old Barry Loukaitis shot three students and a teacher in Moses Lake, Washington, just east of Seattle, leaving all but one of the students dead.[15] His defense attorneys played the *Jeremy* video in court, insisting that the song "triggered" the shooting.[16] The song, released in 1991, describes a boy ignored by parents and taunted by classmates. The lyrics themselves are not nearly as apocalyptic as defense attorneys insisted. The song begins with Jeremy "at home drawing pictures" of himself on the top of a mountain, as "dead lay in pools of maroon below" in the drawing. The violence in school consists of "a surprise left," not a shooting spree.

Barry was clearly troubled; defense attorneys used his bipolar disorder as the basis for an insanity defense. His family life also appears to have been unstable. His father testified that the boy witnessed many arguments between his parents, who were separated at the time of the killings.[17] His mother testified that she shared with Barry her suicidal fantasies of killing herself in front of her estranged husband and his girlfriend.

Barry was sentenced to life for the murders. Just as in the suicide cases of the 1980s, courts have continually rejected "the media made me do it" as a defense.[18]

The Media Made Me Do It (Again)

Nonetheless, many adults remain convinced that music can directly cause violent behavior in young people. In February 2000, sheriff's deputies in Iberia Parish, Louisiana, confiscated sixty CDs from Skate Zone, a local roller rink, allegedly because rap music incited a fight in the rink earlier that month.[19] The fight was blamed both on the music and the "several hundred youth bused in from neighboring St. Mary Parish."[20] Although the racial ethnic composition of the two parishes is similar, the St. Mary youth are portrayed as a rowdy out-group, easily incited to violence by rap music.

Skate Zone's owner was arrested for allegedly contributing to the delinquency of minors for playing the music, which included rappers Snoop Dogg and Master P, but also CDs by Britney Spears, Whitney Houston, and assorted Christmas music. To gain support for the arrest, the sheriff sent letters to all local churches, stating that "The lyrics of songs breed violence in the minds of our children, then unfortunately they act out what was planted in their minds."[21] The arrest warrant charged that the CDs contained obscene language and claimed that "This type of music is the principal cause of the large gang fights that often break out at this business."[22] This is a prime example of adult beliefs about music's negative influence. As a local minister said, "it does ring true to a concern we all have."[23]

In addition to blaming rap music for inciting violence, others condemn rap lyrics because they are often sexist, fearing that rap will lead to violence against women. Rap is certainly not the first musical genre to contain overtly sexist lyrics. Country western, heavy metal, and even mainstream pop all have a history of misogyny. Take one of the most revered bands of the twentieth century (and one of my favorites, by the way), the Beatles. In a rather catchy song called *Run for Your Life*, John Lennon sings: "I'd rather see you dead little girl/ than to be with another man." Of course there were calls to ban the Beatles too, but certainly not because of sexist lyrics. *Run for Your Life* and songs like it reflect a traditional belief that violence against women is justified in the case of betrayal. This doesn't make it acceptable, but we have to acknowledge that the Beatles did not create disparities in power and gender. This song both reflects patriarchy and perpetuates it, making violence against women seem more normal and justifiable. We *should* criticize lyrics like these to raise awareness of the prevalence of sexism in our culture and to challenge the ease with which some young men adopt very misogynist views. But too often discussions stop at music's "effects" without exploring violence or sexism in their broader contexts. This tendency is fueled by the prevalence of "the music made me do it" news reports that suggest music by rapper

Eminem and the heavy metal band Slayer, for instance, inspired violence against women.

Eminem Inspired Misogyny?

Eminem (so named based on the initials of his given name, Marshall Mathers) has become a major figure in rap, sold millions of albums, and is regularly the subject of controversy. In 2001 he was invited to perform at the Grammy Awards, which led to a protest by gay and lesbian activists who argued that his lyrics promote homophobia. Other concerns have arisen over the depiction of violence against women. The performer told *Rolling Stone* in a profanity-laced August 2000 phone interview that he is tired of responding to critics of his lyrical content.[24] He uses his song *Stan* as an example of his criticism of those who take his lyrics too seriously. "'Stan' is about a sick f—ing kid who took everything I said literally—and he crashes his f—ing car, kills his bitch and dies," Eminem explained.[25] "The kids listening to my music get the joke. They can tell when I'm serious and when I'm not. They can tell the entertainment of it."

I have to confess, I am not a fan of his music nor do I agree that we should write off his prolific use of the words "fag" or "bitch" as a joke. These words draw on existing feelings of homophobia and misogyny that both Eminem and his fans apparently find compelling. But while I am not a fan, I recognize that Eminem has received much critical acclaim. "He is a genuinely brilliant rapper," said British music critic James Delingpole, citing his clever rhymes, rife with complex metaphors and humor.[26] Robert Hilburn, music critic for the *Los Angeles Times*, noted that Eminem's albums have "a power and complexity almost unrivaled on the contemporary pop scene."[27] Others note that the characters he creates within his lyrics do not necessarily reflect beliefs he is promoting, but rather criticizing.

What is problematic here goes beyond Eminem's propensity to offend the genteel. My central concern is that misogyny and homophobia only seem to enter public discussion in response to youth culture, especially rap music. The fear centers around what the music allegedly might "do" to its listeners, demanding that it go away or at least become less available to its youngest listeners. Here's the problem: we seem to presume that music is responsible for creating hatred and resentment in youth and fail to take a look in our societal mirror to see how sexism and homophobia are built into other social institutions.

We have a long and deep history of ambivalence towards both women and sexuality in American society. So while discussions of misogyny and homophobia are often started via music lyrics, music remains virtually the only topic of discussion. We rarely talk about how cultural values of women still focus on appearance and sexuality, but easily criticize music videos for being overtly sexual. We chastise women for focusing on careers instead of mothering and blame women for being so misguided as to try to "have it all" (which basically means parity with men). Boys are raised to understand masculinity as distinctly non-female and non-gay, both being common ways that boys chastise each other and adult men shape their identities.

But it is more convenient to avoid even starting this conversation, which has been derided with the "politically correct" label to discredit its introduction into serious public discourse. We instead focus on the plight of women in faraway places (most recently Afghanistan) and ignore the existence of inequality here. The notable exception is in critiques of rap music. Without rap music very little would be different in regards to the overall status of women and tolerance towards gays and lesbians—we need to stop pretending that music is the cause, rather than the symptom.

News reports continually evoke the music-made-me-do-it motif. Two domestic assault cases in 2001 brought attention to Eminem's *Stan*, the song about a troubled fan who drives off a bridge with his girlfriend tied up in the trunk. A British man who was apparently a big fan of the rapper and this particular song attacked his ex-girlfriend with a padlock and chain while she was working at a hair salon.[28] The eighteen-year-old woman had stopped seeing the nineteen-year-old man months earlier because "he was becoming too obsessive and possessive," and he had assaulted her before the attack in the salon. The brutal beating took place in front of terrified co-workers, who tried to pull him away from her.

For those who work with victims of domestic violence, the story sounds familiar: possessive boyfriend lashes out when woman attempts to end the relationship and free herself from control. The Eminem angle probably explains why the case made the news; in that sense it may even help raise awareness about the danger some women face when trying to escape abusive relationships. But the news report is more about Eminem than the ongoing problem of domestic violence. The article began with a shocking opening line: "A teenager who believed he was the rap star Eminem brutally assaulted his former girlfriend."[29] Referring to a nineteen-year-old (a legal adult) as a teenager draws on the fear that "kids" will imitate lyrics in pop music. The article reported that his home was "crammed with Eminem posters, albums and merchandise," which was used in the story to imply the man was obsessed. Further, there is no evidence that the man actually *believed* he was Eminem (which would be a serious psychiatric condition). It appears that the man was instead a big fan, drawn to angry lyrics against women, who bleached his hair in similar style to the rapper.

A similar case made headlines in Canada. A judge asked to hear the lyrics to Eminem's *Kim*, a song about a man abusing his wife, which was alleged to have sparked a domestic assault.[30] In the spring of 2001, a thirty-five-year-old man was accused of assaulting his common-law wife. Apparently the assault occurred one evening after the man played *Kim* for the couple's guests, who included friends and their children. The beating allegedly happened after the woman begged him not to play the song, which she said contained "abusing lyrics." In this case, the music may have been used to humiliate the woman in front of their friends, as part of what was clearly a violent relationship. According to reports, it was a relationship "she was afraid to be in but also afraid to end."[31]

Clearly, these two men were troubled and found a sense of connection with songs containing lyrics that tell of violence against women. They were likely drawn to misogynist imagery because it validated their angry worldview. The problem with focusing so much on the music is we avoid asking why violence against women persists and why themes of misogyny resonate with so many men (and sometimes women) of all ages. Eminem's lyrics, as offensive as people may find them, are a good starting point to begin exploring why violence against women has been and remains so widespread. But the music is the symptom, not the disease. Music alone cannot create violence: violence against women is often a way for people who feel powerless in some regard to assert their power over someone they feel entitled to control.

While cases that appear to be related to Eminem's music grab the headlines, millions of domestic assaults do not; critics of music's negative "effects" get far more national attention than advocates against domestic violence do. If we are truly concerned that young people not adopt misogynist attitudes or engage in violent behavior, we would be better served to focus on the behavior of the adults in their lives than focus so much on Eminem. However, his music and others containing troubling lyrics should not be ignored.

Slayer: Instructions for Murder?

Violence against women exists on a continuum—abusive language is where it begins, and at the extreme end of the spectrum lies murder. That's what happened in 1995 to fifteen-year-old Elyse Pahler of San Luis Obispo, California. Elyse was lured to a remote area where three teenaged boys brutally stabbed and killed her. News of the killing was sparse nationally—only a brief description appeared in the *Washington Post*'s "Around the Nation" column.[32] But when her parents filed a lawsuit against the heavy metal band Slayer and their record company the story gathered media attention; the *Los Angeles Times* ran a story on the front page of its business section.[33] The suit claimed that the band and the record company were responsible for "unlawfully marketing and distributing 'harmful' and 'obscene' products to minors," and that the lyrics served as "an instruction manual for disturbed adolescent fans," like the ones that killed Elyse.[34]

The story went on to describe how one of the killers "idolized Slayer," a heavy metal band, and reported that the boys "stayed up several nights in a row taking drugs and listening to Slayer."[35] The fact that both the victim and the killers were heavily involved with drugs (Elyse met one of them through a drug treatment program and he lured her to the desolate area with the promise of marijuana) is downplayed. Instead, the shocking lyrics of Slayer's *213* are reprinted, a song detailing what appears to be an erotically charged murder of a woman. One of the teens said that the music "gets inside your head . . . it's almost embarrassing that I was so influenced by the music."[36] Despite drug problems, this suspect encouraged others to believe that he was influenced to kill because of the music. By focusing on the culpability of the music, the story ignored other causal factors. Letters to the editor the following week echoed the importance of holding Slayer and their record label accountable for the murder.[37]

The three boys pled guilty, thus avoiding trial, and the claims that "the music made them do it" were never put through the scrutiny a trial would have brought. An August 2001 story in *Entertainment Weekly* provided details about the case left out by the *Los Angeles Times*.[38] First, one of the killers had been expelled from school for possessing marijuana and a knife. His mother, however, did not seem to take this development too seriously. "He had less than an ounce on him . . . they didn't need to kick him out," she told the magazine.[39] Another one of the convicted boys had an older brother who was also serving time for murder. Their mother recognized a major drug problem, but had no luck in getting them into treatment. Two of the boys vehemently denied any connection between the murder and Slayer. "We never listened to the lyrics before the murder. . . . The fact is Slayer music didn't have anything to do with the murder. The police went into my house and saw some Slayer posters and records and they made up a motive."[40] Instead, the two convicted murderers interviewed acknowledged that their drug use was the central influence on their behavior. "The music had zero influence on me going out to kill somebody. . . . Those allegations were put together by lawyers to make money," claimed one of the teens, who were sentenced to twenty-five years to life in prison.[41] Ultimately, just like lawsuits against Ozzy Osbourne and Judas Priest in the 1980s, this lawsuit didn't get very far. In October 2001 it was thrown out. The girl's parents vowed to appeal.

I can certainly understand why the girl's family would feel outraged after their daughter was so savagely and senselessly killed. An investigator from the San Luis Obispo district attorney's office described the boys as "evil little psychopaths," which is perhaps what is most frightening: the fear that white boys from a small town can become killers counters the logic behind where we think "safe places" are.[42] This case defies our typical understanding that delinquency is only an urban minority problem. Further, these boys raise questions that go well beyond their music of choice; they force us to ask how small-town life, like suburban life, may create boredom with few ways for young people to channel excess energy. I point this out not to simply exonerate Slayer or argue that their music was not at all influential, but as a way to expand the scope of explanation beyond *only* looking at the lyrics.

Instead of seeing the music as the proverbial smoking gun, there are many smoking guns here, particularly drug abuse, family context (what would make two siblings both commit murder?), and, as discussed earlier, the broader social context of misogyny. What kind of anger towards girls and women must these disaffected boys have harbored to plot for months to kill? Writers Jane Caputi and Diana E. H. Russell call murders of women "motivated by hatred, contempt, pleasure, or a sense of ownership" "femicide," which may apply here.[43] They explain that violence against women rises in response to the increase of the status of women and is the most extreme form of reactionary backlash. Those who fear being left behind, who sense a loss of status themselves, may be those most likely to act out. White working-class males, particularly those who may feel disempowered at work or in school, are most liable to feel that all of their opportunities have been taken away by women and minorities. This may be why references to women as "bitches" in music and lyrics describing violence against women are so prevalent and resonate with many young male listeners. While "femicide" may be relatively rare, cases like Elyse Pahler's murder highlight the danger of a society that is still deeply ambivalent about the changing status of women. We *should* talk about Slayer's lyrics, about Eminem's lyrics, about how they draw from the deep well of hostility that women face in the world and often in their own homes. But we can't stop with the music; it can get the conversation started, but what lies beneath is crucial.

Making Noise: The Fear of Rap Music

While public outcry over heavy metal and now shock rock appear sporadically, rap music has received sustained steady criticism since its introduction to the mainstream in the 1980s. President George W. Bush called rapper Eminem "The most dangerous threat to American children since polio."[44] Others decry "the worst kinds of images emanating from a postmodern society" and believe that rap is "sugar-coated poison."[45]

It is true that rap lyrics are occasionally shocking, sometimes brutal, and rife with misogyny and obscenities. Rap music details a large variety of experiences, but most attention is placed on lyrics depicting sex, drugs, and violence. Taste is not only what is at issue here. Adults may not like the sexualized teen pop of the early 2000s, but rarely is there public demand from politicians for self-censorship. The musical genres that garnered this sort of attention recently, first heavy metal and then rap, on the surface appear to be criticized for explicit lyrics. But underneath concerns about sex or violence in music lies fears of *politically* explicit language which challenges more than adult sensibilities, but the current power structure as well.

Complaints about lyrics periodically enter public and political discourse because it is easier to target youth culture than examine problems within the *adult*-created social structure. If we are truly so disturbed by the lyrics and imagery in some musical genres, we ought to examine where these themes are rooted, rather than simply demand they go away. Complaints about music have little to do with music. Targeting popular culture enables us to restrict and condemn young people—often young people of color—without appearing to discriminate.

Warning: Politically Explicit Language

Rather than focus on what lyrics may "do" to listeners, it will best serve us to first consider why rap music has elicited so much fear. As writer Terry McDermott described in the *Los Angeles Times*, country music has historically been peppered with stories of violence and misogyny, yet no political movement has tried to censor and prevent its performance with the same vehemence as with rap.[46] Race and politics make this musical genre more than just offensive to "polite" society; rap music serves a threat to the social order as well. This is the fear that motivates public and political outcry beneath the Trojan horse of foul language.

Rap music started in a decidedly populist fashion in the 1980s, not courted by traditional record labels but popularized through local clubs.[47] With no radio or video play, its popularity grew through word of mouth. Public concern seemed to erupt when rap made it to white suburban audiences, who are estimated to now be rap's largest audience.[48] In fact, the first rap album to go platinum was *License to Ill* by the white suburban-raised Beastie Boys. This was the turning point. It was one thing for African-American youth in urban New York and Los Angeles to rap about their anger towards police. But it was entirely another thing for *white* kids to hear such strong anti-authority messages, to learn about the violence and drugs in urban areas that resulted from economic divestment from central cities in the 1980s, and to co-opt the music themselves. Fears of rap draw on anxieties similar to those in the early 1950s when white parents feared what influence "black" rock and roll would have on their kids; fear of rap is a way to displace anxieties about race without having to talk about race directly. Music is a socially acceptable way to indirectly condemn a group without appearing bigoted.[49]

The threat to polite society involves more than using the "f" word and other profanities, though use of language to shock is one tactic used to disrupt mainstream norms.[50] In fact, as authorities worked harder to silence the seminal rap group NWA ("Niggas with Attitude") in the late 1980s (via an FBI letter and arrests after concerts), their record sales skyrocketed. Writer Terry McDermott explains:

> The content of youth culture today is, to a significant extent, hip-hop. . . . Just as rock music was a vehicle for counter-cultural attitudes that provoked social upheaval among the middle classes in the 1960s, hip-hop in general and gangsta rap in particular have carried urban underclass sensibilities to the wider society—which has reacted with equal parts enchantment, imitation, and outrage.[51]

Author Tricia Rose writes in "'Fear of a Black Planet': Rap Music and Cultural Politics in the 1990's" that the discourse surrounding rap is a way to further construct African Americans "as a dangerous internal element in urban America—an element that if allowed to roam about freely will threaten the social order."[52] She goes on to describe how rap concerts have been portrayed as bastions of violence in order to justify greater restrictions on black youth from public spaces.[53]

Music serves as a proxy, an excuse to marginalize and condemn its fans as potential threats while obfuscating the real fear: in this case critiques of the white power structure. Concerns about rap serve to further demonize poor African-American youth living in urban ghettos and to frame them as a potential threat based on music, while ignoring the structural undercurrents of their experiences, like lack of opportunity and racism. Songs like Ice-T's *Cop Killer*, which led to public outcry about its apparent promotion of violence against law enforcement, are based on the feelings of resentment that have built up over generations from racial profiling and the history of police brutality in minority communities. When the anger is co-opted by white middle-class audiences, it ironically both creates fear and loses its potency; to a large extent gangsta rap today has become more about style than about politics. Yet the fear stems from the threat that white middle-class youths will also challenge the power structure and dominant social institutions. Rap can be far more than linguistically obscene; its messages threaten business as usual. Yet white middle-class adults need not fear: rap's co-option has made mainstream media conglomerates rich and its suburban listeners feel cool without really changing a thing.

Turning It Down: Rethinking Fears of Music

Not everyone in the news media or the public accepts the music-made-me-do-it discourse on violence. In response to the Pearl Jam song *Jeremy* described earlier, a reader wrote to the *Seattle Times* charging that the reporter had misrepresented the Pearl Jam video. The reader went on to say, "We tread a dangerous line when we start implying that a music video, or rap song, or a rock concert can somehow take the blame for the world's evils."[54] This is particularly salient in post-Columbine America, where we continually scrutinize popular culture instead of looking more deeply at other factors. Dick Weissman, chair of the University of Colorado's Music and Entertainment Studies Department, writes of the irony that public concern following the massacre focused on the music of the shooters instead of on their obsession with Adolph Hitler, for instance.[55] The boys allegedly chose the day of their attack to coincide with Hitler's birthday. These were extremely alienated boys; we need to examine what creates such deep resentment, and we must look beyond the lyrics to their favorite songs to understand this. Sociologist Donna Gaines, author of *Teenage Wasteland: Suburbia's Dead End Kids*, a study of teens in suburban New Jersey, found that deep divisions between peer groups was the most salient problem facing teens. In response to the Columbine shootings, Gaines told the *Washington Post* "what we can draw from Columbine is the school is not taking responsibility for dealing with status inequality. They reinforce it at every turn."[56]

Richard Corliss of *Time* was critical of the immediate focus on popular culture in the days following the Columbine murders as well. "There is a lapse in parental logic that goes from 'I don't get it' to 'It must be evil,'" Corliss contended, arguing that parents and concerned adults need to look deeper than just popular culture to understand why some young people feel disaffected.[57] Music critic Ann Powers of the *New York Times* wrote that "even the rawest extreme music offers adolescents a symbolic language with which to express the confusion they already feel."[58] That same week Hilary Rosen, then president of the Recording Industry Association of America, wrote in *Billboard* magazine that "You can try to ban music that expresses the views of the alienated and unhappy . . . (but) you won't ban the angst or the anger."[59] *Rolling Stone* founder Jann Wenner worried that crackdowns on popular culture would "make the geeks even more isolated and

humiliated" and that the real problem we need to address is the proliferation of guns in the United States.[60]

Unfortunately, our only large-scale action as a society has been to
attempt to keep music with lyrics that many adults find objectionable
away from young people. We have to question who gets to decide
when lyrics are inappropriate, and for whom? By lumping minors together we indirectly argue that six- and sixteen-year-olds have the
same needs. I'm not saying that parents should not know or care what
music their kids listen to, but at relatively young ages parents cannot
have total control over what music their kids hear. Parents can use
music they may find objectionable to attempt to learn more about their
children and open a dialogue about issues parents may find troubling.

Our other traditional plan of action has been to threaten record
companies with legislation, banning and restricting certain music, or
we admonish them for producing music some groups find objectionable. I'm not suggesting that we totally abandon this tactic; as citizens
and consumers we have the right to openly protest with our voices and
our dollars. In addition, I advocate looking more critically at the corporate role in the music industry. For instance, what music gets air-
play? What artists *don't* get record deals? With consolidation amongst
both record companies and radio stations, our musical choices are becoming more limited and more profit-driven. Further, we need to look
at how the companies benefit from sexist ideas, like the ones in some
of the lyrics previously discussed. If we look deeper we will see that
their benefits are more than simply profits from the music itself, but
that both sexism and racism are often embedded within traditional
corporate structures of the industry. Nonetheless, the more a product
sells the less effective any protest over moral obligation will be.

So what should be our focus? We need to first recognize that music
is not the sole cause of violence, misogyny, or alienation and that by
paying so much attention to music we lose the opportunity to look
deeper. Instead, we ought to explore where themes of rage and alienation originate and why people may be drawn to music that reflects
these issues. For instance, Jesuit priest David E. Nantais uses popular
music in his youth retreats to spark discussions about spirituality.[61]
He also views music as potentially community building and observes
that music provides a "therapeutic release," which helps young people
deal with "strong emotions."[62] Instead of criticizing musical tastes or
condemning lyrical content, he uses music to build connections.

"Teenagers who are troubled are going to listen to pop music just as much as teenagers who are not," Nantais writes, arguing that looking only for causal links between music and behavior is "problematic at best."[63] The questions need to move away from censoring music towards an understanding that music and other cultural forms are firmly rooted in social realities. We ignore this simple truth by focusing *only* on the music.

Part Three

7

Fear of Advertising
and the Young Consumer

How Much Is That Psyche
in the Window?

Along with turkey sandwiches and leftovers, the day after Thanksgiving has become associated with a major shopping marathon; at least, that's what retailers hope. The obligatory news reports of crowds eagerly awaiting pre-dawn openings of toy stores return each year as adults do battle to get the hottest toys of the year first. Last year was no different; the news featured an argument between two parents over "cuts" in line as they waited for the 5 A.M. opening of a Toys R Us. At another store a woman was shoved so violently she sustained a black eye.

Stories of out-of-control adult shoppers are common when the holiday buying season starts, but concerns about consumption and advertising usually focus exclusively on children and teens, because many of us believe that they are easily influenced. Fears persist that young people are easily swayed by advertising, will be parted from their (and their parents') money, and are in need of protection from advertisers. But are young people really the naïve consumers we often presume them to be? This chapter explores two central fears associated with advertising and consumption: first, that children are the victims of the advertising industry; and second, that today's children are excessively materialistic as the result of advertising.

147

Consumption represents a step away from parental control and serves as a way of creating an identity distinct from parents. We will see that concerns about advertising and consumption reflect an ambivalence towards our consumer-driven culture. Rather than seriously question the nature of our consumerist society, we instead choose to focus anxiety exclusively on children. Advertisers speak directly to kids, sometimes working against parents' attempts to curb their material desires. Fears about advertising are based on this perceived intrusion, as well as on the difficulty parents have controlling information their kids get from media sources.

Fear #1: Children Are Victims of Advertisers

There is no shortage of people who believe advertisers have an unfair advantage over children, as a variety of news reports reveal. A spring 2000 *USA Today* article reported that psychologists have considered sanctioning colleagues who consult with advertisers.[1] A *Boston Herald* story described an advocacy group called "Stop Commercial Exploitation of Children," which calls for the federal government to create new regulations like those in Norway and Sweden, which ban advertisements targeted at children under twelve.[2] The group describes advertising as "A $12.8 billion-a-year industry that targets society's most vulnerable minds and deliberately excludes parents."[3] Articles in *The Nation* and *The American Prospect* describe children as "exploited" by marketers and in need of government protection because they are vulnerable to "being programmed" and are "too young to understand . . . that advertising may be harmful."[4]

Advertising is frequently described by its detractors as "emotionally harmful" to children, created by "corporate exploiters of children."[5] During her campaign for the Senate, Hillary Rodham Clinton called for limits on "advertising that is harmful to children," which begs the question: when is advertising "harmful?"[6] Are we living "a toxic cultural environment," as author Jean Kilbourne says, created by advertising?[7] Harm is rather loosely defined. For some, the fact that teenagers can easily identify brands of beer from advertisements is cause for alarm.[8] The concept of danger is difficult to empirically demonstrate but is instead described anecdotally to support demands that advertising is a clear hazard to children. Children are threatened, the logic goes, and therefore some adults ask the government (or have anointed themselves) to protect children from allegedly all-powerful advertisers. Kids are often targets of aggressive marketing campaigns, and this creates worry and anger.

Fear of advertising is peppered with language of assault and exploitation of a wide-eyed, simple-minded unsuspecting child. Children are presumed helpless in the face of advertising, described as "sacrificed for corporate profit" by manipulative, greedy Madison Avenue executives.[9] Parents are encouraged to "combat the effects of advertisements" and protect their children.[10] There's a big problem with this line of thinking, and it stems from the sentimentalized caricature of children and childhood. These advertising fears feed on this stunted, oversimplified view of children's knowledge and abilities. Of course young people (and adults) can be influenced by advertising campaigns and enjoy partaking in consumer culture. But before we assume children are always naïve consumers, it would be wise to find out what children already know, what capabilities and limitations they possess. We can work to create competency in dealing with advertising, but instead we often struggle to maintain the belief that children are weak and in need of protection. Competency building threatens the power adults hold over children and is seldom the focus of advertising fears.

Advertising does represent a challenge to parental boundaries. Advertisers don't ask parents' permission to speak with their children; they bypass parents and tell kids about things parents sometimes don't want them to know about, like candy and sugary cereals. The fact that children are a viable target market upsets many adults because it reminds us that children's influences have expanded beyond their parents alone, and that television is a major part of childhood. A *Los Angeles Times* article noted that "parents face (competition) in shaping their children's values," which is certainly true, but advertising and mass media are by no means the only competing factors when we consider the influence of peers, teachers, and other adults. Fears of the "danger" of advertising reveal adult anxieties about being unable to control children's interests and identities, which are in part demonstrated through consumption. Adult concerns about the nature of our consumption-driven society are more easily deflected onto children, because it's easier to worry about someone else's material desires than to question our own. Parents are charged with the responsibility of teaching kids how to be responsible consumers, which can feel overwhelming.

But while many adults jump to conclusions about what children can and can't understand, advertisers' use of research enables them to have a better understanding of central issues important to young people. In fact, advertisers describe marketing to children as a bigger challenge than selling to adults. By talking with kids within market research, advertisers learn about the power struggles many children feel between themselves and their parents and reflect this back in their ad campaigns. Marketers see young people of all ages trying to create separate identities from their parents, and thus food, toys, and fashion are all marketed as ways to be distinct from adults, yet similar to their friends. Public discussions describing young people as incapable of making informed decisions enhance the tensions they feel towards adults. Of course, advertisers are certainly not child advocates, and only attempt to address these feelings in order to sell things. The imbalance of power, as well as the desire to feel grown up, to be independent yet part of the crowd, are real elements of children's lives that many adults overlook when focusing only on children's shortcomings as consumers.

What Advertisers Know

Advertisers spend a great deal of their financial resources studying their target markets and learning about their values, beliefs, and their lifestyles. They are some of the only people who want to learn about children's fantasies and beliefs before making decisions about them. I am certainly not suggesting we celebrate market research departments because they listen to children; their main interest lies in co-opting youth culture and transforming it into a commodity, and the information they gather is not used to improve children's lives in a serious sort of way. Nonetheless, advertisers cannot afford to make assumptions about children like many of us do; there is simply too much money at stake.

So how do advertisers know what they know? They rely on research in the form of surveys with older groups, but more often than not researchers become anthropologists of "kid culture."[11] This is accomplished through the use of methods like focus groups, where a group of about a dozen is selected from the targeted age range and meets to answer a facilitator's questions. A good facilitator puts aside the role of omniscient adult long enough to let the young participants become the experts and inform the researchers about specific trends and their opinions about a product or other more general issues. As an episode of PBS's *Frontline* titled "The Merchants of Cool" detailed, marketers are constantly struggling to pin down what is currently "cool," something constantly shifting.[12] To discover the mystery of "cool," researchers rely on "cool consultants," or a panel of fashion-forward young people who report on trends within their peer groups for a fee. Very young (or young-looking) marketing staffers sometimes go out in the field themselves to mingle with teens to spy on them and co-opt any new trends. Of course the preeminent goal is selling a product, but marketing research is one of the few instances where adults treat kids as the experts of their own culture, and offer a chance for them to be heard (and paid).

Based on their research, advertisers create ads that they think will reflect central concerns that will resonate with their audience, be they children or adults. Marketing executives make a priority of finding out what kids in their target demographic are most concerned with. Sociologist Michael Schudson explains that "advertisements pick up and represent values already in the culture . . . [and] pick up some of the things that people hold dear and re-present them . . . assuring them that the sponsor is the patron of common ideals."[13] Advertisements for children thus appear to be sympathetic to kids and at times critical of adults. They mirror back whatever the target market wants to hear, and this message is clearly threatening to adults.

Here's what market researchers have found: not surprisingly, children often long for freedom and independence and feel constrained by adult authority while still wanting to know that they will be loved and cared for. Jane Hobson, associate director of Research International, notes "The trick is to aim a product just high enough so that older kids pick up on it and then it can filter down."[14] Jane Mathews, a British advertising specialist, similarly reports, "Children want to seem older and in control in an adult world . . . and they want to be accepted by their friends."[15] In fact, peers are more important sources of information for young people than advertising and influence their purchases more directly. Teens are also less likely to watch television than adults, particularly if they are from affluent families.[16]

But simply understanding a target group's central concerns doesn't guarantee sales.[17] In fact, an ad campaign is considered successful not simply based on sales but on whether brand awareness and market share increase. Advertising has been relatively unsuccessful in changing the size of a market and is instead most effective in obtaining a larger market share of those *already* consuming a product. If we consumers have an image to associate with a product, it may make us more likely to choose one particular brand over another, yet research demonstrates that brand awareness does not necessarily lead to acceptance of a product or a purchase.[18] This does not mean that advertising is unimportant or inconsequential. On the contrary, it reveals a great deal about relevant issues within American society. But advertising doesn't work the way many of us think it does. Commercials don't necessarily make anyone—child or otherwise—immediately think "I have to have that." Instead, advertising often works to remind us of a brand name and to link a particular image with their product. That's why most of us would feel more comfortable brushing our teeth with Crest toothpaste than a generic tube. We think we know something abut Crest, based on experience and from advertising.

Even liking an ad doesn't mean a child will want a product. For instance, an article in *Marketing*, a British trade magazine, described a ten-year-old boy who loves a yogurt commercial yet says he dislikes yogurt and does not plan on eating any.[19] The report went on to note that children are often entertained by ads, but this does not mean they are interested in the product. So children, like adults, are not necessarily tricked into buying things by slick ads that they may enjoy. Consumer behavior is more complex than cause-effect; persuasion is multifaceted and advertising is merely part of this process.

And advertisers know this. "They may be young, but they're not dumb," wrote Kristina Feliciano in *Mediaweek*, an American trade magazine.[20] "Kids don't want to be spoken down to, and they know from 'lame'," she warned advertisers.[21] This information shouldn't come as a big surprise, but it is indicative of advertisers' attempts to understand children from their own perspective, rather than consider children as simply less competent than adults. Jane Mathews, the British advertising specialist, reminds her colleagues that ads that seem patronizing to children do not work. A marketing textbook offers similar "timeless rules" of advertising to the youth market: never talk down to youth, be totally straightforward, and treat youth as if they are rational, thinking people.[22] Too bad when we adults complain about children's incompetence we don't realize these simple truths.

Unlike most adults, advertisers do not consider their young targets particularly gullible. "If there were a magic formula, we'd all be rich," an ad executive reports.[23] Instead, trade publications often speak of children as especially skeptical and difficult to address. *Marketing* writer Patrick Barrett notes that children are not necessarily "a

gullible soft target, but in fact are hard to hit and quick to switch off
. . . ad messages."[24]

Advertisers are fully aware of the knowledge they possess that
other adults, particularly parents, do not when it comes to understanding children. Marketing executive Andrew Marsden finds kids skeptical and knowledgeable about the communications world, and noted
that children are often more independent than their parents are willing
to admit.[25] "There is an element of naivete from parents. The world
they grew up in no longer exists," he remarked in *Campaign*, a marketing trade magazine.[26] He also finds teenagers to be particularly good
at manipulating parents. In spite of the popular (and tautological) belief that advertising must be highly effective since so much money is
spent doing it, advertisers are not overly confident about their ability
to reach young target markets. In fact, because children are seen as a
challenge, some companies such as Burger King have hired specialized
agencies to handle their children's campaign. It seems it may be easier
to influence the parents.

What advertisers know is not earth-shattering. It is not surprising
to learn that young people are interested in connecting with peers,
that popular culture is important, and so is the chance to feel heard in
an adult-centered world. These ideas surface throughout advertisements created for young people. Instead of focusing on advertising's
influence, we can use it to learn about our relationship with both children and consumption rather than only blaming media for kids' consumer behavior.

Advertising Revelation #1: Kids Fantasize About Triumphing over Adults

Recurring themes in children's advertising include the triumph of children over adults, freedom and adventure, and the desire to appear
older. Part of what may upset adults about advertising for children is
that it draws on the hostility that children often feel towards them. A
"good" child is obedient, conforming, and accepts adult authority. Parents' central struggles with their children are about kids' resisting
parental authority, which parents fight to maintain. Advertisers are
well aware of the centrality of these battles. Several Saturday morning
TV ads feature kids prevailing and outsmarting adults.[27] For instance, a
Toys-R-Us ad presents a boy of about twelve who is told in no uncertain

terms that he can only have one new toy. His eyes move excitedly across aisles and aisles of toys as a smirk fills his face. He runs outside as his confused parents haplessly chase after him. He has apparently outsmarted their one-thing-only challenge—his one thing is the whole store, which he attempts to drag with a rope. "I'm gonna need a really big bag," he says to his bewildered parents.

The fantasy of outwitting adults and subverting limits prevails in this and several other ads. While the Toys-R-Us ad promises an endless supply of toys, an ad for Pillsbury offers non-stop chocolate chip cookies, which the kids in the commercial two-fist with reckless abandon in an adult-free zone. One could certainly argue that ads like these promote gluttony and greed, but the fantasy of plenty is certainly part of many adult ads as well—see any lottery commercial and it becomes clear that having it all is a widespread American preoccupation.

Advertising offers the possibility of getting around adult-placed limits, addressing the desire for kids to make their own decisions and challenge parental restrictions. Several ads go beyond children merely outwitting adults and feature direct attacks on authority figures:

- A fast-paced M&M's candy commercial involves mischievous animated M&Ms climbing into a tube that is tossed off the side of a building. We see two elderly men (dressed in suspenders and bow ties, no less) sitting on a bench below, next to a large Dumpster. "Put the old men in garbage!" an M&M shouts, while a chorus of candies chants "Do it! Do it!" The men sit on the bench, motionless, and are splashed with garbage. Here the older generation appears helpless, foolish, and at the mercy of the child-like M&Ms.
- A similar spot for Oreo cookies involves another pair of hapless elderly men playing chess in a park. They hear rumbling. The ground begins to shake. They see other adults running in a panic as a wave of white cream explodes behind them. Cars are carried away by the cream before a bewildered meter maid can write parking tickets. Coffee-drinking cops are oblivious to the mayhem, which is taking place out the window right behind their backs. Cream explodes through a building, carrying a wealthy female socialite lounging in bed into the chaos. What is causing this pandemonium? Two twelve-year-old boys sit on a bench and survey the creamy disorder. "Whoa, do that again!" says one to the other, as he

mischievously twists open another Oreo. In this scenario kids have the power to create mayhem for the purpose of their amusement. They are separate from the chaos, as they sit above the creamy mess.

- A Cinna-Crunch cereal ad features a teenage boy in a Hawaiian shirt daydreaming in class, in defiance of an authoritarian teacher. Spinning a globe, the maniacal teacher (dressed in traditional tweed with elbow patches) asks the errant boy how the continents were formed. Busted? Not hardly. The boy draws inspiration from the box of cereal he has been snacking on and imagines Fred Flintstone and Barney Rubble on the sand with surfboards. The powder from the cereal magically breaks apart the continents and brings the ocean to Fred and Barney, who can surf at last. The ad concludes with the daydreamer lounging on the beach (with Cinna-Crunch cereal, of course) while the teacher is buried to his neck in sand.

All of these commercials feature the victory of youth over authority, a reverse of the typical social order. In these worlds, it is adults who are foolish and kids who have taken over. The linkage with snack food is almost incidental; rather than attempting to sell the product, each ad communicates a re-balance of power and a major shift of control. However in each of these ads it is a teen or pre-teen *boy* who challenges the mostly male authority, so the age order is challenged but the gender order is left intact. Adults may complain that these are the "wrong messages" for advertisers to "send" to children. But advertisers are not the originators of this message; they are instead projecting what they have learned from their research.

Advertising Revelation #2:
Kids Desire Freedom, Independence, and Adventure

When adults aren't being covered in Oreo cream filling or garbage and tricked by all-powerful kids, they are essentially absent. An ad promises that "nothing is easier" for kids to cook for themselves than Easy Mac, a microwave version of Kraft's Macaroni and Cheese. Kids visit restaurants alone in an ad for Burger King and in a candy ad, where kids converge alone at a diner. No adults are present in either restaurant—a child's dream. Cartoon children walk alone through a park and buy their own Trix yogurt. With each spoonful the park becomes more and more colorful. Part of children's fantasy is to live in their own world, free from adult regulation and restriction, while at the same time they take comfort in knowing parents are there for them.

In addition to power and independence, children's advertisements focus on adventure. "Let's go save people and stuff!" shouts one of the Power Puff Girls action figures. A Burger King ad features ten- to twelve-year-old boys and girls mountain-climbing, skateboarding, and playing soccer within its first fifteen seconds. A Universal Orlando theme park ad shows families riding a roller coaster together, but the twelve-year-old boy "explores the real life Jurassic Park" alone. And two boys (who look about fourteen and probably too old to really like Pokemon dolls) run through a field, quickly digging the Pikachu doll out of the woods as the voice-over proclaims that they now "can command Pika-power like never before." They become kings of their own adventure, reflecting both the creativity of play and a sense of mastery.

Advertising Revelation #3: Kids Want to Seem Grown-up

Although the teens shown would probably not find much interest in Pikachu dolls, advertisements commonly use older actors than the actual target audience. As market researcher Jane Hobson noted, advertisers presume that if older kids appear interested in a product it will seem cooler to younger kids.[28] Actors in commercials also are older than the would-be consumers because children want to appear more grown-up. After all, older kids have more freedom, and children are frequently told to wait until they are older for certain privileges or even answers to their questions. While adults tend to view childhood as a time of carefree innocence that should be retained as long as possible for the child's own good, we rarely question what adults gain from struggling to maintain childhood "innocence." It is no wonder that children want to be more like those who hold power, freedom, and independence. This desire is evident in several commercials where older children are used to sell products to younger ones.

In addition to the teenage boys seeking out Pikachu dolls, a Burger King ad asks directly, "What do big kids want?" The question is quickly answered: "Big kids want to be treated like big kids," the child announcer reminds us as a small group of preadolescents eat kids' meals (yet still play with the included Pokemon toys) alone in the restaurant. This ad clearly addresses a central concern of kids by inferring that their meals have grown-up appeal. Several candy ads feature older teenage boys and girls. Push Pops and Ring Pops are brightly colored lollipops licked by actors in their mid-teens, with fifteen- and sixteen-year-olds proudly wearing the Ring Pops on their fingers. This clearly appears to be a mismatch, but makes sense when we realize that if something looks "babyish" it loses its appeal to elementary-school-aged kids. Age thus serves to validate a product as acceptable.

The most interesting use of age was for a candy called Baby Bottle Pops, which presented infantile images with an undercurrent of sexuality. Freud would have a field day here; the candy is shaped like a baby bottle, and users are told they must first lick the top, turn it upside down into the bottle, and shake it until the nipple-like part is covered in a sweet powder. In essence the consumer appears to be sucking a baby bottle, but the commercial still attempts to link the product with teens and thus coolness. The ad begins with a group of teenaged girls entering a diner that appears to be a high school hangout. As they walk in they catch the eye of a group of similarly aged boys licking baby bottles. "They look like babies!" the girls shout as both groups begin singing (and flirting) while licking their bottles. The product is thus associated with older kids in spite of the infantile imagery, revealing the complexities of children's desire to be both "big kids" and babied at the same time.

Media fear has unwittingly drawn a line in the sand, as those who fear the power of advertising often underestimate children's abilities. Marketers, however, try to appear to be on the kids' side, acknowledging their central struggles in commercials with a wink and a nod. Advertisers also know that children derive both a sense of individual identity and group membership through consumption, which adults all too often dismiss when criticizing advertising and consumption. The anti-authority themes in advertising were not invented by crafty advertising executives—they were learned through research and mirrored back. Adults do not like to hear this message, but they are blaming the wrong messenger. We need to better understand how the imbalance of power between adults and children can create tension and the desire to rebel. If we don't like that advertisers use anti-adult themes to sell products adults may want to give them less ammunition and stop publicly condemning kids.

What Kids Know

So how effective are advertiser's techniques? The voices of panic seldom seem interested in what kids *do* know, how critical they may be, or how they think about advertising. Adults tend to view themselves as seasoned enough not to be vulnerable to advertising, which is referred to as the "third-person" effect; we rarely think that *we* are influenced by advertising, but are certain others are. A great deal of research points out that children are more capable than many of us realize. It shouldn't be a big surprise that people raised in a media-saturated society would have the ability to think beyond simply see-want-buy. Research indicates that children under six may be critical of ads and by the age of eight nearly all children are skeptical of advertisers' claims.[29] Pre-school children may be less critical, but they are also far less likely to recall advertisements later.[30] Marketing scholar Deborah Roedder John's review of twenty-five years of advertising research suggests that preadolescents' (ten- to twelve-year-olds) knowledge about advertising tactics and skepticism level is similar to that of young adults.[31] This finding reflects psychologist Jean Piaget's theory of cognitive development, which argues that critical thinking skills appear around the age of eleven, and thereafter kids are capable of analytical reasoning. In any case both children and adults can become more critical consumers, but we have to keep in mind that adult competencies are not dramatically better than adolescents and even most preadolescents.

Within the shrill debate about children, advertising, and consumption, children's abilities are often downplayed to invoke sentimental images of innocence corrupted. Calls are made to parents to "protect" kids from advertising and to limit children's "media diet" to the extent possible. But according to a 1998 study, teens who watch more television tend to be more skeptical and have more marketplace knowledge.[32] Nonetheless, media fears continue to insist that we view children's minds as blank slates that advertisers easily manipulate. Adult power is reinforced, since they are needed to "defend" the allegedly weak from harm. Protection can be used to restrict, to censor, and to deny children's right to desire. It is too simple to view kids as helpless victims instead of as decisionmakers with varying levels of critical ability—like adults.

Kids also know how to influence the adults around them, which drives a lot of parental anger towards advertisers. Apparently many parents find their children's powers of persuasion irresistible, or at least annoying. As Juliet B. Schor describes in *The Overspent American: Why We Want What We Don't Need*, parents are more likely to buy items for their children when there is a sense that not doing so would impair their chances for success or popularity.[33] Schor suggests that parents collectively agree to end the "upward creep" of consumption. While this is better than asking advertisers to simply stop marketing products that parents prefer their children did not have, it reveals that children do in fact hold power within families, and this challenges the traditional age order.

Do Kids Know Too Much?

Children's increasing consumer knowledge and power clearly make some adults uneasy. A 2001 *Time* magazine article titled "Who's in Charge Here?" cautioned that the shift in the balance of power could be deadly.[34] The story starts by describing how an overindulged seventeen-year-old crashed her Mercedes into another teenager while driving drunk and killed the other teen. Anecdotes about spoiled kids abound in stories such as these. Marketplace knowledge is also portrayed as a sign of overindulgence; the story describes a pre-schooler who told her teacher she was wearing a Calvin Klein dress. "Kids shouldn't know about designers by age four," the teacher laments. "They should be oblivious to this stuff." I'm guessing the child was aware of designer names because they are important to her parents. Yet the problem here is considered the child's, not the adults'.

Children continue to be the focus of our fears of hyper-consumption, especially when it appears that children's consumer knowledge is greater than that of their parents. Kids are thought to be especially influential when parents are purchasing computers or other technology products, and estimates of the amount of purchases children influence range from 100 to 300 billion dollars annually.[35] This leads those who fear advertising to insist that advertising teaches kids to "nag" too effectively—a pejorative way to describe communication between parents and children. A July 2001 *U.S. News & World Report* article uses the term "kidfluence" to describe the power children have to influence their parents' purchasing decisions. Kidfluence challenges the conventional notion that children are either nags or easy prey who need protection from "premature consumerism."[36] So perhaps the power of persuasion held by advertisers is not nearly as important as *children's* power to persuade adults. This power threatens traditional notions of adult-child relations and repositions children as sources of knowledge. Adults are often reluctant to acknowledge the degree to which children influence us—we are more accustomed to thinking of children as learners and adults as teachers, but it also works the other way around.

A *Boston Herald* article described a child's relationship with her grandfather.[37] "Grandfather . . . is putty in her seven-year-old hands," the article chided. "She knows what she wants; she works me," grandpa admitted. The article went on to describe how parents can combat their persuasive kids—by using "the ultimate weapon: the word 'no.'" A mother interviewed for the piece was described as such an example, as a mom who "doesn't fall prey to pressure from her son." The language here is that of battle; words like "weapon" and "falling prey" connote a rather antagonistic relationship between children and parents in the "war" of consumption. A *Los Angeles Times* article described advertising's "blitz upon us" as a menace to unprepared adults, who must learn to "combat the effects of advertisements."[38]

Who is the battle really between? While many adults outwardly claim that the conflict is between powerful advertisers and vulnerable kids, it appears the real struggle is between adults and children, and parents don't exactly know what to do. That's probably because they are fighting a battle that should instead be negotiated and serve as an opportunity to teach and learn about setting limits. Perhaps advertising creates a sense of inadequacy in parents because they can't possibly meet all of their children's material desires. The reality of advertising is that selling to kids is not nearly as simple as many of its detractors would have us believe. Advertisers know this and work to understand children on their terms—something the rest of us might try and do more often.

Fear #2: Children, Corrupted by Marketing, Are More Materialistic Now Than Ever

The fear that children are lured into our hyper-consumerist society too soon draws on romantic notions of childhood innocence, in which children are perceived as somehow untainted by consumer culture until advertisers enter their allegedly pure space. In reality, consumption often precedes birth. Parents with the means to do so spend thousands on branded nursery furniture, the right stroller, car seat, and brand-name clothes. But while blaming affluent parents for our culture of consumption may seem like the answer, the truth is our highly consumerist society has been created and sustained by a large shift in the American economy following World War II. Economist Daniel Bell described this as a "postindustrial" economy based on surplus and driven by consumption.[39] We live in a consumption-oriented society not simply because parents can't say no, but because our economy has been built on consuming abundance. Instead of recognizing these broad economic forces we tend to blame individual consumers, and usually other peoples' consumption at that.

Some fear that parents now spend "guilt money" on children to make up for the time they can no longer spend with them because they are so busy working to buy more stuff. But Ellen Galinsky, director of the Families and Work Institute, challenged the common belief that "selfish, greedy parents . . . sacrifice their children at the altar of their own materialism."[40] In her book *Ask the Children: What America's Children Really Think about Working Parents*, Galinsky notes that parents are in fact making family time an important priority. Suzanne Bianchi, a University of Maryland sociologist, supports this contention. In her 1998 study, Bianchi found that on average parents spend *more* time with children now than in the past.[41] Mothers spent an average of 5.8 hours with their kids each day in 1998 (compared with 5.6 hours in 1965), and fathers spent an average of four hours a day with children in 1998, a sharp rise from 2.7 hours in 1965.[42]

Nonetheless, other people's parenting skills remain an easy target. Blaming other parents enables the rest of us to avoid looking at our broad economic system that has created a culture of consumption. For example, in a *Chicago Sun-Times* op-ed, Betsy Hart facetiously wrote that she and her husband would like to be reincarnated as their own children "because of all the neat stuff they have."[43] But she insisted that it is *other* parents who cross the line: "our kids' stuff pales when compared with the indulgences enjoyed by many children and teens," she explained. A San Diego *Union-Tribune* headline warned parents "Don't Give Your Kids Too Much," and claimed that overindulgence is a problem in "any income bracket."[44]

By this logic, children as a group have too much—it's not just a handful of choice examples, as such stories present, but allegedly a large-scale problem. In a *Time*/CNN poll conducted in the summer of 2001, 80 percent of parents agreed with the statement that kids are more spoiled than ten to fifteen years ago.[45] For many adults, materialism appears to be a widespread problem among today's youth. A 1997 PBS special supports this belief, warning parents that "affluenza" has become a national "epidemic."[46] An anti-advertising group blames childhood affluenza on advertisers, proposing that "no advertising (should be) directed at kids that promotes an ethic of selfishness."[47] Betsy Hart concurred in her *Chicago Sun-Times* piece: "We have a serious problem of a generation of kids who don't know what it means to be told 'no.'"[48] A whole generation? While this is quite a sweeping generalization, Hart's opinion is clearly shared by many. Each generation tends to believe that the next is worse than their own, but this is more than benign age-centrism. By continuing to believe that greed is a characteristic of youth today, we can overlook that an estimated one million children suffer from neglect each year and that in any given year about one in five American children are living in poverty. Is affluenza really their biggest problem? Probably not, but believing that children are categorically overindulged diverts our attention from funding programs to assist those in need. After all, if kids have so much, why give any more?

Consuming Schools

Another way we stiff children is by underfunding public education to the degree that many schools now accept various forms of corporate involvement. In her *Toronto Star* column, writer Rachel Geise charged that "Advertising has invaded all of children's 'safe spaces' like schools and playgrounds."[49] While advertising did enter schools as never before during the 1990s, it may be better to ask who left a vacuum for corporations to rush in and fill. Instead of looking at who is invading, we need to take a good look at why the rest of us ran away.

Advertisers have stepped in to fill the void left behind by a society that has steadily divested from public education. California, for example, changed property tax laws in 1978, which led to a sharp drop-off in the state's overall rank of expenditures per student.[50] In some communities the local tax base has been decimated by tax breaks to lure corporations to relocate there. So as distasteful as corporate-sponsored schools, beverage contracts, and in-class market research may be, we have to acknowledge that as a society we have created a situation where schools are faced with few other options. In 1993, a Colorado Springs school district became the first in the country to court advertisers; this district had been unable to pass a school levy for nearly twenty years at that point.[51] This occurred four years after Channel One was introduced in classrooms across the country, a news-like program containing advertisements that students in host schools had no choice but to watch. In exchange a school could receive up to $50,000 in audio-visual equipment.[52] Other examples of corporate America's entrance into public schools abound:

- Coca-Cola and Pepsi each provide six-figure signing bonuses and cash advances to schools signing exclusive contracts;
- A company called ZapMe! offered thousands of dollars worth of computer equipment and high-speed Internet access in exchange for constant ad streams and tracking students' browsing habits;[53]
- Corporations like Exxon, Kellogg's, and Domino's Pizza mail free "educational" materials like videos, posters, booklets, and software directly to teachers.

Money, lesson plans, computers, and audio-visual equipment are all things that schools need that we all too often fail to provide. If this angers you, you are certainly not alone. At the time of this writing, legislation is pending in both Maryland and California to ban sales of soda and junk food in schools. On a smaller scale, groups such as the Center for Commercial-Free Public Schools have convinced some school board members to reconsider accepting corporate funding. But until school districts receive adequate public funding, school boards will feel pressure to take corporate money. Advertisers appear to value children as consumers more than our society values them as students, and advertisers are fronting the money to prove it.

While we need to acknowledge our own responsibility in creating the void that advertisers seek to fill in schools, we also need to recognize that young people can develop the ability to think critically about advertising. Some teachers report using the ads from Channel One or the corporate-sponsored curriculum materials to teach about propaganda and bias. Ironically, the omnipresence of ads may itself serve to drain the influence out of advertising. "They just fade into the background," a high school student remarked about the ads in his school, which are so widespread he barely noticed them anymore.[54] This is what advertisers call "clutter," turning ads into white noise that we become so accustomed to that we cease to see them after a while. Schools are beginning to look like the rest of American society, where public space is branded space.[55]

Simply banning in-school advertising or corporate sponsorship ignores schools' lack of adequate resources. Additionally, public education policy has increasingly mirrored a business model, trying to foster competition between schools via standardized tests and using funding as a reward rather than a right. This model of education makes students themselves a product. The logic of school vouchers is much the same. It seems that many adults have a hard time understanding success outside of the logic of consumption . . . yet we think *children* are especially vulnerable to corporate influence?

Rethinking Childhood and Consumption

While we should be concerned that corporations seem more interested in funding public education than the public does, participating in consumer culture doesn't necessarily mean that children (or adults) are inordinately materialistic. Researcher Ellen Seiter found, in a study of preschool children, that consumption is used to create both group and individual identity.[56] The children wore T-shirts with recognizable logos and carried lunch boxes with Disney characters to create a shared culture and let their peers know that they were "in on" kid culture. I recall that in my own childhood, consumption was used in much the same way. When I was in the third grade, having a mini wind-up doll called a "kidalong" meant you could play kidalong mom with the other girls. We also bought mini desk organizers with tiny drawers for our desks at school and colorful binders to hold our schoolwork. I chose a green pencil holder and a binder with a plaid cover that at once set me apart and marked my group membership. Consumption is a social act: buying may be an individual activity, but the types of purchases we make can create a sense of shared identity. Children's play with particular toys or knowing about the latest fad is a way of creating a shared culture. Adults use consumption in the same way, of course, buying cars, gadgets, and clothes that indicate we are members of various groups.

Maybe we should question why consumption is so much a part of fitting in with other kids, but curiously few adults ask the same question about our own behavior, like why we desire a $50,000 car when the $15,000 one works just as well or better. It's too simple to say we are all just fodder for advertising genius. We consume what we do for a number of reasons: we need things, we are making statements about who we are as individuals, and we are affiliating ourselves with certain groups, making status distinctions. Children are no different in this regard.

We therefore need to take caution when we criticize children for exhibiting buying habits similar to our own. The key difference between children's consumption and our own is that as adults we tend to be outsiders in the world of children's culture. Their consumption is an easy target for us because their culture may not hold meaning for us and may even seem silly. Some parents cite the fervor over fads like Pogs or Pokemon as proof that children are easily duped into throwing money away on items adults find useless. Scott Donaton wrote in *Advertising Age* of his disgust after taking his kids to see *Digimon: The Movie,* which he called "an unimaginative wholesale rip-off."[57] I'm not sure what his kids thought, and of course he is entitled to his opinion, but too often adults judge children's culture based on our own tastes. When adults view children's tastes pejoratively it is easy to proclaim that slick advertisers have hoodwinked kids, rather than recognize that children may enjoy things we adults don't get.

Kid culture creates anxieties amongst adults when it becomes apparent that their children's sources of influence have expanded beyond the family. Children's consumption decisions are shaped by peers, teachers, and other adults—no longer do parents have the ability to fully influence their children's tastes. Creating separate identities signifies a loss of control, a wedge between parents and children. Advertising's power is more symbolic than real, but to many parents it signifies a very real loss of power.

Children use consumption to begin to assert their independence from their parents, as being a consumer in American society is a step towards maturity. Cultural anthropologist Cindy Dell Clark found in her interviews with elementary school children and their parents that money left by the "tooth fairy" serves as an important rite of passage.[58] A child may begin to earn an allowance at this age, and thus they learn to become consumers in their own right. Clark notes that this time is often difficult for parents, who must come to terms with the fact that their child's "babyhood" has ended. So while the step towards independence is important, parents may indeed feel a powerful sense of loss that accompanies a child's entrée into the world of consumer culture. Advertisers get blamed for "luring" children out into the world, but within a consumerist society this is in fact an inevitable and in some respects necessary step away from total parental control. Anxiety about young children's consumption coincides with their first steps towards independence and the decreased centrality of their families.

Of course an identity *only* based on consumption is rather empty, and concerns about advertising often stem from the fear that consumption is making this generation more superficial than children of the past. But learning to be a responsible consumer means learning that simply having things will not fill all of our needs. This may be a hard lesson to teach. Yes, in part because advertisers do insist their products will cure what ails us, but more importantly because lots of us have yet to master this lesson ourselves. *Los Angeles Times* fashion writer Valli Herman-Cohen gushed that she "love(s) (her) insanely expensive purse . . . and everything it says about me."[59] Although tongue-in-cheek, the author explained how good it made her feel to buy the deeply "discounted" bag (marked down from $2,000 to a bargain $1,500). At the same time we need to recognize that consumption can be pleasurable—who am I to judge how a person spends $1,500 of her own money? My point here is that we adults haven't done a great job resisting advertisers' claims that a newer new car is the answer or that we can lose ten pounds this weekend by swallowing some magic powder.

These are all serious issues to address in a consumer-oriented society, where we are told by government leaders that if we stop consuming people will lose their jobs and where interest rates are lowered to encourage us to buy things we can't afford and to discourage saving. Yet public discussion tends to focus exclusively on children's consumption and seldom turns a critical eye on advertising for adults. In fact, if adults do question capitalism or our culture of consumption, they tend to be viewed as radical extremists. But adults can safely charge the next generation for being overly materialistic or pawns of advertisers without challenging the status quo. Rather than address consumption head-on, we deflect our concerns onto children and their consumption.

We adults are very much a part of a consumption-oriented society, where we show people we love them with material goods and are asked to shop to show our patriotism. Children are regularly rewarded with gifts and learn that special holidays means special consumption, that happiness can be found in a store. Consumption is the building block of a capitalist society and has become the hallmark of American culture.

If people have a problem with capitalism and consumption, fine. Just don't leave yourself out of the circle of responsibility: if kids are overly materialistic, it is because the rest of us are.

Critical Consumerism

Instead of simply trying to eliminate children's relationship with consumer culture, I advocate critical consumerism, a mode of behavior that acknowledges that we are part of a consumption-based society. This means admitting that the experience of consumption can be fun and enjoyable but can also be empty and ultimately cannot fill every emotional need, as it often promises.

Parents and teachers ought to focus on preparing children to be members of a consumer-driven culture, or, if truly concerned about our consumption-based society, attempt to change the nature of the culture itself. This, of course, is a much more difficult task, since many adults have no intention of changing their own behavior. So rather than continually attempting to shield children from the pervasive culture of consumption, which eventually fails, we should work to create more critical consumers, starting with ourselves.

To do so we must first acknowledge the pleasurable aspects of our own consumption and recognize that children experience the same feelings. This process must be reflective rather than authoritative; people don't want to be told they have bad taste, including children. Adults should move beyond only controlling what children purchase and seek to learn what meaning children give to products. Both adults and children would benefit from challenging the belief that consumption and happiness go hand in hand.

Additionally, we need to understand that advertising is just a piece of a big puzzle, that consumerism is built into the fabric of American economic and cultural life. Trying to safeguard against "premature consumerism" is a tactic that is doomed to fail. Learning to be wise consumers is far more useful than attempting to keep children away from commercial contact.

The Real Fear: Losing Control

The fear of advertising stems from adult ambivalence about the nature of our consumer-based culture, but also from children's power to influence adults. Additionally, children use consumption to create cultural experiences separate from their parents, by aligning their tastes with peers. All of these things represent a loss of adults' control over children's worlds and thus a perceived reduction in adult authority. A child with independent tastes and desires represents a step away from conventional adult power. But rather than recognize the autonomy children may express, we are quick to blame advertisers for imposing "false" needs on children. To deny any influence of marketing and media culture would be naïve, but so too is any view of children that negates the complex process of peer culture and identity in negotiating desire.

Until we deal with the tension created by the imbalance of power between adults and children, advertisers will be able to continue to utilize this tactic to gain the trust and attention of young people. The answer is not to totally eliminate adult authority, but instead to take a closer look at where adult power is used arbitrarily. Discourse that uniformly condemns children as ignorant consumers easily swayed by advertising is one such abuse of power, a sweeping generalization that deepens the rift between generations. Adults cannot legislate taste or identity, nor can we ensure that kids grow up to be exactly whom we hope they become. Both children and adults can be empowered by learning to become more critical and knowledgeable about consumption, but this can't happen with a "you-first" attitude. Adults need to take the lead by examining our own relationship with consumer culture.

8

Fear of Sex

Do the Media Make Them Do It?

When I was twelve I did something I never had done before: I snuck into an R-rated movie. My friend and I told our parents we would be seeing a PG film playing at the same complex and bought tickets for that movie, so when they dropped us off and later picked us up they would have no idea. When the lights went down we walked into another theater to see *Young Doctors in Love*, which promised to feature a racier version of our favorite daytime soaps.

In spite of feeling that any minute an usher would appear and kick us out, it seemed remarkably easy to enter this forbidden zone. But aside from a few more four-letter words, the movie was no different than any television show I'd seen except it was longer. This of course did not stop us from embellishing what we saw when we returned to school on Monday. I was finally part of the group who had seen an R-rated movie, and for a day that felt good.

My story is not unique, of course. At one point most young people take a peek behind the iron curtain of adulthood. Knowledge about sex is often kept from children as long as possible, considered the final frontier separating adults from children. It is a hard-fought battle that is almost never won by adults, in part because sex permeates our media culture. Sex becomes associated with maturity and with status largely because adults define it that way and our popular culture appears to be obsessed with sex. It only makes sense for young people to be curious, and media culture threatens to satisfy all sorts of sexual curiosities.

Sex is feared almost as much as violence, and the belief that sexuality in media culture will increase teen sexual activity is quite common. Headlines like "Don't Let TV Be Your Teenager's Main Source of Sex Education," "Grappling with Teen Sex on Television," and "Racy Content Rising on TV" have created an atmosphere of anxiety amongst adults who fear that the "rules have changed" and that young people are becoming more promiscuous.[1] The truth is, young people are a lot more responsible than *Jerry Springer*, *Ricki Lake*, or MTV's *Spring Break* and *Real World* might have us believe from shows like "help, my daughter is a slut!" and the like. Topics like "my teen is going on a date" might be more applicable to regular kids, but probably not a big ratings grabber. Horror stories of teen promiscuity make the media rounds to demonstrate the popular hypothesis that kids now are morally depraved (note stories about equally promiscuous adults aren't considered newsworthy) and imply the media are at fault. Has media culture created a sex-crazed generation? While yes may be the simple answer, this chapter critically assesses common beliefs about media, youth, and sex and demonstrates that the relationship between the three is more complex than we are often told. As we will see, changes in economics and demographic shifts during the past century have driven changes in sexual attitudes and behavior. But sexuality has always been part of coming of age, and parents have always felt anxious about this passage. The declining ability of adults to control children's sexual knowledge has created a high level of fear and that fear is often focused on popular culture. When we take a closer look at how young people make sense of sexuality in media, we see that they are not simply influenced by popular culture, but use sexual representations to create identity and status within their peer groups.

Teenage Sex: New Media, New Mores?

While attending a seminar about issues concerning contemporary youth, a man who appeared to be in his early to mid-fifties said with certainty, "People didn't have sex before marriage back when I was a kid. It just wasn't done." He was very sure of himself and it was clear he wanted to set the younger expert straight. "You weren't there," he told her. "Now things are totally different. Kids today just don't have the same morals."

I wasn't there either, but then again neither was he. The time he spoke of did not exist. The history he remembers is likely television and film history. On that count, he would be right. It just wasn't done—on TV.

Sexual behavior steadily changed throughout the twentieth century. During the "good old days" adults shared many of the same fears that today's parents have, that young people were engaging in behavior they never did at their age, and that kids today have too much freedom and not enough sexual restraint. Chances are, if history is any indicator, in about fifty years people will look back at today as an age of innocence too. When it comes to young people and sexuality, the past has always seemed more innocent because it is viewed through the lens of nostalgia.

Sexuality in media has always been a cause for concern. Film content in the 1920s reflected changes in sexual mores, featuring Rudolph Valentino's passionate kissing and sometimes even female nudity. Hollywood's early stars created scandals just like those in our own era; their wild parties, frequent failed marriages, and sex scandals made conservative groups weary. Movies were a new source of influence that religious leaders feared would bypass the family, school, and religion in importance in young people's lives. Politicians and the Catholic Legion of Decency called for government censorship. Instead, the new film industry guaranteed self-regulation by what came to be known as the Hays Office, led by prominent political figure Will Hays, to monitor movie content and ensure it met the standards of a new code, formally implemented in 1934.[2] As the country took a more conservative turn at the end of the 1920s, the Hays Office restricted film content to what was deemed "wholesome entertainment." This included censoring any content that appeared to criticize "natural or human" laws so as not to incite "the lower and baser element" of American society.[3] Rules governing film production were overtly racist—no interracial relationships were allowed—and any criticism of the status quo was interpreted as a violation of the "moral obligation" of the entertainment establishment. An extremely reactionary ideology of filmmaking was justified in the name of preserving children's "innocence."

The Hays Code dominated film production until 1966. In an attempt to compete with the rise of television, films started presenting sexuality more frankly beginning in the 1960s, particularly as European "New Wave" films by directors like Federico Fellini and Jean Luc Godard helped redefine movies as art. Twenty years later, cable television and videos brought more sexually explicit programming into the home. Sex has become another product of contemporary society, circulating more rapidly and difficult to control and regulate because highly sexualized images attract attention and profit. Adults now have less control over what young people know about sex, which blurs the perceived distinction between adults and children.

Popular culture *is* different today than in the past and provides an easy (but ultimately misguided) answer to explain social changes. We didn't arrive here on the coattails of television or movies; popular culture incorporates and reflects societal issues and values, many of which some people find objectionable. Instead of targeting attention solely on popular culture, we need to first understand the social context of sex in twentieth and twenty-first century America.

New Century, New Meanings

During a discussion in my juvenile delinquency course a student once volunteered that he was sure teen sex is much more prevalent now than ever before. "We don't hear about teenage pregnancy being a problem during colonial times or anything," he noted.

There is some truth to this statement, particularly because "teenagers" as we now think of them did not exist until about one hundred years ago. Colonial "teens" were likely to be regarded as adults with full familial and economic responsibilities. G. Stanley Hall's 1904 book *Adolescence: Its Psychology and Its Relations to Physiology, Anthropology, Sociology, Sex, Crime, Religion and Education* defined the phase we now largely think of as an inevitable stage of life. Hall described adolescent years as a biologically-based time of "storm and stress." However, cross-cultural and historical studies have not found adolescence as we know it to have existed in all societies, suggesting the teenager is more of a social than biological creation.[4] Thus, it is hard to compare the teenagers of today with those of the past. This new phase of life emerged as the outcome of industrialization and the diminished necessity for people in their teens to join the labor force. Previously, the group we now know of as teenagers often functioned as adults: they worked instead of attending school and may have been married with children. The time before adulthood steadily lengthened throughout the twentieth century, as did the gap between sexual maturity and marriage. Socially and sexually we expect teenagers today to function partially as adults and partially as children. The roles and expectations of adolescents today are far different from their counterparts a hundred years ago.

New Sexual Freedom

It is nearly impossible to understand changes in dating rituals without considering the economic context. Courtship began to change with the rise of industrialization and was marked by the gradual decrease of adult control. In rural life work was concentrated in the home, so supervision of courtship was much simpler: a suitor might call on a potential mate at her home with parents or chaperones very close by. Industrialization led to the growth of cities and took adults away from the home for longer periods of time. The possibility for supervision decreased, as did the amount of space a family might have had in which courtship could take place. Dating thus moved from the parlor to the public sphere, and progressively became more of an independent pursuit with less family intervention. Highly populated cities offered more anonymity and the expansion of suburbs following World War II created even more space for young people to congregate away from adults. The new affluence of the postwar era brought more leisure time for teens, and teenagers could do what they wanted with less fear of getting caught or punished. Economic changes led to higher rates of high school and college attendance, which increased separation between adults and young people. In my own suburban teen life, affluence sometimes led parents to travel and ultimately "my-parents-are-out-of-town" parties. I was never left home alone, and I still won't rat out my friends who were, but let's just say that traveling parents created all sorts of opportunities for teens to do things they wouldn't if their parents were home.

The 1950s economic boom created the possibility for many people to experience youth as a time of leisure, while a generation before teens were much more likely to be in the labor force. Young people were likely to have fewer responsibilities than their parents had before them, and childhood and adolescence were increasingly seen as time for fun.[5] Dating became associated with recreation rather than procreation, as the search for a spouse became a more distant concern. Historian Beth L. Bailey describes how remaining chaste before marriage gradually lost its economic value in the marriage market, particularly as women had more opportunities to become self-supporting.[6]

Additionally, technological changes created more freedom for young people. The widespread availability of electricity at the beginning of the twentieth century enabled nightlife to emerge away from the family home, and the automobile became an important part of

American dating. Courtship grew even more difficult to monitor, as having a car provided more privacy, opportunities for sexual experimentation, and the ability to travel even farther from parental supervision. Drive-in restaurants and movies as well as lovers' lanes are examples of semi-private settings where teens went to be away from parental supervision.

Contrary to nostalgia, premarital sex did occur before the so-called sexual revolution of the 1960s; it was the *reaction* to premarital sex that changed. In mid-century, for instance, if sex resulted in pregnancy, it was more likely to remain secret through a quick marriage, a forced adoption, or, for the affluent perhaps, an abortion disguised as another medical procedure.[7] The main difference now is that we are more likely to acknowledge both premarital sex and teen pregnancy compared with in the past, and it is certainly talked about in public forums and in the news media. Teenage girls today are less likely to be pressured into early marriage and more likely to have access to birth control.

Premarital sex and pregnancy have always been part of the contemporary social landscape. As noted in Chapter 1, American culture has extended childhood while physical maturation is reached earlier than a century ago. Yet we still often hope that people who are sexually mature don't engage in sexual behavior before socially defined adulthood, if not marriage. A full 72 percent of adults responding to the 1998 General Social Survey agreed that teen sex before marriage is "always wrong," yet a large proportion of people engage in sex before their teen years end.[8] In all likelihood many in the survey had premarital sex themselves, but help build a generation gap by insisting teens do as we say, not as we did.

Asexual Children?

Movies, daytime soap operas, talk shows, and the Internet are often filled with sexualized imagery. If only children were not exposed to so much so soon, popular thinking goes, they would maintain their "innocence" instead of becoming sexually active. In a *Los Angeles Times* commentary, radio talk show host Dennis Prager claimed that children are by nature "asexual beings" who would never know anything about sex if it weren't for media.[9] Prager's view of childhood is one of complete sentimentality: in his opinion a boy looking up a classmate's skirt is completely devoid of sexuality. Even teaching children about sexual harassment is a form of sexual abuse, according to Prager. Of course a talk show host earns a living by presenting outrageous ideas, but the belief that children are inherently asexual until "corrupted" by media is one many adults believe.

Adults often attempt to deny the importance of sexuality within childhood, because to do otherwise is kind of scary. After all, America was largely founded by Puritans. Sexual innocence serves as a major marker in the way our society presently defines children and distinguishes them from adults. Interestingly, the term "adult" tends to connote sexuality rather than responsibility. "Adult" books and "adult" films indicate sexual content, not emotional maturity. We like to believe that knowledge of sex represents the last remaining dividing line between childhood and adulthood.

But does it really?

Sexual exploration is and has been a big part of childhood, but perceptions of how parents should deal with sexually curious children have shifted during the past century.[10] Before World War II, American child-rearing practices reflected the belief that controlling children's behavior could prevent any "inappropriate" sexual exploration. In the postwar era the influence of Sigmund Freud and Benjamin Spock altered perceptions about sexuality and childhood. Both Freud and Spock considered children inherently sexual, so sexual curiosity was natural, even necessary for healthy development. Unlike the prewar notion that control created a well-adjusted child, postwar advice urged parents to avoid shaming their children lest a fixation develop. Parents were encouraged to provide information about sex, a major shift from prewar practices.

Starting in the early 1970s a backlash against the new openness began.[11] The 1960s tends to get the credit for being a time of sexual freedom, but actually the 1970s was the time when much experimentation happened. This new sexual openness led to fears that a more accepting approach to childhood sexuality had gone too far, that the lack of discouragement in early childhood led to less restraint against premarital sex. But think back to your own "facts of life" talk, if your parents had one with you. If it was anything like mine, it was tense and embarrassing for all parties involved—certainly not a pep talk. Concerns about parents' being "too open" blamed behavioral changes on the availability of information and did not take into account the demographic, economic, and political changes of the twentieth century. Our

contemporary ambivalence about sexuality was born, as were complaints that the media make them do it. Today American adults want
young people to be both psychologically healthy and sexually re-
strained, which is why we are at best ambivalent about providing children with information about sex; sex education now is often just
abstinence education.

Sexuality, as much as adults may like to convince themselves otherwise, is not only a part of adulthood and adolescence but also a part
of early childhood. We often dismiss things like childhood crushes as
innocent puppy love, but the reality is that the development of sexual
identity is an important component of childhood. Instead of young
people simply learning about sex in the media and then acting on what
they watch, preteens and teens try to make sense of what they see in
the context of their other experiences. Seeing all these images of sex
does not necessarily mean that children interpret them by having sexual intercourse, but instead that coming to terms with sexuality in
popular culture and their lives is a major part of adolescence and
preadolescence as well.

A Tale of Two Studies

A 2001 Kaiser Family Foundation study of sex on television is a great
example of the traditional American approach to understanding sex,
youth, and media.[12] The study received a great deal of media attention
because it follows the conventional wisdom that there is even more
sex on TV than ever, presumed to be a potential danger to youth. This
study's assumptions are in direct contrast to a 1999 British study that
received no American media attention. The British study critically examines how children make sense of representations of sexuality and
romance on television.[13] Comparison of these two studies reveals our
tendency to underestimate youth and overstate the power of popular
culture.

Assumptions of the Kaiser Study

While the authors of this study insist that television is not the most important factor in sexual socialization, television is the main focus of
their study. Researchers analyzed over a thousand television pro-

grams, counting incidents they deemed sexual in nature.[14] By using content analysis, researchers determined what they believe to be the central messages of these programs, yet they interviewed no young people to ascertain how they actually interpret these messages. This method isolates meaning from the context of both the program and the audience, a problem the researchers don't seem to be worried about. Additionally, this study broadly defines sexual messages to include flirting, alluding to sex, touching, kissing, and implication of intercourse. When the incidents get boiled down into statistics, hugs and handholding appear the same as more explicit representations of sex.

Perhaps most troubling are assumptions about youth that are never tested empirically. The researchers seem to presume that young viewers will be heavily influenced by television, completely negating young peoples' ability to interpret media images on their own.[15] The authors presume that media are an important source of information about sex for teens, but media sources are not where young people get most of their knowledge. Within the report, authors noted that only 23 percent of teens say they learn "a lot" about pregnancy and birth control from television, while 40 percent have "gotten ideas on how to talk to their boyfriend or girlfriend about sexual issues" from media.[16] We focus on media when other sources are clearly more important because media is the feared spoiler of innocence—it is always there for us to credit with social influence and enables us to overlook the complexity of the history of sexuality and social change.

In the third paragraph of the Kaiser Family Foundation study the authors note almost as an aside that many teens feel they do not get enough information about sex from parents or teachers. Rather than focusing on this point, we belabor the media issue. We fear that popular culture is filling the void that nervous adults have created and beg Hollywood to teach kids about sex more responsibly. Here's an idea: how about we initiate a dialogue about sex ourselves, where young people are not just preached to but heard. We ought to stop whining about what young people shouldn't know and start dealing with what they *do* know. Adults should focus on enriching, rather than restricting young people's knowledge about sex. Media gets flak for leaking what we like to think of as adult information, which we are either too embarrassed or unwilling to share ourselves.

The authors cite the risky sexual behaviors some adolescents engage in to support the need for their research, but they fail to provide real context.[17] In emphasizing negative behaviors, important statistics get buried. Prime example: the majority of teens under fifteen (80 percent of girls and 70 percent of boys) reported *not* being sexually active.[18] Most of those sexually active reported using condoms, yet the authors of the Kaiser Family Foundation report chose to invert these statistics to tell the negative story. Dangerous behavior is of course important to examine, but perhaps the biggest problem here is that we focus on adolescent risk and fail to put it in the context of *adult* behavior. For instance, the 1998 General Social Survey found that just 20 percent of adults used condoms during their last sexual encounters. By ignoring adults within the media-sex panic we pathologize teen behavior even if it is consistent (or even better than) that of adults.[19]

In sum, this study found that sexual content (as the researchers define it) on television rose from a similar study two years before, but so what? We are left with no information about how young people actually interpret and make sense of these programs. It is important that we find out how young people interpret sexual images in advertising, music, and television in their context, and in their own words. If we are so concerned about teen sexuality we need to talk with them, not just about them, to learn more. The British study did just that.

Talking "Dirty"

Initiating conversations about sex with children is not just frowned upon, in some situations it is considered morally questionable or even illegal. Likewise, providing sex education in schools is frequently the subject of fierce debate. Maybe that's why studies like the one conducted by the Kaiser Family Foundation only focus on television. Talking about sex is considered indecent where children are concerned, enabling us to maintain the illusion that they can be separated from the rest of the world.

No doubt, this is why the British authors chose a provocative title for their study, which takes a rather different perspective on media and young people than the Kaiser Family Foundation study. "Talking Dirty: Children, Sexual Knowledge and Television" was published in the journal *Childhood* in spring 1999 with no American fanfare. Not surprising, considering that the authors challenge our assumptions about childhood and sexuality at every turn. First, the authors critique the belief that television is responsible for the loss of childhood "innocence" and argue it is best to find out what children *do* know rather than continue to focus on what adults *want* them to know. To that end, the researchers were more concerned with how the children they studied made sense of the programs they watched, and how they understood the content in the context of their own lives. Unlike the Kaiser Family Foundation study, which presumed heavy influence, these researchers were interested in how children negotiated their social roles as children dealing with a subject that is regarded off-limits for them. The research team sought to find out what the children knew and how they made sense of it on their own terms, avoiding value judgments in the process.

Secondly, in contrast with traditional views that we need only pay attention to teenagers when it comes to sex, these researchers talked with six-, seven-, ten-, and eleven-year-olds in small groups, asking them to talk about what programs they liked and disliked. Children were then asked to sort a list of program titles into categories, which enabled researchers to see how the children defined adult content compared with programs that the kids considered appropriate for children, teens, or general audiences. Sex itself was not brought up by researchers but by the children, often used by the kids to define adult programs.

Researchers found that although most children felt that programs with romantic themes were "adult" shows (like *Ricki Lake* and *Blind Date*), the ten- and eleven year-olds were quite familiar with these programs and others like them. Kids reported that adult shows were appealing because they knew that they were supposed to be off-limits. I know when I was that age I was very curious about sex and attempted to read a book a friend said contained "everything." *Forever*, written by Judy Blume, was the perfect gift to ask my grandparents for because they knew that I read all of Blume's books for kids, yet they did not know that my parents wouldn't let me read it (which made me want to read it even more). But sadly, when I got the gift, my mother confiscated it. For a fleeting moment I was the envy of all my friends at my birthday party. Likewise, the authors of the *Childhood* study note that claiming interest or knowledge of an "adult" program elevates one's status amongst peers. It was not uncommon for some kids to claim knowledge of a show when they clearly hadn't seen it. Other research has found similar results when studying children's interest in horror films; the more restrictive rating the film earned, the greater mark of status kids attained by watching.[20]

Gender was also central in identifying children's interest in the television programs discussed. The younger boys in particular were likely to deny any interest in shows with kissing or romantic themes. That was "girl stuff," which they wanted no part of. The authors also observed that children feigned shock or disgust about romantic scenes, a response common amongst preadolescents in adult company.

Rather than advance the narrow view that sexual content does something *to* children, this research informs us that it is used *by* children to build peer connections and to make sense of sexuality from a safe distance. Children use adult themes from television to try to demonstrate adult-level competence and knowledge. The researchers concluded that neither television nor audiences "hold anything approaching absolute power. Television obviously makes available particular representations and identities. . . . In defining and debating the meanings of television, readers also claim and construct identities of their own."[21]

In my own research with high school students, I found that sexuality in media is used differently depending on the context: in groups comprised of mostly males, sexuality was collectively defined as the celebration of women as objects, while mainly female groups tended to challenge the objectification of women's sexuality.[22] One male student (whom I'll call Scott) stood out the most. Scott appeared to be sixteen, slender, and perhaps the class intellectual, and I got the impression that his remarks were less heartfelt and more for the benefit of his male peers. After viewing an Evian commercial with a nubile woman swimming alone in a pool, Scott eagerly announced that he wanted to "buy this girl." In truth, it seemed his intention was to fit in with his more athletic peers than it was to demean women. As his male classmates laughed, he continued, saying "I just want to go buy Evian with that girl swimming in it . . . I just like her commercial!" His peers met Scott's comments with supportive amusement. Interestingly, boys in predominantly female groups tended to agree with their female classmates that the ad's use of a scantily clad woman was offensive. The teens I studied clearly demonstrate how the meaning of popular culture is created collectively in the context of peer culture, a negotiation process that goes way beyond simple cause-and-effect.

As the above example demonstrates, sometimes the way people talk about sexuality is a way to bolster their status among their friends. Rather than only criticize the quantity of sexual images in the media, providing more opportunities for young people to critically discuss these images is a way to better understand underlying beliefs about sex and gender. Young people use media imagery in their struggle to fit in with each other while developing individual identities.

They also try to fit into the larger society, where issues of sex, gender, and power are deep seeded.

Sexuality and Children's Culture

Several recent American studies demonstrate the importance of sexuality within elementary and middle school children's peer groups. Traditionally, studies of children have focused only on social and cognitive development, or on how close kids are to being like adults. However, recent sociological thinking has sought to understand children as creators of their own experiences who need to be understood in their own contexts without only considering them adults in the making.[23] Rather than devise surveys to get answers to the questions adults think are important, these researchers immersed themselves into the daily experiences of children's lives. Schools provide a useful setting to understand how peer groups create and maintain their own unwritten rules that shape children's behavior.

These studies detail that young people may borrow issues from adult culture and from the media, but children's culture does not completely emerge from either.[24] Instead, an interactive negotiation process takes place as children seek acceptance and status from their peers. While popular culture is an important part of this undertaking, it is not the all-powerful force many adults fear.

Adults tend to view children as imitators, sponges who soak up the language, behavior, and attitudes of the world around them. But sociologists Patricia and Peter Adler studied children's peer groups for eight years and concluded that we need to recognize the power of preadolescent peer culture. According to their research, children negotiate individual identities while striving to maintain status amongst peers, and sexual themes are interwoven into this process. Adults somehow fail to acknowledge (or remember) that curiosity about sexuality is a big part of growing up.

In her study of elementary school students, sociologist Barrie Thorne discusses how games like "kiss and chase" demonstrate that children are actively involved in the construction of their own sexuality.[25] We might deem this sort of behavior "innocent child's play," but that would ignore how children themselves define their experiences. I can remember the excitement of chasing a boy I liked; of course I had no clue what I'd do if I caught him. Thorne details how children's play incorporates heterosexual meanings into everyday occurrences and shapes male-female interactions. Accusing someone of "liking" a student of the other sex is used to police boundaries between genders. This happened in my elementary school experience if a girl and boy got too chummy and didn't pay as much attention to their same-gender friends. Also, popular rhymes ("Susie and Bobby sitting in a tree, K-I-S-S-I-N-G") amongst girls highlight the importance of romantic connections within children's games.

Children use popular culture to negotiate meanings from the world around them within their peer groups. When *Saturday Night Fever* first came out, most kids my age couldn't see it because it was rated R, but those who did would brag about it in school so the rest of us wanted to see it too. In a study of middle school students, researchers found that sexually explicit scenes from movies are often repeated in peer groups in order for the storyteller to solidify his or her rank in the group.[26] For example, researchers observed a group of boys talking about a scene from the 1982 movie *Quest for Fire*, a sci-fi adventure they saw on video, which the authors coincidentally had also seen. The boys discussed the female characters as passive sexual objects (in much the same way they discussed their female classmates), but the authors' interpretation of the same scene was somewhat different. Yes, this is a very troubling filter about women that the boys used, but their frame of reference was not entirely created from popular culture. This is the sticking point: while the movie was used to reinforce their viewpoint, we must also consider the broader context of the sexual objectification of women and male dominance, which of course predates film and television. So to change their frame of reference we have to address the full social context in which the film itself was created. The boys attempted to maintain status in this group through reinforcing ideas of male sexual dominance.

This example demonstrates that young people are not simply influenced by popular culture, they negotiate meaning within the context of their friends and within the larger structure of social power. There *is* a problem when boys must adopt very narrow versions of masculinity to fit in. But if we were to somehow totally succeed in keeping children away from these sorts of films, or even do away with all such representations of sexuality in popular culture, we will have done nothing to address the real issue. The media did not initiate women's objectification, but we see it most clearly there. Popular culture is where we see reflections of power and inequality. It is naïve to think that the next generation only reproduces this shallow form of sexuality because they see it in movies or on TV. They are part of a society where gender inequality is replicated in many social institutions, including education, religion, government, and economics. Our popular culture shows us some of the ugly realities of our society and we focus on media as if that's where these realities originate.

There is tremendous anxiety that kids are becoming sexually aware too early, before adults think they are ready, and the blame is placed squarely on media. While this is tempting, we must realize that sexuality is not just a consequence of media culture, but also a part of growing up. As if they were on a shopping trip, young people try on new identities to see how they fit, to see if they feel right, and how others respond to them. Some identities young people try on bear resemblance to "adult" identities. If we want to change the identities young people experiment with, we must provide more, not fewer, choices for them.

The Danger of Innocence

The myth of childhood innocence is not simply a benign fantasy, it can be a dangerous one. First of all, it does not match the reality of children's experiences. Secondly, sexually curious or sexually knowledgeable kids are defined as "lesser" children, or, as media studies professor Valerie Walkerdine put it, "Virgins who might be whores."[27] A child with knowledge of sex is considered damaged, spoiled, and robbed of his or her rightful "childhood" when in fact their knowledge may stem from sexual abuse.[28]

Clinging to the notion of childhood innocence serves to further entice those who exploit children. Defining children as pure and powerless ironically sets some children up for abuse. Abusers are often titillated by innocence, which our cultural construction of childhood unconsciously supports. Instead of only focusing on perpetrators who take advantage of children, we must also reevaluate how our culture unwittingly contributes to this eroticized definition of childhood innocence.[29] Even though most of us are not pedophiles and do not directly harm children, the insistence on children's inherent innocence can create danger for children. Albeit unintentionally, the idealized version of childhood that many of us actively construct may do more harm than good.

Adding to the confusion is the manner in which innocence is eroticized, particularly within girls and women. When Britney Spears proclaims she is a virgin, she is both a role model and enhances her sexual appeal. Virginity has served as a sexual commodity for centuries, increasing female value on the marriage market in the past and fueling male fantasies in the present. Cultural critic Henry Giroux described a film called *Kids* in which the hypersexual male character is called the "virgin surgeon," and for this he is a hero amongst his male peers.[30] Innocence serves as a sexual marker denoting increased desirability, reflecting the traditional gender order where women's passivity and lack of experience are prized and reproduce patriarchal power. Beauty pageants are a good example of the contradictions between innocence and sexuality projected onto the female child's body. While young girls in pageants are made to look like women, women are encouraged to look like girls.[31] The teenage female body is fetishized as the ideal against which adult women are measured.

Our culture creates and reinforces inconsistencies, asking us to see children as pure and untainted by the adult world when in fact sexuality is part of the human experience. This of course does not mean people of all ages ought to engage in sexual intercourse, but instead that we must recognize that self-awareness, curiosity, and some knowledge of sex are a part of childhood. When we acknowledge that media alone do not create curiosity and knowledge about sex, we begin to recognize the complexity of children's experiences. Our anxiety is rooted in the fear that adults cannot control children's knowledge or identities. One of the ways our culture defines childhood is the absence of knowledge of sex, yet its presence in popular culture serves as a reminder that our ideal childhood is merely an illusion. While adult guidance is useful to help young people navigate this terrain, we must also recognize that sexuality is partially rooted in peer culture, which by definition excludes adults.

More Promiscuous Than Ever?

Just as sexuality seems like a new invention for each generation of teens, the fear of teen sexuality is renewed in each adult generation. When I was in high school, we were sure that my sister's class, just three years behind us, had completely different morals than we did. Teenage sex is frequently associated with irresponsibility, disease, promiscuity, and unwanted pregnancy. We claim that teens have trouble controlling themselves due to "raging hormones," implying that adolescents are ruled by sexual impulses. Ironically, we blame powerful forces of nature for shaping teen behavior, yet at the same time we condemn young people for this allegedly biological and natural behavior. Meanwhile, we ignore the majority of teens who are responsible or do not engage in sex, and we don't stereotype promiscuous adults as hormone-crazed animals. When it comes to young people and sex, we tend to hear only the negative side of the story. We hear about the kid who makes a sex video and shows all of his friends. The teens frequently on tabloid-style talk shows speak freely of their ample sexual experience. Let's face it, these kids make the news and the talk shows because their stories are lascivious and sensational. Chastity just isn't dramatic.

Consequently, a false impression exists, created in part by media culture, that young people are sexually out of control at earlier and earlier ages. Even teens themselves think their peers are having sex more than they really are. A survey conducted by the National Campaign to Prevent Teen Pregnancy found that more than half of teens overestimated the percentage of their classmates who are sexually active.[32] Sociologist Mike Males dispels such faulty perceptions in *The Scapegoat Generation: America's War on Adolescents*. Based on his analysis of public health statistics, Males found:

- Between 1970 and 1992 there was just a 7 percent rise in the number of junior high school aged boys claiming to have had sex and a 6 percent rise amongst girls;[33]

- Adult men (aged nineteen to twenty-four) are far more likely than teen boys to father children born to teenaged girls;[34]

- Adult men, not teenaged boys, are most responsible for spreading HIV and other sexually transmitted diseases to girls;[35]

- For 40 percent of girls under fifteen who report being sexually active, their *only* sexual experience was rape.[36]

In addition, Males points out that we must consider any claims of sexual activity with skepticism. In spite of the belief that teens now are far more sexually active than adolescents of previous generations were, any data must be analyzed through the context of the sexual mores of the time. Simply put, people are more likely to *under-report* behavior that is considered deviant and more likely to *over-report* behavior that they perceive as elevating their status amongst peers. The fact that claiming sexual experience is treated differently now than fifty years ago makes accurate comparisons difficult. While boasting may be a factor, we must also consider that surveys rarely distinguish between forced and consenting sex. The small proportions of young teens who report having had sexual experiences quite possibly have been victims of sexual abuse.

The second and third points made above highlight the inadequacy of the term "teenage sex." We overlook the role adults, particularly adult males, play in teen pregnancy and the spread of sexually transmitted diseases. Adult men are responsible for seven out of ten births to girls eighteen and younger.[37] Also, because the HIV infection rate for teen girls is so much higher than for teen boys (a whopping disparity of 8 to 1), it is unlikely that teen boys are responsible for a large proportion of new cases.[38] In a way, our society enables adult sexual involvement with teens, as thirty-six states consider fifteen the age of sexual consent.[39] In these states teens cannot vote, drive, or purchase alcohol but adults can have sex with them without legal recourse. The numbers indicate that we cannot ignore that adults are very much a part of the "teenage" sex equation.

Nonetheless, politicians and public health officials try to steer this conversation away from adults and onto teens. In Males' analysis, he found that the teen birth rate can be predicted not by changes in media or pushes for abstinence, but by adult birth rates and poverty rates.[40] It is far easier to blame media than to study the effects of poverty. Studying poverty is dangerous: we uncover structural problems that can't be blamed on individuals; we find reasons to question the viability of our current economic policies. It is much easier to simply charge poor people with personal failure without examining why the link between teen motherhood and poverty is so strong.[41] We let policymakers off the hook and give the media bashers something to complain about.

We are all too eager to point out the bad behavior of a few teenagers and hold them up as symbolic of an entire generation. Imagine if we saw a story on the news about a child molester followed by a commentary on how the middle-aged generation is completely without moral grounding. Of course this would never happen—we would say the molester was a sick individual, different from the rest of us. Yet we never afford young people this same explanation. Teens are accused of participating in risky sexual behavior, allegedly coaxed by sex in media. Adults tend to ignore the fact that a large proportion of young people report very little or no sexual experience, but instead focus on those that do.[42] We also hear very little about the fact that the teen birth rate has been steadily *falling* since 1990 and that the teen abortion rate fell 39 percent between 1994 and 2000.[43]

Finally, and perhaps most significantly, we overlook the role of sexual abuse in the discussion about teens and sex. For many young people, sex is not a choice they have made but it was forced upon them. Adolescents who have been sexually abused as children are also far more likely to engage in riskier sexual practices in the future.[44] Rather than focus so heavily on popular culture leading to sexual activity, we see that *adult* behavior must be taken to task. We need to pay more attention to adults who impregnate, infect, and sexually abuse children and adolescents. They are the problem here, not the media.

Why Lie?

So how is it that in a society that claims to put young people first, we ignore the good news and highlight the risky behavior of a few? The answer is by no means simple, but one that has become a recurring theme in the way our society has treated disempowered groups. Immigrants, racial ethnic minorities, women, and the poor at varying times in history have been perceived as sexually out of control and in need of tighter social restraint. Adults project the aura of danger onto teen sexuality, which elicits both concern and fascination.[45] When groups are considered a danger to themselves or to others, restricting their freedom seems justifiable. We rationalize social control of young people based on the few who are held up as promiscuous bad examples, insisting that these teens prove most adolescents are incapable of making responsible decisions or are too easily influenced by media. In the next section we will see the parallels between the treatment of young people now with historical perceptions of immigrants, racial ethnic minorities, women, and the poor.

Fear, Sex, and Social Control

It is difficult to think of sexuality as anything but personal and individual, but the way we understand sex is socially constructed. Sexuality is a central site where struggles over social power take place.[46] The regulation and control of sexuality have served as ways to maintain dominance over disempowered groups. One such power struggle in the United States has emerged following demographic shifts of the past hundred years. Historically, fears that the population is becoming less Protestant and less white have led to attempts to control the reproduction of immigrant and non-white groups. This has been accomplished by policies promoting sterilization, removing girls from their families if juvenile courts believed they were likely to engage in sex, and, more recently, demonizing mothers of color.[47] Due to this fear, during the early part of the century white women's pregnancies were encouraged, and their access to birth control and abortion was restricted. So while sexuality is personal, the uses and meanings attached to the practice are decidedly social and linked with broader systems of power.

No Sex As a Weapon

The sexuality of groups perceived to be a threat is labeled dangerous and serves to legitimate public policies that restrict members' behavior. Many African-American men were lynched by whites allegedly protecting white women's virtue; black male sexuality came to be defined as a threat to the racial order. Miscegenation laws were enacted for much the same reason. They were created to prevent a union of a non-white man and a white woman, but were certainly not enforced when slave owners fathered the children of black slave women. This double standard reveals how the dominant group maintains power by controlling the sexuality of the "other."

We see similar trends today as population estimates suggest that there will be no racial majority in the near future. Instead of passing laws that overtly discriminate, today we operate with more socially pleasing buzzwords that allow us to think we are beyond racism and more enlightened than our predecessors were. The "welfare queen" symbol stereotypes young mothers of color and has been invoked within political discourse in attempt to restrict funding for children's poverty programs. Demonizing black and Latino mothers creates the perception that their children are an economic drain on society.[48] Yet in reality federal funds spent on food, housing, and unemployment assistance comprise only 5 percent of the budget, while subsidies to corporations represent anywhere from 75 to 200 billion dollars in lost revenue each year, or approximately 4 to 10 percent of the federal budget.[49] If the issue were really about economics, why do we ignore where the big money goes? Measures like California's Proposition 187, which sought to restrict undocumented immigrant children from obtaining an education or medical care, represent the same kind of logic, that our society just cannot afford any more of "those" children. Contrast the "welfare queen" diatribe to the personal and corporate outpourings to multiple-birth families that have five, six, even seven children at once, which they cannot afford. These families appear on news magazine programs and talk shows to speak of their multiple blessings, while policymakers and pundits rail against the huge cost of other people's children. Concerns about promiscuity, pregnancy, and disease have served as a way for dominant groups to assert control over those whom they feel threatened by, whether the threat is real or imagined.

Gender (Dis)order

In addition to changes in demographics we have been experiencing shifts in the gender order that are closely linked with sexuality. Historically, abstinence has been a female burden, with girls and women supposedly responsible for regulating male sexuality. The social control of women has been secured in recent history by policing female sexuality. Even within the confines of marriage, at the turn of the twentieth century femininity meant not taking too much pleasure from sex. Clinics provided "treatment" to women who suffered from such "unnatural" urges. Women who enjoyed sex were viewed as deviant and considered threats. Even when women's desire ceased to be considered a medical problem, sexual gratification was defined as a socially undesirable quality, one that might reduce a woman's chances for marriage. This was of course a serious threat in a time when women's wages rarely enabled them to live independently. Women were socially and economically constrained by the need for male financial support, as well as by the fear of unplanned pregnancy.

The threat of rape has historically been used to keep women from public spaces, supported by the practice of humiliating rape victims in court and not acknowledging marital rape. Women's sexuality has been a double-edged sword: a woman's worth has been tied to her appeal to men, yet rape has historically been blamed on women for being too appealing. The threat of sexual violence, even if not carried out, serves to limit women's movement and freedom.

In recent decades the widespread availability of birth control and shrinkage in the wage gap between men and women have created more personal freedom for women. But the old sexual double standards, that male sexuality is natural and female sexuality is a threat, are still alive in our fears about teens and sex. Concerns about teens' sexual activity reflect shifts in the gender order: attempts to control teen sexuality tend to focus on girls, on pregnancy, on girls' self-esteem and body image, but usually leave male sexuality out of the conversation. A *New York Times* article even suggested that earlier onset of puberty for girls might be due to "overstimulation" from sex in media.[50] Interestingly, this hypothesis would not apply to boys, since their physical maturation has remained relatively stable over the last century. So why is *female* sexuality so frightening?

Teenage girls are considered a threat when they seek to become more than just sexual objects—when they act as sexual *agents* we worry. I still remember a family member's shock when her preteen son started receiving phone calls from girls and she worried about how brazen this new generation of girls must be. American society still expects girls to hold the keys to chastity, but at the same time they are held up as the ideal form of female desire. Open any fashion magazine and chances are good a teenage girl will be pouting back at you. We see this representation of teenage girls in many forms of popular culture, but it certainly does not originate there: its history lies in our tendency to value women who are young and sexually available for men. Rather than only blaming media culture for this representation of teenage girls, we need to take a closer look at the nature of power, sex, and gender in contemporary American society. Underneath fears of teens having sex are concerns about the changing meaning of gender.

The Genie Is Out of the Bottle

Societal shifts spurred by economic changes have altered American life, which has made it more difficult to monitor teens. Knowledge of or engagement in sex reveals that the illusion of innocence cannot be sustained, no matter how hard adults may try. Censoring media will not work, nor will less than complete and honest sex education.[51] This includes dealing with the reality of how sexual content is used and understood by young media audiences. No matter how much we may want to turn back the clock we can't. Teen sexuality *is* a threat: it destroys the unsustainable myth that adults can fully control young people's knowledge or their actions. The media are an easy target, but not the root cause of the changes in the attitudes and practice of sexuality in the twenty-first century.

As we have seen, changes throughout the twentieth century have provided young people with the means to become more independent from their parents, rendering their behavior far harder to control. Generally adults look at this as a sad reality, one that will inevitably lead to the breakdown of social order and the decline of American society.

Adults need to recognize that teenagers cannot be fully controlled, nor should this be our goal. This doesn't mean renting kids hotel rooms and telling them to go for it; instead we must acknowledge that teenage sexuality is not new nor is it necessarily the threat that adults believe it to be. Education that helps young people deal with the realities of sexuality is needed, beyond doom-and-gloom scare tactics. Most centrally, adults need to let go of the illusion that childhood innocence can be maintained through ignorance. We have to begin by understanding how young people make sense of sex, both in media and in their lives.

Rethinking Media, Youth, and Sexuality

Sex on TV, in movies, and on the Internet scares lots of adults. Representations of sex in media expose the reality that childhood does not and cannot exist in a separate sphere from adulthood. Ironically, we use sex as the ultimate dividing line between childhood and adulthood, the line in the sand that adults try so hard to maintain and young people try so hard to cross. We define sex as a ticket to adulthood, so we should not be surprised when teens do, too. In my family, maturity was in part defined as seeing an R-rated movie with sexual content; it was a big deal when I was allowed to see *An Officer and a Gentleman*. Sex in popular culture reminds us that we cannot sustain the lengthened version of childhood we have idealized since the mid-twentieth century. The realities of sex dispel myths about childhood and media remind us such myths cannot be upheld.

We often associate changes in sexual behavior with changes in media. Historical shifts are difficult to see and understand, while media are by nature visible and always trying to grab our attention. And yes, frank exploration of sexuality is more prominent in popular culture now than it was at mid-century. But sexuality within popular culture has changed in conjunction with other social changes. Media are not the sole cause, but a messenger, jumping into the social conversation about sex, not starting it. To paraphrase Syracuse University's Robert Thompson's explanation, media do not push the envelope; they merely open the envelope that has been sitting under our noses.[52]

That being said, we should not ignore representations of sexuality in media. They provide useful clues about power and privilege and can launch greater exploration of contested meanings of both sexuality and gender. Rather than seek to censor, we should study media representations to analyze the taken-for-granted nature of relationships and sexuality in our culture. But instead of using these representations for cultural criticism, we often condemn the images and fail to critically challenge what they represent. If we really are concerned about the meanings young people make from such images, we ought to encourage people to critically address them, not simply call for self-censorship.

The truth is there aren't *enough* representations of sex in popular culture: not enough exploration of the depth of emotion that comes with sexual intimacy and not enough representations of regular-looking bodies.[53] Depictions of sex in media offer a prime opportunity to open up important discussions about gender and power within society as well. Of course, if we could have conversations like this there wouldn't be so much fear about sex in media in the first place. Instead of fearing the "negative effects" of sex in media and demanding that it go away, we need to keep learning about how young people make sense of sex in both media and in their lives.

We can choose to cling to old fears and old ways of thinking and try and make ourselves believe in the whimsical myth of innocence. Of course, that will leave us complaining from here to eternity, because the fear is based on faulty beliefs about both media and children. On the other hand we can get real and try to better understand how young people make sense of what they do know, rather than bemoaning *that* they know. The choice is ours: we can either try in vain to put the genie back into the bottle or open our eyes and create a deeper level of understanding of both media and youth.

9

Fear of the Internet

Information Regulation

I imagine that someday my generation will be asked the same kinds of questions about the Internet as my grandparents were about what they did before television. Children may wonder how we did our homework, listened to music, or shopped. Sad to say I'm no longer sure either.

I picture this child of the future looking upon us in awe for having survived such antiquated times. It's interesting how new technologies seem totally unnecessary until we get used to them and then think we can't live without them. I didn't understand why I would want to get e-mail in the early 1990s. I thought I managed just fine with my phone and the post office, but now it seems impossible to go more than a few days without checking my inbox. I still used an old first generation IBM PC when the Internet took off, and when a friend showed me how fans put up Websites of their favorite television shows I thought it was a big waste of time. That was then, of course; much of the information for this book was accessed through the Internet. So I became a convert to the Internet age, an age so many young people today were born into, as I was born into a world already saturated with television. Much of how people interact has evolved in recent years. For those who can remember life before both television and the Internet, things must feel radically different, perhaps even scary. This may happen even though, according to the 2000 U.S. Census, adults over sixty utilize home computers more times per week than any other age group, so the Internet is not just the domain of the young.

While the rise of the Internet has changed a lot within American society—the way we do business, the way we interact with others—it is also the product of change. Using technology developed for Cold War purposes, the Internet was shared with the public due to political changes after the demise of the Soviet Union. A growing economy and cheap production of the microchip made the purchase of home computers more affordable as well. In the past decade the Internet has gone from a somewhat obscure university-based tool for computer scientists to a mainstay within American commerce and culture. And lately, a mainstay in American fear.

Because no one owns the Internet, and it is impossible to regulate, Internet usage is hard to control. The walls adults try to put up around childhood had already begun to crack with the creation of more private media like television, cable and satellite transmission, VCRs, the Sony Walkman, and the like. With the Internet the boundaries are more fluid, threatening to move information to children at full speed, and further reduce adult ability to slow them down from venturing into places we'd rather they not go. At the same time, we want kids to be able to take advantage of the technology to enhance their schoolwork. But as home computers and Internet use has grown, so has the fear that it will somehow harm children and childhood.

Stories of pedophiles lurking in chat rooms, pop-up porn, and recipes for building bombs have helped generate these fears. How can we save kids from online predators? Warnings appear about young people being seduced (and seducing) people they met online, with dozens of news stories providing suggestions for parents about how to keep children safe from cyber-stalkers. The biggest fear, that children will be sexually assaulted or even murdered, comes to us in dramatic headlines.

This chapter explores the fear surrounding the Internet, assessing the nature of the threats many people fear cyberspace contains and the calls for regulation that have followed. Like many other fears pertaining to media, fears of online danger outweigh the actual risk and divert energy and attention from more viable threats. The likelihood of sexual abuse from a non-cyber acquaintance is far greater than from an online predator. Concern over "cyber sex" and online pornography represent fears that information can no longer be filtered through parents; it is no surprise that Internet-blocking software companies imply that their product can act as cyber-parent. We fear what children may access without much thought about those that don't have access at all.

In truth, lack of access does not provide protection. As we will see, the biggest problem isn't porn or pedophiles (although they are the most dramatic), but the growing divide between those who are computer literate and have computer access and those who don't. As the economy shifts towards a two-tier information/service base, those without appropriate skills—namely low-income children—will have trouble competing with the Internet savvy economically in the future. Nonetheless, we are continually reminded by the news media of the potential dangers of the Internet because it gets our attention and makes headlines.

Cyber-Stranger Danger

In May 2002 a thirteen-year-old Danbury, Connecticut, girl was killed by a twenty-five-year-old man she met online.[1] This tragedy was widely reported as yet another example of the dangers awaiting children when they log on to the Internet unsupervised. In spite of the fact that the vast majority of children's killers are their own parents or someone they know, the Internet has awakened long-existing fears of stranger danger. News accounts regularly advertise the alleged risk—"Web Puts Kids in Peril" and "Instant Message to All Parents: Watch the Kids"— and many stories present ways of "Saving Kids from Online Predators."[2] The Internet is characterized as a site of risk, be it from adult predators waiting to lure kids into offline danger, or cyber-porn threatening to create sex-obsessed young people. But how big of a risk does the Internet really pose to young Web surfers? The answers are far less dramatic than news reports would have us believe. Most law enforcement agencies do not keep track of Internet-related violent crimes, largely because there aren't that many to track. Nonetheless, Jan D'Arcy, one of the directors of the Media Awareness Network in Canada, commented, "One of the greatest ironies about online dangers is the fact that children see the virtual world as safer than the real world."[3] The kids are right—it is!

The non-cyber world is a far more dangerous place for children. According to the U.S. Department of Health and Human Services, of children who were abused in 2000, 84 percent were abused by their parents.[4] Family members were responsible for 71 percent of sexual abuse, and revelations of numerous incidents of molestation by Catholic priests reveal that sexual abuse is not only committed by strangers lurking on a playground or in an Internet chat room. Of children murdered, the largest proportion are under six (85 percent of all fatalities), and almost half are infants under one; neither group is likely to be killed by people from cyberspace.

This is not to deny that the Internet has been used as a vehicle for pedophiles, but that danger is far greater in the home than in cyberspace. But we place our attention on the more dramatic dangers, just like the age-old "don't talk to strangers" mantra so many of us heard growing up. News stories continually warn how to "protect kids from an invisible enemy."[5] "On the Internet, everyone is a stranger," a *St. Petersburg Times* story ominously began, implying that danger is only a mouse click away.[6] A Canadian detective told the *Ottawa Citizen*: "If we went on the Internet in an undercover capacity as a thirteen-year-old girl we'd be hit on so fast we could hardly get our hands off the keyboard."[7] An Australian newspaper warned, "As soon as you get online they hit you with all kinds of propositions."[8] These comments are somewhat vague, as the threat allegedly comes from simply being "online" or "on the Internet." But a study by the Center for Missing and Exploited Children estimated that only about one in thirty-three kids, or about 3 percent, are "aggressively solicited for sex."[9] This is a rather small number in comparison to the amount of coverage the issue gets.

Nonetheless, junior Internet users are all portrayed as potential victims who are "dangerously naïve," according to the *New York Times*.[10] We obviously need to pay very close attention to the people who are trying to victimize children and provide young people with skills to deal with predators both on and offline. But we also need to recognize that the risk of being lured offline is not universal. A survey by the Crimes Against Children Research Center at the University of New Hampshire found that the danger of online solicitation was higher for kids already troubled and likely to engage in other risky behaviors.[11]

This may help explain the tragedy of the thirteen-year-old murdered Danbury girl. Although the *Los Angeles Times* ran the story under the headline "Internet is Blamed in Death of Altar Girl," she appears to have had some serious problems that went undetected, or at least unreported. The Associated Press described her as a girl next door, who "received good grades, led the cheerleading squad and was an altar girl."[12] To read the story one might believe that she was an American everygirl without a care in the world until she went online. "On the Internet," the story reads, "she used provocative names in chat rooms and arranged sexual liaisons."[13] Sounds like it could happen to anyone? Actually, a closer look leads to more questions about the non-cyber life of the young teen. We learn from the AP that she lived with an aunt, not her parents, and was described as having a "tougher side." A teacher called her "streetwise," and cryptically, "torn in both directions." But the story and those that followed focused almost exclusively on the Internet, rather than looking more deeply into the girl's life. Even more disturbing is the lack of information about the killer; the real question is why adult men are interested in young girls sexually and then kill them. But follow-up stories focused more on Internet safety, sending the message that there were no special circumstances here, and that anyone's daughter could be next. In the quest to tell the most sensational side of the story that will grab readers and ultimately heighten fear, the more mundane elements of tragedies like this tend not to make headlines.

Perhaps the real risk is in focusing on the well-publicized, highly dramatic accounts of cyber-stalking and ignoring the less dramatic but equally tragic abuses that go on in places we believe kids to be safe: their homes, their friends' and families' homes, and their places of worship.

Cyber Promiscuity?

When we're not worried about cyber-strangers waiting to prey on children, we fear that the kids themselves will become sex-crazed consumers of cyber-porn. Online pornography has been one of the few consistently profitable Internet business ventures, and because of the bugs in search engines it sometimes presents itself when you're not looking for it. This has lots of adults worried; if it's so easy to find when you aren't looking for it, it must be plentiful when you are. A *Los Angeles Times* article warned, "With Teens and Internet Sex, Curiosity Can Become a Compulsion," although a 2002 Congressional report found that less than 10 percent of young people admitted that they actively seek out porn.[14] Calls for filtering software in libraries and admonitions to parents stem from the fear that the Internet will make porno-heads out of kids. In my pre-Internet 1970s childhood, pornography wasn't exactly impossible to see, even if you weren't seeking it out. While walking to school one day, some friends and I discovered a stack of discarded magazines on the side of the road. When word got around my elementary school that we found porno magazines, hardly a kid took the bus home and instead all wanted to see the contraband pictures. Another incident occurred at one of the hallmarks of childhood—a slumber party. We stumbled upon my friend's father's *Penthouse* magazines in the study, where we had camped out for the night. I suspect that many children's first exposure to pornography was not on any computer but the result of a family member or neighbor's own purchasing habit.

But we fear the Internet makes pornography even more readily available, more interactive. To try to avert accidental or intentional contact with pornography or material parents might find objectionable, several companies have created software meant to block access to such sites. The problem with the software has been its overly literal response to certain words like "breast" to prevent access to health or medical-oriented sites. Computer-savvy users have learned to hack around the blocks as well. Aside from the software problems, the truth is that Internet access is becoming so readily available, particularly in middle-class and affluent communities, that filtering one computer will not do much.

The fear of Internet porn rests on the assumption that teens are not just curious but sex-crazed. "In cyberspace, adolescents and teenagers flirt, talk dirty, send each other photos and have 'cyber sex'," reported the *Los Angeles Times*, although the article stated that less than 3 percent are considered "addicted."[15] "Cyber sex" heightens the fear that adults cannot entirely control kids' sexuality or information about sex, that seeing and talking about sex will make young people more promiscuous, more apt to want to meet people offline for actual sex. This may occur in some cases, but as I detailed earlier, kids are actually *less* sexually active now than they were ten years ago, before the rapid growth of cyber porn or cyber sex. Perhaps the Internet is an outlet for curiosity rather than a push towards promiscuity. There are, of course, examples of young people who do get sexually involved with people they meet online, like the Danbury girl, but cyber-promiscuity is more anecdotal than a trend. For instance, when the *Pittsburgh Post-Gazette* reported on this topic, their sources were teens who "heard of someone" or "know people" or "have friends" who engage in lots of cyber sex.[16]

Parry Aftab, author of *The Parent's Guide to Protecting Your Children in Cyberspace*, recommends that we avoid the tendency to simply restrict kids' Internet use or to spy on them. Instead, she argues that we teach them to be skeptical, in order to help them learn to protect themselves. She suggests that rather than banning all offline meetings that parents provide guidelines, like bringing an adult or a group of friends, and meeting in a public place, to discourage kids from sneaking off to secret meeting places without telling anyone. She also notes that while "spam" (unsolicited e-mail advertisements that sometimes contain sexual content) is very common, "it doesn't mean kids have been visiting porn sites."[17] "Spamming" is a cheap form of advertising and often a way marketers use the Internet to make money. Proposals to limit spam have been made, but it is rather difficult to control. Nonetheless, Aftab believes that "kids handle it very well, most ignore it or block it," and she thinks "It's the adults who don't handle it well."[18]

Internet pornography and sexually charged communication do exist, a logical progression from pay-per-view porn and phone sex lines. It was impossible to completely keep these things from young people then and it is unfortunately impossible to keep all Internet porn from them now. Rather than focus only on protection, regulation, and control, we would be better served to follow Aftab's advice and provide more empowerment through teaching young people how to navigate the Internet. Problem is, we adults are still grappling with how to make sense of the Internet ourselves.

Information Regulation

Almost from the Internet's inception, some politicians have called for more policing and regulation. After the Columbine shootings, the Clinton administration stepped up calls to keep online violent and sexual content from children. Vice President Al Gore wanted to "ensure that children aren't surfing into dangerous waters when they surf the web."[19] During the 2000 presidential primary race, Republican candidate John McCain called for all publicly funded libraries to use Internet filtering software. And in 2001, Senator Hillary Rodham Clinton sought $25 million in federal funds to create a task force targeting Internet crimes.[20] Reflecting the anxieties many people have of this new and still somewhat-unknown medium, Congress has also tried to regulate the Internet. Politicians have responded to widespread fears of online predators and Internet porn by enacting legislation that the courts have found is in violation of First Amendment rights, rights we are ambivalent about when it comes to children.

In 1996 the Communications Decency Act (CDA) made it a crime to send "indecent" material to minors or to post anything "obscene" that could be viewed by children. The Supreme Court considered CDA a serious violation of free speech and struck it down because of its broad nature. The 1998 Child Online Protection Act (COPA) followed, also seeking to limit postings where minors have access. COPA also created a commission to study ways of keeping pornographic material away from children, which ultimately advocated education over mandatory blocking software.[21] In any case, parts of CODA were also struck down by the Supreme Court and sent back to lower courts for review.

While these acts of Congress focused on Internet content, the 2000 Child Internet Protection Act (CIPA) took a new tack. CIPA would instead require that institutions that receive public funding, like libraries and schools, use filtering software or lose their funding. Proponents argued that pornography has no place in public institutions, that just as you won't find *Playboy* on the library's magazine rack, so too should pornography be unavailable online in libraries. No big argument here. The problem, which led to rejection by the U.S. Third Circuit Court of Appeals, is that filtering software blocks more than just pornography. The American Library Association (ALA) argued that filters both over-block and in some cases under-block content, which ultimately prevents people from accessing legal, "non-obscene" material like information about reproduction, sexuality, and relationships— topics found in books libraries regularly have on their shelves.[22] The ALA also argued that CIPA would interfere with local decisionmaking, as different communities would no longer be able to set their own standards of "decency" and continue to receive public funding. U.S. District Judge Edward R. Becker questioned how CIPA could be followed in earnest, since "The filtering programs bar access to a substantial amount of speech on the Internet that is clearly constitutionally protected for adults and minors."[23]

In essence, CIPA has been challenged because the software works like a "sledgehammer instead of a surgical scalpel," as sociologist Amitai Etzioni described, acting less like a filter and more like a series of blocks that lets some pornography slip through and denies access to some non-pornographic material.[24] Considering the sheer volume of material available online, even software that is 99 percent effective will still block out thousands of sites. Still, arguments against CIPA do not suggest banning the use of blocking software, but instead keeping the decision local. In 2000, about 15 percent of all libraries nationwide used blocking software on at least some of their computer terminals; in suburban communities the rate is even higher, at 22 percent.[25]

CIPA has created a strong response from both sides. Will Manley, author of *The Truth about Reference Librarians*, argued vehemently that "if you are against filters on computers . . . you are against children, unless you think pornography is not particularly harmful to children."[26] If the real issue were pornography there would be little debate—I don't think the American Library Association challenged CIPA to ensure children could have access to pornography. The problem is dealing with a new medium that is nearly impossible to control. Thus, comparisons to other media like magazines, videos, and books fail to capture the essence of a medium that by its nature is a bastion of unregulated information. Clearly this reality is less utopian than some may have hoped; some of the images and ideas freely shared, like pornography, are objectionable to the sensibilities of many, at least where children are concerned.

Since regulation is practically impossible, the House of Representatives approved a new domain, "kids.us," that would only contain Websites and links to pages certified "appropriate" for children under twelve.[27] While the question of what is in fact "appropriate" is a sticky one, creating more, not fewer options is a more productive way of dealing with content we may not like but can't control. We should be wary of too much government control of any medium, particularly the Internet, even in the name of "protecting" children, but a small piece may turn out to be a suitable compromise. It will be interesting to see what is considered acceptable and who will make that decision. Clearly porn sites won't be on kids.us, but what about educational information about sex? As Marjorie Heins, author of *Not in Front of the Children: "Indecency," Censorship, and the Innocence of Youth* points out, any attempt to restrict information on the grounds of protecting children:

> is an avoidance technique that addresses adult anxieties and satisfies symbolic concerns, but ultimately does nothing to resolve social problems or affirmatively help adolescents and children cope with their environments and impulses or navigate the dense and insistent media barrage that surrounds them.[28]

Rather than focus on blocking, filtering, and restricting, a 2002 report to Congress by the National Research Council, titled "Youth,

Pornography, and the Internet," found that no single tactic will alone prevent children's access to pornography and instead supports education and training to provide kids with skills to navigate the Internet safely.[29] The report details how solutions and strategies must fit different situations and community needs, criticizing a one-size-fits-all approach to dealing with the Internet.

Pornography and pedophiles exist both online and off, and as much as they instill fear in parents, this is not the only reason that the Internet scares many adults. The Internet represents a loss of adult control and regulation over young people, a loss of power to control what kids know and how and when they know it.

While news reports may have us fearing that the Internet is mainly a vehicle for porn and pedophiles, it is of course much more than that. It is a site for exchanging ideas, for commerce, a warehouse of information—sometimes educational, sometimes trivial or personal. Yes, there are people looking to exploit others and we need to expose them, just as people need to be aware of this possibility offline. But fears about the Internet are not only about pornography, not just of pedophiles in chat rooms pretending to be teenagers. The Internet serves as another challenge to the fantasy of childhood innocence, one in which information can be kept away from children until adults decide the time is right. The Internet makes it more difficult to wall off children from the realities of the world around them and enables them to find answers to questions adults may not want them to ask.

So while pornography and sexual exploitation gain public attention, it is the information about sex and its discussion that feels threatening to childhood. Most young people may not steal a credit card to enter a porn site or be accosted by a pedophile, but information is available if they want to know about sex before their parents want them to. The Internet is the next step in the century-long process of adults' reduced ability to keep information about sex from children. I'm not just talking about pornography—information about reproductive health, sexual identity, and sexual practices have been moving from their underground Victorian hiding places into public discourse. Although concern centers on children's exposure to this information, the anxiety also reflects the shift in social mores that puts knowledge and discussion about sex and sexuality more in the open. From the Comstock era of the early twentieth century, when sending information about birth control and reproduction through the mail was illegal and considered immoral, we have arrived at the point where this information and more is directly available through the Internet. To deal with this shift we have tried to curtail access rather than face the reality that information about sexuality can no longer be contained.

As with older obscenity laws, attempts to regulate Internet access seek to decide what is obscene and what is appropriate for children. These are both slippery slopes. For some, explicit information about sexual health and behavior may be considered obscene. For others, chat rooms for gay and lesbian teens may be found inappropriate. Who gets to decide what is obscene or inappropriate? For an embarrassed young person, the Internet may be the only source of information about sex, particularly for gay or lesbian youths afraid to come out but able to find an online community that lets them feel less alone. Access may be a matter of life and death, as gay and lesbian teens are more likely to commit suicide than their heterosexual counterparts. Information about sexual health may prevent a sexually transmitted disease or provide sources of support for a victim of sexual abuse afraid to tell those around them what happened.

The Internet contains information that many of us may feel uncomfortable with and perhaps even believe is best kept from children and teens until we decide that they are ready. In reality, they may need this information before we would like them to have it. Just as we have been afraid that they will get the wrong information from movies and television, there are those who fear that the Internet may provide misinformation or conflict with a family's particular set of values. I think the way to handle this possibility is to provide more, not less information about sex and sexuality, to be able to have frank and honest discussions of what those values are, rather than only trying to keep competing information or values at bay. True, these are often uncomfortable conversations, but the information is out there—we can choose who we want kids to hear it from first.

The Internet makes regulation of information very difficult, if not impossible. While we can't assume that kids are "naturally" computer literate, this power shift is especially present when kids are more computer savvy than their parents. This imbalance is at the heart of Internet fears; yes, pornography may be distasteful and predators may be frightening, but underneath it all lies anxiety about a new medium and the changes it has accompanied to society. Changes to the economy and commerce were certainly not entirely or even mostly created by the Internet, but the Internet has come to represent the computer age, an age in which personal information is digitized and stored in computers that can sometimes be accessed by criminals. Credit card numbers, Social Security numbers, birthdays, addresses, and private medical information are out there for the gifted hacker's taking. This lack of privacy, the ubiquity of public and private information, has made us understandably concerned. Much of this anxiety gets deflected onto children and the information they may encounter online. In truth, it is our own personal information that we need to worry about keeping private. We also need to help young people deal with sexual content and other information we may be uncomfortable with that has become more available through the Internet.

Digital Disempowerment

All the talk about porn and pedophiles and protecting kids from online dangers has crowded out a very important conversation about those children with no access at all. Rather than simply "protected" from potential online perils, these are kids who are not developing the same sort of computer skills as their peers. The digitally disempowered are most likely to be from low-income families and may live in communities with libraries that have no computers, no Internet access, or no public library at all.

According to a 2002 Annie E. Casey Foundation study, having access to a computer at home increases educational performance, even when factors like income are taken into account.[30] Not surprisingly, income is a major factor in determining who is likely to have a computer in their home. Census data from 2001 indicate a huge disparity between home computer access: two-thirds of children in families earning under $15,000 have no home computer, compared with just 5 percent of those in families earning more than $75,000.[31] Of the poorest children, just 14 percent have Internet access at home, compared with 63 percent of their affluent counterparts. Access is also a factor of race: while more than 80 percent of white and Asian American children have home computers (and about half have Internet access), only 46 percent of black and 47 percent of Latino families have home computers. Just 25 percent of blacks and 20 percent of Latino families have Internet access, and for residents of inner cities these numbers are even lower.

Clearly low-income families have more pressing needs, like food and rent, before buying a computer or subscribing to an Internet service provider. But can't these kids use computers at school? The Annie E. Casey Foundation report cited a 2001 study that found that only a quarter of kids without home computers had access at school.[32] Even when schools do have computers, they may not be up to date and the time students can individually spend using them is limited. Over time, this disparity in computer usage translates into less time to do homework assignments on a computer, less ease with computer software, fewer Internet research opportunities, and an overall educational disadvantage. Those without computer skills today already face serious employment setbacks, which are bound to multiply.

The Internet represents a strange new world, one that is still segregated by income and race, much to the dismay of those who once saw the Internet as inherently democratizing. Rather than creating a new cyber world, the Internet has largely been created in the image of our traditional non-cyber society. Conventional businesses are still the ones most likely to find success online, not the mom-and-pop cyber shops or individual 'zine sites, as was once believed. Like the non-cyber world, the Internet contains information that some adults prefer children not know about, such as information about sex, drugs, hate, and violence. And like the rest of the world, there are people who seek to take advantage of others, possibly bringing financial or physical harm. We need to deal with these cyber realities just as we do with the outside world: through becoming aware of what the dangers may be, what the warning signs are, and what strategies can help us all.

Conclusion: Rethinking Fears of Media and Children

Media: A Sheep in Wolf's Clothing

Fear is a powerful emotion. To deal with our fears, we often seek more information to both justify that our concern is real and to figure out what we can do to minimize our personal risk. This is one reason why stories of risk and danger play out over and over in the news media, why cop shows and hospital dramas are a mainstay on television, and action movies become blockbusters. We want reassurance that our fears are legitimate, that they are heard, shared, and respected, and we want to gain competency to deal with them.

In no instance is this truer than when fears concern children. To adults, children often represent vulnerability and innocence, which is why we respond so viscerally when we are given information on how we may best "protect" them. As representatives of the future, children remind us that the world ahead is yet unknowable, and perhaps more unnerving, uncontrollable. The media remind us of and represent this uncontrolled, unknown future. We often fear media's influence on children because kids serve as both powerful symbols of the future and of change, and we are anxious about both.

So while our fears are very real, quite often the actual threat is not. The media may always be visible, often unavoidable, and sometimes downright annoying, but the real things we should be concerned about are less visible and thus easier to overlook. I have discussed the widespread impact of child poverty—children comprise a majority of the nation's poor, and poverty is closely linked with many of the problems that we usually blame the media for, like violence, alienation, and teen pregnancy. While "the media made me do it" stories grab headlines, we avoid confronting childhood enemy Number One: the fact that nearly twelve million American kids live in poverty.

We don't like to talk about poverty in America; it is rather depressing and doesn't make an exciting headline. It is our badge of shame that amidst great wealth and prosperity so many children have no health insurance and attend deteriorating schools. When we do talk about poverty we tend to only blame the poor themselves; we tell them they aren't educated enough, are too lazy, lack ambition, and depend on welfare. We decided in 1996 that welfare was the problem, not poverty, not the untenable minimum wage. Children of course are in the middle of this politically charged debate. To face this problem, we will have to rethink public policy choices and consider using more resources to bring more families out of poverty. If we truly want to reduce violence in America the answer will not be found in a v-chip.

But this is no easy task, particularly when it comes time to foot the bill for solutions. Blaming media is a cheap campaign decision—it costs relatively little to hold hearings and pass unconstitutional legislation compared with getting at the heart of what causes violence. Blaming media takes us all off the hook: we can point our fingers at media producers and parents we don't find restrictive enough.

We should also focus our attention on the state of public schools, some of which are barely fit for human occupants. Standardized tests are not necessary to predict the disparity in educational outcomes when kids have no books or computers. Even well-funded schools merit a closer look to examine how well they can meet the needs of their students, how well they inspire rather than alienate the young people they are meant to serve. Schools tend to focus on conformity—both academically and socially—and need to take responsibility to support those who don't quite fit in. This, of course, can only be accomplished when the public provides better support for school systems and teachers.

Families also need more support, through affordable, quality day care and after-school programs. Instead of simply placing the blame on parents for their kids' media preferences, we need to acknowledge the strain many people face trying to support their families both economically and emotionally. And let's be honest, many people have no training in creating an emotionally supportive environment; how many of us boast, albeit facetiously, that we come from "dysfunctional" families? While I want to avoid the all-too-easy tendency to blame parents for everything, we should recognize that violence is often first learned in the family. Of children exposed to violence first-hand, the vast majority see it in their homes and communities. Stranger danger is scary and its warnings circulate nationally, but parent danger is far more prevalent. Abuse is often a hidden problem, so prevention, not only punishment, should be our focus. Parenting classes need to be more commonplace, not just court-ordered or the bastion of the middle class. Just as Lamaze and birthing classes have become widely available, so too should support groups and training classes for parents.

In addition to recognizing what I have termed the big bad wolves of childhood—poverty, inequality, abuse, and under-funding of education, we should take a closer look at why the news media have been crying wolf.

First, fear sells. As sociologist David Altheide writes in *Creating Fear: News and the Construction of Crisis*, the press is central in the development and perpetuation of fear. Things that scare us make for good drama, draw us closer, and create a sense that we need to watch or read more for our safety, and, most compellingly, for the safety of our children. But too much fear tends to backfire, particularly if we feel we can't gain control of the threat. This is one reason that aviation accidents are highly represented in news accounts, but automobile accidents are not. It is much easier to choose not to fly, or to only fly rarely, but most Americans are rather dependent on regular car travel, so thinking about its danger is simply overwhelming. As social psychological research demonstrates, scary messages work best if the fear they create is only mild.[1] When people feel too scared, too out of control, they tend to go into denial and ignore the frightening information. So providing low doses of seemingly manageable fear draws viewers in, but presenting complex problems may make people want to avoid the news. This is why the things that we need to be concerned about, the social problems without easy solutions, are not as compelling news stories. They scare us too much.

Media fear resonates with preexisting anxieties about youth culture and new media technologies. It would be too simple to say that this fear is only the press's fault. As I have emphasized throughout this book, both youth and youth culture are symbolic of change, of a loss of adult centrality and control. Popular culture is often the bastion of the young and in many ways reflects the contemporary experience of youth, which could seem frightening to adults. We often prefer to deny both the aggression and sexual curiosity young people feel, so when we encounter these themes in popular culture we often blame media for their existence.

In its quest for ratings, local news in particular is heavily focused on giving the public what the news executives think we want: sensationalism. The news itself often becomes secondary. Stories are often selected because of their emotional appeal rather than newsworthiness. For instance, Los Angeles network affiliates each offer about three to four hours of local news broadcasts a day, and of course the handful of twenty-four hour cable news channels offer a constant stream. To fill so much airtime, dramatic attention-grabbing stories are needed, to make us feel that thirty or sixty minutes of news a day isn't enough. Unfortunately, the expansion of news channels has not led to much expansion of in-depth reporting of the substantive issues I have discussed. Local news stories are brief, sound-bite journalism without much time for context or analysis. As we have seen in previous chapters, reports of studies that appear to justify our media fears are often presented as conclusive or dramatic without much analysis or critical investigation into the validity of the studies' findings.

Rather than simply blame reporters, news directors, or editors for being lazy, this type of reporting—brimming with drama and emotion, low on depth, context, or analysis—is indicative of what sociologist Todd Gitlin calls an endless torrent of images and sounds with increasingly less and less actual information.[2] According to Gitlin, we have become accustomed to a rapid stream of images, and to slow down for a moment of analysis threatens the possibility of a moment of boredom. True, the twenty-four-hour cable news networks do offer discussion on a selection of news topics, but they too are laden with emotion; the guests are aggressive within the crossfire-style format, mostly on the air because of the drama, rather than because of the information they may add.

Finally, the news media promote media phobia because as corporate entities they have a lot vested in the status quo. If culture is the problem, even culture their company may take part in creating, then we stay focused on media content rather than public policies. For instance, the 1996 Telecommunications Act (which is rarely scrutinized as harshly as popular culture) enabled behemoth media conglomerates to become even bigger, to create even larger monopolies in the production of media culture. These corporations also benefit from a tax structure that minimizes their liability. They (and the politicians they have funded) benefit from our tendency to view poverty and lack of opportunity as the result of individual failings rather than a public problem. Currently, our federal budget is comprised of taxes mainly collected from individuals; only 10 percent came from corporations in 2001, compared with 17 percent in the 1980s and 39 percent in the 1950s.[3]

Media conglomerates have a lot to gain by keeping us focused on the popular culture "problem," lest we decide to close some of the corporate tax loopholes to fund more social programs. More and more, the news is just one arm of an octopus designed to feed shareholders, so the more laissez-faire our public policy remains, the better for them. It's a win-win situation for the corporations: attention is deflected away from public policy solutions and on to media culture, which the First Amendment largely protects from regulation. While we are busy clamoring for more restraint and changes in content, there is little threat of any real change in social structure or challenge to business as usual. In short, the news media promote media phobia because it doesn't threaten the bottom line. Calling for social programs to reduce inequality and poverty would.

That said, there are ways that we can cope with an increasingly media-driven society. While social forces may seem uncontrollable, they only truly are if we ignore them in favor of what we think we can control: children and media. Although each may truly worry us in some regard, neither is at the heart of the central problems plaguing American society. There is much that journalists, policymakers, educators, parents, and everyone else can do.

Journalists

To a large extent, journalists' hands may be tied. They are compelled to tell dramatic stories, to continue preexisting narratives like the fear-the-media theme. But they can still introduce a new angle, try to add depth within a tight deadline and word-count restriction. I have had several good conversations with journalists who are interested in broadening the boundaries of the media-and-children story but have to work to convince editors that telling this story differently is important. I have a lot of respect for journalists—my critique of news media throughout this book does not mean that their work isn't important or difficult. Journalists are usually truth-seekers and most do want to learn about the subjects they cover, often for very little pay. They are often highly motivated to use their skills for the public good, but frequently the reality of the business gets in the way. On several occasions I have had reporters ask for a quote in order to support a preexisting conclusion; even when told that research may contradict their angle they prefer to seek out another quote rather than rethink their story. Sometimes this is laziness or bias, but more often I suspect it is due to pressure from editors, deadlines, or a combination of these and other factors.

But good reporting must somehow overcome these limitations. Journalists need to be the curious eyes and ears of the public, open to learning new, even counterintuitive, ideas. Many reporters do carry a healthy dose of skepticism, but I think even more is needed. For journalists who report on research of any kind, some basic training or a refresher course in research methods will enhance their ability to be skeptical of research as well. It is easy to defer to expert interpretation and opinion, but journalists should cast a critical eye on the studies they report. God knows professional journal articles can be dry and dull, but reporters need to be familiar with their content when reporting on research, not just with the press releases sent in their stead.

Writing grounded in context often dilutes drama, but emotion often replaces real information. Editors may gripe that stories that calm instead of trigger fears don't grab the reader's attention. Ideally, good writing would remedy this problem, but in order for stories to get the green light the topic itself needs to be considered dramatic. News organizations also need to ask deeper questions about their purpose, whether they exist to simply excite or to inform the public. Of course, within an increasingly corporatized climate it is the accountants and shareholders, not the journalists, who often have the final say of what constitutes news.

Idealistically, journalism could shine a bright light on the key issues at the root of social problems. Of course this isn't how people get ahead in news organizations, which are more about excitement and ratings than social change. The news media have become increasingly powerful in shaping what issues rise to the top of the national agenda, so it would be great if journalists were free to expose the problems children face living in poverty, attending under-funded schools, and trying to obtain health care. In an ideal world journalism would be a beacon, leading us to face the most difficult of social problems and steering us away from the pseudo problems based in collective anxiety.

But of course we do not live in an ideal world, nor is a mostly for-profit press necessarily going to advocate for major changes to our society. These are big questions we should all be asking, rather than blaming the news media for entertaining us and catering to our worst fears. But with influence comes responsibility, and journalists need to be sure they are covering stories about children's issues in their proper context with sufficient depth and analysis to do children justice.

Policymakers

I'd like to hope that most policymakers and elected officials believe that their work will make a positive difference. I even believe that the politicians who have focused a lot of energy blaming media mean well. I don't think that there is a grand conspiracy to avoid facing tough social issues; the politicians who have participated in cultural criticism truly believe that they are attacking a serious problem. So when I say that they have diverted both their and our attention away from the most important issues, I don't mean that it is intentional. All too often, politicians operate in order to face the least opposition from colleagues and constituents. The media are a rather safe target. Unfortunately, this safety is based on the fact that culture is not the basis of the problems we often think regulating media content will solve. I have spoken with politicians who agree that media blaming is a misguided policy turn, but feel frustrated in attempts to get their colleagues to refocus. This is where the rest of us come in; write your senators and representatives (find them at www.congress.gov) when they get on the media-blaming bandwagon and tell them what we prefer they focus on with our tax dollars. Politicians need to take a leadership role on this issue too. Remind fellow lawmakers that violence is far more likely to result in high poverty areas, that crime rates and media usage have nothing to do with one another, that unemployment rates in the poorest areas are a more worthy target than slasher films or video games.

Policymakers can choose to lead or to be led by seemingly safe choices like media-blaming. They can make a difference by reminding all of us that the foundation of our fears lies in problems rooted in social structure, like lack of opportunity, not media culture. I'm not going to pretend that the solutions to these problems are easy, but this is the arena in which elected officials can make a difference. Sure, legislation trying to restrict kids' access to the Internet may be politically popular and receive bipartisan cooperation, but history will not look kindly on a society whose leaders ignore the big issues to appease their constituents' fear of change.

Attempts to regulate taste and culture may play well with those most likely to vote, but this policy turn ultimately alienates young would-be voters, both from policy issues and from the older generation. If we want to change the terms of debate, both young and low-income people need to vote in larger numbers to let politicians know that media culture is not the problem. Grassroots organizations can help leaders refocus on the problems of poverty, corporate crime, job insecurity, and other issues that they tend not to pay much sustained attention to. Of course everyday people can rarely afford huge campaign contributions, as corporations can, or afford lobbyists to get attention, but without votes politicians will be out of business. Lawmakers can choose to take this difficult, but meaningful, uphill road towards the real domestic problems facing the United States or continue down the path of least resistance and least real change.

Educators

Educators also have a very important role in our media-saturated culture. Media analysis is a great tool for exposing the complexities of issues like gender and sexuality, for instance. Our media culture provides a great text for both artistic and social criticism. We can ask questions like what *Buffy the Vampire Slayer* tells us about contradictions within gender and power, or how the relative absence of non-white professionals in a drama series reflects inequalities of race. Our media culture is a great starting point to explore our society, using references young people are already familiar with. Being media savvy alone does not necessarily lead to critical analysis, which should be a part of being educated in the twenty-first century. Media literacy education, the kind that seeks to increase critical awareness of how texts are produced and how they represent (or fail to represent) real social issues, is essential. But adult-introduced discussions of media culture can be problematic, particularly if they are designed to create taste and promote adult value judgments, thus serving as another vehicle for media bashing. This will not engage young students, but will only alienate them further.

Educators need to include analysis of popular culture as part of critical competency building, not as taste promotion. Some people fear bringing popular culture into the classroom. After all, the argument goes, it is everywhere else; is no place sacred? But critical media literacy skills are a contemporary necessity for living in our media-saturated culture. Just as novels (once thought frivolous themselves) are analyzed, evaluated, and critiqued in literature courses, so too should twenty-first century students have full awareness of how electronic texts are produced and learn to critically discuss and evaluate them. The benefits of critical media literacy education are threefold: we help students apply critical thinking skills to popular culture they encounter every day, enhance traditional curricula, and in the process perhaps mitigate adults' fears that kids will be overwhelmed by media culture. Finally, critical media literacy could be a subject that students connect with, as they already come to the topic with experience and expertise. This may increase their commitment and connection to education. Within critical media literacy, education ceases to only be a top-down authoritative experience, but instead one in which students' knowledge and skills are valued and incorporated. This challenges traditional approaches to both education and media culture, as well as our assumptions about young people. Incorporating media analysis within the educational experience can therefore be empowering in several ways.

To succeed, critical media literacy must recognize that young people are more than blank slates that teachers fill, but instead are capable of making sense of popular culture in unique and sometimes counterintuitive ways. It is too simple to conclude that a violent film only inspires violence, or that a romantic movie will make kids more likely to have sex. To create critical skills, we must recognize that young people may interpret media in more complex ways than cause-effect logic suggests. Good media education isn't an inoculation against feared effects; it is necessary to understand the complicated, often contradictory ways that media audiences make sense of content. American educators are often tethered to the cause-effect media fears, but a growing media literacy movement provides many divergent viewpoints and resources that teachers can access. For a place to start, see the Center for Media Literacy's website at www.medialit.org.

Parents

Parents constantly face pressure to curb and control their kids' media use. Within the fear of media, parents are implicitly blamed for not "protecting" their children from allegedly dangerous media exposure. We need to be much more considerate of the challenges that many parents face, like the time crunch and economic challenges of everyday life. As I have detailed, we have been caught in a wave of trying to legislate parenting; we need to trust parents' judgment to raise their children as they see fit. The rest of us get too involved telling other people how they should be raising their kids.

This is not to say that parents should ignore what their kids are watching or listening to. But parents do need to recognize that kids' taste in popular culture is not necessarily an indication that their values are different, but that, for instance, their needs may be met through listening to music that parents may not approve of. To some degree, growing up happens with peers and away from parents. I think that many parents understand this, but it is sometimes difficult. For this reason, parental conversations with their kids about why they like what they do may not always be fruitful. But kids, especially as they become older, do need some space to enjoy popular culture on their own without having to explain themselves. Parents need to understand that teens in particular play with imagery from popular culture as they try to form their independent identities. That being said, a supportive parent who can listen without judging will understand their kids better and have a much greater impact than popular culture ever can. Informed trust and supportive monitoring will be much more productive than attempting to heavily regulate and control teens' media choices.

Discussions about popular culture, with both teens and young children, need to be supportive. Parents have to be careful to avoid condemning or judging their children's taste in popular culture, which will make kids defensive or even feel bad if their interests are criticized. To some extent parents will always find popular culture a threat: it is providing kids with something that they cannot. In many ways, media culture connects with kids in ways parents wish that they could, provoking a sense of incompetence within parents. Parents need to realize that popular culture provides an important stepping stone towards an independent identity and creates a connection with peers. Popular culture affords its consumers a chance to indulge in fantasies, some of which adults may feel uneasy about. Parents have been blamed for not policing their kids' popular culture enough, but the rest of us need to recognize that too much restriction may prevent young people from being able to deal with issues media culture assists them in confronting on their own.

Youth

It must be very overwhelming to be a kid now, with all that media culture has to offer beckoning on one side and the voices of fear and doom on the other. Kids first need to realize that adults have always worried about the movies, music, and books that their kids enjoyed. I think that some adults fear that kids' media consumption is out of balance, replacing other activities. Many of our lives are out of balance too, and we have trouble dealing with that. Although it may be frustrating for young people at times, adults are concerned about kids' media use because adults care about kids, and in some ways aren't sure how to best guide them to adulthood.

Kids also need to be patient with adults who don't understand their games or music. Many of us are scared, not necessarily because of anything that they did, but because the world is becoming a very different place from the one we were accustomed to. One of the biggest mistakes we make as adults is that we don't listen to kids enough. No, not to set their own curfews or allowance, but we often tell kids we are the experts of what is best for them without at least asking for their perspective first. Young people deserve at least that.

The Rest of Us

There is much that the rest of us need to do to cope with the preponderance of media culture and our tendency to fear it more than we need to. We can let our elected officials know that they must address the roots of problems facing children, like making sure that all children have access to decent health care and a quality education before worrying about video games they may play or Websites they may visit. But we can challenge some of these problems on our own without waiting for the government to do it for us by doing the following:

- Donate our money and time to keep low-cost clinics open
- Start book drives for poorly funded schools
- Donate to food banks and homeless shelters
- Volunteer time at a local public school or daycare center
- Start a political affairs discussion group
- Create a grassroots organization to support children's issues
- Run for public office

Some of these are small individual actions, but collectively small acts make a big difference. We can also work to empower kids in other ways too, by valuing their ideas and by consulting them, particularly when making decisions about their competency. But unfortunately the logic of media fear leads us towards more restriction and less empowerment.

We shouldn't ignore our media culture either. Kids aren't the only ones who need to work towards becoming critical media consumers. Adults often believe that kids don't know the difference between fact and fiction, but adults could stand to question whose viewpoint a news report or political pundit represents. This means questioning what we are told are facts by the news media and challenging the logic of hyperconsumption, that more is better and that fulfillment and good citizenship is accomplished by spending.

Instead of media phobia, where we complain about media content, we should engage in more media analysis. This means critically exploring representations of gender and race, for instance, and considering how these representations may reflect social inequality. What we ought to be discussing about media is who produces it, and for what purpose. In the United States especially, most media are produced for profit and are often created for some audiences and consumers but not others. While green is the only real color of interest, there is more green to be found in some racial/ethnic groups than others, and these groups are more likely to have media produced with them in mind.

We can learn a lot about race, class, gender, sexuality, and age by studying media representations and linking them to systems of power. It is simply not enough to spot these patterns within media, but we also need to implicate other social and historical factors that create such conditions. Sexism, for instance, wasn't born with the advent of movies or television, but it does live and breathe there. By paying sexism a "visit" within media culture, for instance, we learn a lot more about it.

Media content is a poor predictor of future behavior, but an excellent window through which we can understand social relations of power. As with any form of self-scrutiny, we often tend to avoid looking at media culture in this way. But like media analysis, societal analysis doesn't mean America bashing, but instead an honest look at what may need to be improved. Change is only possible when we dig below the surface, below media content, to critically explore issues of power in America.

Media: A Sheep in Wolf's Clothing

While media may reflect and remind us of social problems, media are not the central cause of violence and the other things that truly scare us. But because media culture may not be too important in creating violence or promiscuity, it is nonetheless very powerful. Its power shapes how we schedule and fill our days and influences how we interact with others. Its content often shapes what we talk to each other about and how we think about ourselves and the world around us. Its emergence has certainly altered other institutions, such as education, government, and religion. Keeping this in mind, media merit critical analysis, as do all social institutions. If we analyze media we will better understand society, but only if our energy regarding media is not expended on maintaining illusions about childhood. The news media in particular cast a very powerful spotlight, directing our attention onto some issues and away from others. Its power is feared harmful, but is much more complex than that. The biggest harm media power can yield is not in creating killers, but in creating complacency.

This complacency is not due to fictional entertainment, as we so often fear; it is created from news reports based on emotion and drama rather than citizenship. We are lulled not by music or movies or video games, but by programs passing as news that only skim the surface of what we need to know about our government, our corporations, our society. I say that media is a sheep in wolf's clothing because it gets our attention, seems scary, but underneath is much more of a follower than a real leader or creator of change. This is no accident—as I noted at the beginning of this chapter, media conglomerates are heavily invested in keeping things exactly as they are. That's why we continually hear reports from the news media that popular culture is the problem. Media phobia challenges nothing and fails to address the central problems that do affect millions of American children. The media sheep play follow the leader.

It doesn't have to be this way. Because media culture is so enchanting, so attention-seeking, it can be used to redirect our attention to the sources of social problems and to provide us with a wake-up call. We need to demand that the public-owned airwaves be used proactively, rather than reactively.

Fear can be crippling, especially when we fear something that poses no major threat. While changing media culture may truly concern us at times, we need to be sure to keep our real challenges in sight. It would be a mistake to only focus on the negative in these changing times and overlook the positive aspects of both media culture and the next generation. Fear prevents us from fully embracing either.

Notes

Introduction

1. Maxwell E. McCombs and Donald L. Shaw, "The Agenda-Setting Function of the Mass Media," *Public Opinion Quarterly* (1972): 176–187.

2. National Center for Children in Poverty, *Young Children in Poverty: A Statistical Update* (New York: NCCP, 2003).

3. The Children's Defense Fund, *The State of America's Children Yearbook, 2002* (Washington, D.C.: CDF, 2002).

4. The Children's Defense Fund, ibid.

5. U.S. Department of Health and Human Services, Administration on Children, Youth and Family, *Child Maltreatment 1999* (Washington, D.C.: Government Printing Office, 2001). U.S. Department of Education, *Indicators of School Crime and Safety* (Washington, D.C.: Government Printing Office, 2000). The most recent data on fatalities in school available is from the 1998–1999 school year.

6. For further discussion of Plato's concerns, see David Buckingham, *After the Death of Childhood: Growing Up in the Age of Electronic Media* (London: Polity Press, 2000).

7. John Springhall, *Youth, Popular Culture and Moral Panics: Penny Gaffs to Gangsta-Rap, 1830–1996* (New York: St. Martin's Press, 1998).

8. For further discussion see Springhall, chapter 5.

9. Frederic Wertham, "Such Trivia as Comic Books," in *The Children's Culture Reader*, ed. Henry Jenkins (New York: New York University Press, 1998).

10. Grace Palladino, *Teenagers: An American History* (New York: Basic Books, 1996).

11. Tom Brokaw, *The Greatest Generation* (New York: Random House, 1998).

12. Laura Sessions Stepp, "Why Johnny Can't Feel; Poor Relationships With Adults May Explain Youth Alienation," *Washington Post*, April 23, 1999, p. C1.

13. Matthew Ebnet and James Rainey, "It's Hard to See the Line Where Alienation Turns to Violence," *Los Angeles Times*, April 22, 1999, Orange County Edition.

14. Ebnet and Rainey.

15. Ebnet and Rainey.

16. U.S. Department of Education, *Indicators of School Crime and Safety* (Washington, D.C.: Government Printing Office, 2000).

17. Kelly L. Schmitt, *Public Policy, Family Rules and Children's Media Use in the Home* (Washington: Annenberg Public Policy Center, 2000).

18. Cynthia Cooper, *Violence on Television: Congressional Inquiry, Public Criticism and Industry Response—A Policy Analysis* (Lanham, Md.: University Press of America, 1996).

19. James Bates and Faye Fiore, "Hollywood Braces for a Showdown on Capitol Hill," *Los Angeles Times*, September 24, 2000, p. A1.

20. Abigail Goldman and Joseph Menn, "Wal-Mart Halts Gun Sales After State Laws Broken," *Los Angeles Times*, April 5, 2003, p. A1.

21. In 2002 Wal-Mart did implement more stringent handgun purchasing policies, angering the National Rifle Association. The chain later agreed to temporarily stop selling guns in California, following the investigation conducted by the attorney general's office.

22. U.S. Department of Health and Human Services, *Youth Violence: A Report of the Surgeon General* (Washington, D.C.: GPO, 2001). For more discussion of the research on which the statement was based, see Chapter 2.

23. Jeff Leeds, "Surgeon General Links TV, Real Violence," *Los Angeles Times*, January 17, 2001, p. A1. Jesse Hiestand, "Media Dodges Violence Bullet; Poverty, Peers More To Blame," *Daily News*, January 18, 2001, p. B1.

24. Sally Beatty, "Kids Are Glued to a Violent Japanese Cartoon Show," *Wall Street Journal*, December 3, 1999, p. B1. Gregory Lang, Letter to the Editor, *Wall Street Journal*, December 29, 1999.

25. United Nations, *Demographic Yearbook, 1993* (New York: United Nations, 1995).

26. Howard Karlitz, "Due South of Funny for Kids," *Los Angeles Times*, May 3, 1998, p. B15.

27. Douglas Kellner, "Beavis and Butt-head: No Future for Postmodern Youth," in *Kinderculture: The Corporate Construction of Childhood*,

eds. Shirley R. Steinberg and Joe L. Kincheloe (Boulder: Westview Press, 1998).

28. Susan Linn, "Sellouts," *The American Prospect*, October 23, 2000, p. 17.

29. Ali H. Mikdad et al., "The Spread of the Obesity Epidemic in the United States, 1991–1998," *Journal of the American Medical Association* 282 (1999): 1519–1522.

30. Ronald Brownstein, "As Youths Are Bombarded With Ads, a Pro-Family Group Counterattacks," *Los Angeles Times*, April 30, 2001, Section A.

31. Deborah M. Roffman, "Dangerous Games; A Sex Video Broke the Rules, But for Kids the Rules Have Changed," *Washington Post*, April 15, 2001, p. B1.

32. Roffman, ibid.

33. Barrie Gunter and Jill L. McAleer, *Children and Television: The One Eyed Monster?* (New York: Routledge, 1990).

34. Scott Martelle, Christine Hanley, and Kimi Yoshino, "'Sopranos' Scenario in Slaying?," *Los Angeles Times*, January 28, 2003, p. B1.

Chapter 1

1. For a comparison between children's and women's disempowerment see Barrie Thorne, "Re-Visioning Women and Social Change: Where are the Children?" *Gender and Society* 1 (1987): 85–109.

2. Jenny Kitzinger, "Who Are You Kidding? Children, Power, and the Struggle Against Sexual Abuse," in *Constructing and Reconstructing Childhood: Contemporary Issues in the Sociological Study of Childhood*, eds. Allison James and Alan Prout (London: Falmer Press, 1997).

3. David Buckingham, *After the Death of Childhood: Growing Up in the Electronic Age* (London: Polity Press, 2000).

4. Henry Jenkins, "Introduction: Childhood Innocence and Other Myths," in *The Children's Culture Reader*, ed. Henry Jenkins (New York: New York University Press, 1998).

5. Joe Kincheloe, "The New Childhood: Home Alone as a Way of Life," in *Kinderculture: The Corporate Construction of Childhood*, eds. Shirley R. Steinberg and Joe L. Kincheloe (Boulder: Westview Press, 1998).

6. Kitzinger, ibid., p. 168.

7. Karin Calvert, *Children in the House: Material Culture of Early Childhood, 1600–1900* (Boston: Northeastern University Press, 1992).

8. Stephen Kline, "The Making of Children's Culture," in *The Children's Culture Reader*, ed. Henry Jenkins (New York: New York University Press, 1998).

9. Viviana A. Zelizer, "From Useful to Useless: Moral Conflict over Child Labor," in *The Children's Culture Reader*, ed. Henry Jenkins (New York: New York University Press, 1998), p. 81.

10. Zelizer, ibid., p. 84.

11. Anthony Platt, "The Child-Saving Movement and the Origins of the Juvenile Justice System," in *Juvenile Delinquency: Historical, Theoretical and Societal Reactions to Youth*, second edition, eds. Paul M. Sharp and Barry W. Hancock (Upper Saddle River, N.J.: Prentice Hall, 1998), pp. 3–17.

12. Grace Palladino, *Teenagers: An American History* (New York: Basic Books, 1996).

13. U.S. National Center for Education Statistics, *1900–1985, 120 Years of Education: A Statistical Portrait* (Washington, D.C.: Digest of Education Statistics, annual).

14. Jenkins, ibid., p. 4.

15. Judith Stacey, *Brave New Families* (New York: Basic Books, 1990).

16. U.S. Census Bureau, *Statistical Abstract of the United States*, Tables P60–200 and P60–203 "Current Population Reports" (Washington, D.C.: Government Printing Office, 1999).

17. A fake list of the top ten biggest problems in schools of the 1990s (robbery, drug abuse, pregnancy) compared with the supposed top ten problems in 1940 (gum chewing, running in the halls, improper clothing) was widely distributed and treated as real in spite of evidence otherwise. For a discussion see Mike Males, *Framing Youth: Ten Myths about the Next Generation* (Monroe, Maine: Common Courage Press, 1999).

18. Miriam Formanek-Brunell, *Made to Play House: Dolls and the Commercialization of American Girlhood, 1830–1930* (New Haven: Yale University Press, 1993).

19. James Heintz and Nancy Folbre, *The Ultimate Field Guide to the U.S. Economy* (New York: The New Press, 2000).

20. U.S. Bureau of the Census, *Statistical Abstract of the United States*, "Current Population Reports Series P20–537" (Washington, D.C.: Government Printing Office, annual).

21. National Center for Health Statistics, *Natality, Vital Statistics of the United States.* (1937–); Birth Statistics (1905–1936) (Washington, D.C.: U.S. Bureau of the Census).

22. James E. Côté and Anton L. Allahar, *Generation on Hold: Coming of Age in the Late Twentieth Century* (New York: New York University Press, 1994).

23. Marcia E. Herman-Giddens, et al., "Secondary Sexual Characteristics and Menses in Young Girls Seen in Office Practice: A Study from the

Pediatric Research in Office Settings Network," *Pediatrics* 99 (4 April 1997): 505–512.

24. Michael Emery and Edwin Emery, *The Press and America: An Interpretive History of the Mass Media*, seventh edition (New York: Prentice Hall, 1992).

25. For discussion see Mike Males, *The Scapegoat Generation: America's War on Adolescents* (Monroe, Maine: Common Courage Press, 1996).

26. Ellen Seiter, *Television and New Media Audiences* (Oxford: Oxford University Press, 1999), pp. 58–90.

27. John Fiske, *Media Matters: Everyday Culture and Political Change* (Minneapolis: University of Minnesota Press, 1994), p. xv.

28. John Hartley, *The Politics of Pictures: The Creation of the Public in the Age of Popular Media* (London: Routledge, 1992).

29. For further discussion see Daniel Dayan and Elihu Katz, *Media Events: The Live Broadcasting of History* (Cambridge: Harvard University Press, 1992).

Chapter 2

1. Ann Scott Tyson, "The Role of Washington in Curbing Youth Violence," *Christian Science Monitor*, May 6, 1999, p. 2.

2. Tyson, ibid., p. 2.

3. John M. Broder, "Searching for Answers After School Violence," *New York Times*, May 10, 1999, p. A16.

4. For a discussion of this fear see Franklin E. Zimring, *American Youth Violence* (London: Oxford University Press, 1998).

5. Gabriel Escobar, "Washington Area's 703 Homicides in 1990 Set a Record," *Washington Post*, January 2, 1991, p. A1.

6. Escobar, ibid., p. A1.

7. Mike A. Males, *Framing Youth: Ten Myths about the Next Generation* (Monroe, Maine: Common Courage Press, 1999).

8. For discussion see Thomas Hine, *The Rise and Fall of the American Teenager: A New History of the American Adolescent Experience* (New York: Perennial, 1999), p. 178.

9. Foon Rhee, "Politicians Stepping in Where Parents Once Ruled," *Times-Picayune*, August 24, 1997, p. A31.

10. Rhee, ibid., p. A31.

11. John M. Yonkers, "How Could This Happen? When Children Kill Children, Who is to Blame?" *Plain Dealer*, April 5, 1998, p. 4D.

12. "Teens are an Easy Target for Older Generations," *Toronto Star*, October 10, 2000, "Life" section.

13. Laura Sessions Stepp, "Generation Hex: Stereotypes Hurt Today's Teens," The *Washington Post*, January 31, 2002, p. C10.

14. Stepp, ibid., p. C10.

15. Mike Males, "The Latest Assault on Teens: It's Their Brains," *Los Angeles Times*, February 17, 2002, p. M3.

16. Tracy Allen Jeffrey, "Rearing Down-To-Earth Children," *Chicago Sun-Times*, January 30, 2000, p. 33.

17. Susan Spaeth Cherry, "Handling Teens' Inflated Sense of Self-Importance," *Plain Dealer*, January 10, 1998, p. 2E.

18. Cherry, ibid., p. 2E.

19. Joshua B. Janoff, "A Gen-X Rip Van Winkle: Looking the Part Doesn't Mean I'm a Stereotypical Twentysomething," *Newsweek*, April 24, 1995, p. 10.

20. Kenneth T. Walsh, "Kinderpolitics '96," *U.S. News & World Report*, September 16, 1996, pp. 51–57.

21. Ronald Brownstein, "As Youths are Bombarded with Ads, A Pro-Family Group Counterattacks," *Los Angeles Times*, April 30, 2001, p. A5.

22. Caela Koszewski, "More Teens are Counting Their Blessings After Sept. 11 Attack on U.S.," Milwaukee *Journal Sentinel*, November 19, 2001, p. 4E.

23. Rhee, ibid., p. A31. Virginia Young, "From Here to Washington, Teen Smoking is Targeted," St. Louis *Post-Dispatch*, June 1, 1998, p. A1.

24. Rhee, ibid., p. A31.

25. "Washington's Teen-Ager Curfew to Start Soon," *New York Times*, June 20, 1999, p. 27.

26. Susan A. Sherr, "Scenes from the Political Playground: An Analysis of the Symbolic Use of Children in Presidential Advertising," *Political Communication* 16 (1999): 45–59.

27. "Campaigning in Michigan, Bush and Gore Sound Remarkably Similar," October 6, 2000, St. Louis *Post-Dispatch*, p. A10.

28. "Excerpts from Speech on Education," *New York Times*, June 20, 1999, p. 27. Maria L. LaGanga, "Governor Bush Stresses Safety in Schools," *Los Angeles Times*, November 3, 1999, p. A17.

29. Carla Marinucci, "For Gore, a Day of Word Games, Teen Talk and Cafeteria Food," *San Francisco Chronicle*, May 12, 2000, p. A6.

30. Matea Gold and T. Christian Miller, "Gore, Bush Speak Out Against Youth Violence," *Los Angeles Times*, p. A14.

31. Pamela J. Podger, "Contenders Differ Widely on Gun Control," *San Francisco Chronicle*, February 1, 2000, p. A7.

32. From the 1998 General Social Survey, National Opinion Research Council. The twenty-five-and-under category contains only those eligible to vote in the previous election.

33. John M. Broder, "Dole Indicts Hollywood for Debasing Culture," *Los Angeles Times*, June 1, 1995, p. A1.

34. "Campaigning in Michigan, Bush and Gore Sound Remarkably Similar," St. Louis *Post-Dispatch*, October 6, 2000, p. A10.

35. Mary Leonard, "Gore Gives Hollywood a Deadline," *Boston Globe*, September 12, 2000, p. A20.

36. "Campaigning in Michigan, Bush and Gore Sound Remarkably Similar," ibid., p. A10.

37. *ABC World News Tonight*, September 12, 2000.

38. Claudia Puig, "Bush, Gore Chide Entertainment Industry Report: Kids Lured to Adult Matter," *USA Today*, September 12, 2000, p. A1. "Campaigning in Michigan, Bush and Gore Sound Remarkably Similar," ibid., p. A10.

39. "Hollywood Sells Kids on Violence," *Los Angeles Times*, September 11, 2000, p. A1.

40. Geoff Boucher, "Sound and Fury Signifying What?" *Los Angeles Times*, December 24, 2000, Calendar section 5.

41. "Hollywood Sells Kids on Violence," ibid., p. A1.

42. Brian Lowry, "Culture Warriors, Meet the Parents," *Los Angeles Times*, April 29, 2001, Calendar section 7.

43. Dee Anna S. Behle, "Young Voters' Issues are Ignored," *Los Angles Times*, October 28, 2000, p. B9.

44. Mary MacDonald, "Youths Talk Back to Congressman About Issues," Atlanta *Journal and Constitution*, December 7, 2000, p. 4JG.

45. Brooke Dairman and Amy Marrin, "Is Political Apathy Just a Phase for Teens?" *Newsday*, November 14, 1999, p. H21.

46. Karen Sternheimer, "A Media Literate Generation? Adolescents as Active, Critical Viewers: A Cultural Studies Approach" (Ph.D. dissertation, University of Southern California, 1998), pp. 138–140.

47. See Anna Greenberg, "What Young Voters Want: They're Looking for Help With College and a Reason to Believe in Government," *The Nation*, February 11, 2002, p. 14.

48. William J. Chambliss, "The Saints and the Roughnecks," *Society* (11: 1973), 24–31.

49. Thomas Hine, *The Rise and Fall of the American Teenager: A New History of the American Adolescent Experience* (New York: Perennial, 1999), chapter 8.

50. Bureau of Labor Statistics, "Unemployed Persons by Sex and Age, Seasonally Adjusted" (Washington, D.C.: U.S. Department of Labor, annual). Figures cited include only those seeking employment.

51. National Center for Health Statistics, "Teen Birth Rates Decline in All States During the 1990s" (Atlanta: Centers for Disease Control and Prevention, press release, May 30, 2002).

52. Adolescent and School Health, "Youth Risk Behavior Trends" (Atlanta: Centers for Disease Control and Prevention, 1991–1999).

53. Substance Abuse and Mental Health Services Administration, *Health, 2001* (Washington, D.C.: Government Printing Office, 2002).

54. Marguerite Kelly, "Teens at 14 Are Still Living Self-Centered Life," *Milwaukee Journal Sentinel*, May 28, 1999, p. 1. Independent Sector website: www.independentsector.org/media/Archive/teen_summary.html/teen _volunteers.html.

55. Allison Steele, "Teens Lend a Helping Hand," *Baltimore Sun*, July 9, 2001, p. 2B.

56. Monte Whaley, "Evergreen Teen Among Top Youth Volunteers," *Denver Post*, May 7, 2002, p. B1.

57. Richard Fausset, "Two Students Suspended Over Fliers," *Los Angeles Times*, June 14, 2002, p. B4.

58. Barry Checkoway, "Do We View Youths as Victims, or as Resources?" *Los Angeles Times*, February 3, 1993, p. B7.

59. Caitlin Lovinger, "Violence, Even Before the Internet," *New York Times*, April 25, 1999, p. 18.

Chapter 3

1. See Jonathan L. Freedman, *Media Violence and Its Effect on Aggression* (Toronto: University of Toronto Press, 2002), p. 43.

2. Dorothy Dimitre, Letter to the editor, *San Francisco Chronicle*, September 18, 2000, p. A16.

3. Dimitre, p. A16.

4. Freedman, ibid., p. 200.

5. Todd Gitlin, *Media Unlimited: How the Torrent of Images and Sounds Overwhelms Our Lives* (New York: Metropolitan Books, 2001), p. 145.

6. After publishing an op-ed (Karen Sternheimer, "Blaming Television and Movies Is Easy and Wrong," *Los Angeles Times*, February 4, 2001, p. M5), I received e-mails that presumed that my work must be funded by the entertainment industry, which it is not.

7. Jim Sullinger, "Forum Examines Media Violence," *Kansas City Star*, August 29, 2001, p. B5.

8. Jennifer Blanton, "Media, Single Parents Blamed for Spurt in Teen Violence," *Pittsburgh Post-Gazette*, 2 August 2001, A1.

9. Federal Bureau of Investigation, Violence Index, *Uniform Crime Reports for the United States, 1999* (Washington, D.C.: U.S. Department of Justice, 2000).

10. Federal Bureau of Investigation, Property Index, *Uniform Crime Reports for the United States, 1999* (Washington, D.C.: U.S. Department of Justice, 2000).

11. James Alan Fox and Marianne W. Zawitz, *Homicide Trends in the United States* (Washington, D.C.: U.S. Department of Justice, 2000).

12. Federal Bureau of Investigation, *Uniform Crime Reports for the United States, 1964–1999* (Washington, D.C.: U.S. Department of Justice, 2000).

13. Lori Dorfman et al., "Youth and Violence on Local Television News in California," *American Journal of Public Health* 87 (1997): 1311–1316.

14. E. Britt Patterson, "Poverty, Income Inequality and Community Crime Rates," in *Juvenile Delinquency: Historical, Theoretical and Societal Reactions to Youth*, second edition, ed. Paul M. Sharp and Barry W. Hancock (Upper Saddle River, N.J.: Prentice Hall, 1998), pp. 135–150.

15. Rosie Mestel, "Triggers of Violence Still Elusive," *Los Angeles Times*, 7 March 2001, A1.

16. Wayne Wooden and Randy Blazak, *Renegade Kids, Suburban Outlaws: From Youth Culture to Delinquency*, second edition (Belmont, Calif.: Wadsworth, 2001).

17. Federal Bureau of Investigation, *Uniform Crime Reports for the United States, 1980–1999* (Washington, D.C.: U.S. Department of Justice, 2000).

18. Mediascope, "Copycat Crimes," http://www.mediascope.org/pubs/ibriefs/cc.htm.

19. Caroline J. Keough, "Young Killer Wrestles Again in Broward Jail," *Miami Herald*, February 17, 2001, p. A1. Michael Browning et al., "Boy, 14, Gets Life in TV Wrestling Death," *Chicago Sun-Times*, March 10, 2001, p. A1. "Wrestle Slay-Boy Faces Life," *Daily News*, January 26, 2001, p. 34.

20. "13 Year-Old Convicted of First-Degree Murder," *Atlanta Journal and Constitution*, January 26, 2001, p. 1B.

21. Caroline Keough, "Teen Killer Described as Lonely, Pouty, Disruptive," *Miami Herald*, February 5, 2001, p. A1.

22. "Murder Defendant, 13, Claims He Was Imitating Pro Wrestlers on TV," *Los Angeles Times*, January 14, 2001, p. A24. Later in media interviews, Lionel said that Tiffany was lying down on the stairs and he accidentally crushed her when he came bounding down the steps.

23. Tom Farmer, "Out of Control; Child Stabbing Puts Focus on Violent Movies," *Boston Herald*, February 6, 2001, p. A1.

24. Farmer, ibid., p. A1.

25. Jessica Heslan, "Stab Victim's Classmates Counseled," *Boston Herald*, February 8, 2001, p. 14.

26. "Tackling Violence Puzzle," editorial, *Boston Herald*, February 7, 2001, p. 24.

27. Scott Williams, "Schools Address Bullying Issue," *Milwaukee Journal Sentinel*, March 25, 2001, p. 1Z.

28. Carol J. Smith, Letter to the editor, *Los Angeles Times*, September 17, 2000, Section M.

29. Todd Gitlin, *Media Unlimited: How the Torrent of Images and Sounds Overwhelms Our Lives* (New York: Metropolitan Books, 2001), p. 92.

30. Chris Zdeb, "Violent TV Affects Kids' Brains Just as Real Trauma Does," *The Gazette*, June 5, 2001, p. C5.

31. Jim Sullinger, "Forum Examines Media Violence," *Kansas City Star*, August 29, 2001, p. B5.

32. Marilyn Elias, "Beaten Unconsciously: Violent Images May Alter Kids' Brain Activity, Spark Hostility," *USA Today*, April 19, 2001, p. 8D.

33. I would like to thank Cheryl Maxson and Malcolm Klein for including appropriate measures in their study, "Juvenile Violence in Los Angeles," sponsored by the Office of Juvenile Justice and Delinquency Prevention, grants #95-JN-CX-0015, 96-JN-FX-0004, and 97-JD-FX-0002, Office of Justice Programs, U.S. Department of Justice. The points of view or opinions in this book are my own and do not necessarily represent the official position or policies of the U.S. Department of Justice.All interviews were conducted in 1998. The content of the interviews primarily involved the youths' descriptions of a selection of the violent incidents that the youths had experienced, the major focus of the study. At the end of each interview, youths were asked whether they thought television and movies contained a lot of violence. This question was posed to ascertain their perceptions of the levels of violence in media. Following this, respondents were asked whether they thought that viewing violence in media made them more afraid in their neighborhoods and why or why not they felt the way they did. This topic helped respondents

begin to compare the two types of violence and consider the role of media violence in their everyday lives. Finally, respondents were asked to name a film or television program that they felt contained violence, and compare the violence in that film or program to the violence they experienced and had described in the interview earlier. This question solicited direct comparison between the two modes of experience (lived and media violence). The subjects were able to define media violence themselves, as they first chose the medium, and then the television program or film that they wished to discuss. Definitions of media violence were not imposed on the respondents. The interviews were tape-recorded and transcribed. Data were later coded using qualitative data analysis software to sort and categorize the respondents' answers. Data were collected by random selection by obtaining a sample of addresses from a marketing organization, and households were then enumerated to determine whether a male between the ages of twelve to seventeen lived in the residence for at least six months. (Interviewees were sometimes eighteen at the time of follow-up.) It was determined that if youths had lived in the neighborhood for less than six months, their experiences might not accurately reflect activity within that particular area. They were excluded in the original sampling process.

34. But not necessarily—researchers who study media violence often have backgrounds in communications, psychology, or medicine.

35. No females were included because primary investigators concluded from previous research that males were more likely to have been involved in violent incidents.

36. Rosie Mestel, "In A Wired World, TV Still Has Grip on Kids," *Los Angeles Times*, September 18, 2000, p. F1. The same article also appeared in Montreal's *Gazette* as "The Great Debate: Experts Disagree Over the Extent of the Effects of Media Violence on Children" on September 30, 2000.

37. Susan FitzGerald, "Cutting Back on Kids' TV Use May Reduce Aggressive Acts," *Denver Post*, January 15, 2001, p. A2.

38. FitzGerald, ibid., p. A2.

39. See Gerard Jones, *Killing Monsters: Why Children Need Fantasy, Super Heroes, and Make-Believe Violence* (New York: Basic Books, 2002).

40. L. Rowell Huesman, et al., "Longitudinal Relations Between Children's Exposure to TV Violence and Their Aggressive and Violent Behavior in Young Adulthood: 1977–1992," *Developmental Psychology* 39, no. 2 (2003): 201–221. Kids who regularly watched shows like *Starsky and*

Hutch, The Six Million Dollar Man, and *Road Runner* cartoons in 1977 were regarded as high violence viewers.

41. Based on r=.17.

42. Richard Saltus, "Survey Connects Graphic TV Fare, Child Behavior," *Boston Globe,* March 21, 2001, p. A1.

43. Mestel, ibid., p. F1; Saltus, ibid., p. A1.

44. "A Poisonous Pleasure," editorial, St. Louis *Post-Dispatch,* July 30, 2000, p. B2. Psychologist Jonathan Freedman suggests that the claim of one thousand studies is inflated, and that there have been more like 200 studies conducted. Jonathan L. Freedman, *Media Violence and Its Effect on Aggression* (Toronto: University of Toronto Press, 2002), p. 24.

45. "A Poisonous Pleasure," ibid., p. B2.

46. "Preventing School Shootings," *USA Today,* May 21, 2001, p. 1A.

47. David Buckingham, *After the Death of Childhood: Growing Up in the Age of Electronic Media* (London: Polity, 2000), p. 130.

48. David Buckingham and Julian Wood, "Repeatable Pleasures: Notes on Young People's Use of Video," in *Reading Audiences: Young People and the Media,* ed. David Buckingham (Manchester, U.K.: Manchester University Press, 1993).

49. Buckingham, ibid., p. 132.

50. Buckingham, ibid., p. 132.

51. Buckingham, ibid., p. 137.

52. Joanne Cantor, "Media Violence," *Journal of Adolescent Health* 27 (2000): 30.

53. One incident played itself out in the pages of the *Los Angeles Times.* (Brian Lowry, "More Experts Than Facts on Kids, Media Violence," *Los Angeles Times,* October 24, 2000, p. F1.) Television columnist Brian Lowry introduced some of the arguments against the media-violence connection in an October 2000 column and questioned why the news media rarely challenge the claims of media-effects researchers. Communications studies professor Dale Kunkel, who was senior researcher for the extremely well-funded National Television Violence Study, responded with venom. "Lowry's take on the topic barely scratches the surface," Kunkel charged, as he essentially stated that a mere television critic could never understand the complex findings. (Dale Kunkel, "Evidence on Media Violence Still Stands," *Los Angeles Times,* November 6, 2000, p. F3.) But most of the attacks focused on psychologist Jonathan Freedman, whom Kunkel attempted to discredit by calling his study a "rehash" and "good press but bad science."

54. Megan Garvey, "Washington Again Taking on Hollywood," *Los Angeles Times,* June 2, 2001, p. A1.

Chapter 4

1. Leann Smith, "Cartoon Violence is No Laughing Matter," *Kansas City Star*, November 30, 2000, p. B6.

2. Sally Beatty, "Kids are Glued to a Violent Japanese Cartoon Show—'Dragon Ball Z' is Bringing Impalement, Strangulation to the After-School Crowd," *Wall Street Journal*, December 3, 1999, p. B1.

3. Gregory Lang, Letter to the editor, "Violent Cartoon Show Can Destroy Childhood," *Wall Street Journal*, 29 December 1999, A15.

4. Karen MacPherson, "Children See Most Violence in Cartoons, Study Says," Pittsburgh *Post-Gazette*, April 17, 1998, p. A1.

5. Fumie Yokota and Kimberly M. Thompson, "Violence in G-Rated Animated Films," *Journal of the American Medical Association* 283 (2000): 2716–2720.

6. Amy Dickinson, "Violent Cartoons," *Time*, June 12, 2000, p. 90. Paul Farhi, "Cartoons That Aren't for Kids," *Washington Post*, May 24, 2000, p. C1. Associated Press, "Study Cites Violent Content in G-Rated Films," *Los Angeles Times*, May 24, 2000, p. A8.

7. Jami Bernard, "Reel-World Violence," *Daily News*, May 28, 2000, p. 7.

8. "Animated Objection," Pittsburgh *Post-Gazette*, April 22, 1998, p. A22.

9. For further discussion see Robert Hodge and David Tripp, *Children and Television: A Semiotic Approach* (Stanford: Stanford University Press, 1986).

10. For further discussion see Jib Fowles, *The Case For Television Violence* (Thousand Oaks, Calif.: Sage, 1999).

11. Cindy Kranz, "Wrestling with a Moral Dilemma," *Chicago Sun-Times*, April 4, 1999, p. 34.

12. Kranz, ibid., p. 34.

13. Kranz, ibid., p. 34.

14. Communications scholar George Gerbner is quoted in Jim Rutenberg, "Violence Finds Niche in Children's Cartoons," *New York Times*, January 28, 2001, p. 1.

15. The Disney genre refers to a particular style of storytelling and is not limited to films and products by Disney itself. For further discussion, see Michael Real, *Exploring Media Culture: A Guide* (Thousand Oaks, Calif.: Sage, 1996).

16. Howard Karlitz, "Due South of Funny," *Los Angeles Times*, May 3, 1998, p. B15. Karl Zinsmeister et al., "Wasteland: How Today's Trash Harms America," *The American Enterprise*, March/April 1999, p. 26. Barry Fagin, "Goin' Down to South Park," *Reason*, May 2000, 38–41.

17. James Collins, "Gross and Grosser," *Time*, March 23, 1998, pp. 74–76. Rick Marin, "The Rude Tube," *Newsweek*, March 23, 1998, p. 58.

18. Collins, ibid., p. 74.

19. Marin, ibid., p. 56.

20. Helen Nixon, "Adults Watching Children Watch South Park," *Journal of Adolescent & Adult Literacy*, September 1999, 12.

21. Marin, ibid., p. 56. Collins, ibid., p. 74. Karl Zinsmeister et al., ibid., p. 26.

22. Nixon, ibid., p. 16.

23. For seminal work in this area, see Peter Conrad, "The Discovery of Hyperkinesis: Notes on the Medicalization of Deviant Behavior," *Social Problems* 23 (1975): 12–21.

24. Cindy Dell Clark, *Flights of Fancy, Leaps of Faith: Children's Myths in Contemporary America* (Chicago: University of Chicago Press, 1995).

25. Douglas Kellner, "Beavis and Butt-head: No Future for Postmodern Youth," in *Kinderculture: The Corporate Construction of Childhood*, eds. Shirley Steinberg and Joe Kincheloe (Boulder: Westview Press, 1998).

26. "Bush Barks Up Wrong Tree When He Slams *Simpsons*," *TV Guide*, May 23, 1992, p. 31.

27. "A Rascal Cartoon Character Sets Off Controversy in S.C.," *Los Angeles Times*, March 1, 1994, p. A5.

28. Frank McConnell, "'Real' Cartoon Characters: *The Simpsons*," *Commonweal*, June 15, 1990, p. 389.

29. See Henry Giroux, *The Mouse That Roared* (New York: Rowman & Littlefield, 1999).

30. For more discussion on how Disney markets "innocence" see Henry Giroux, *The Mouse That Roared*, chapter 1.

31. Jacquelyn Kilpatrick, "Disney's 'Politically Correct' Pocahontas," *Cineaste* 21 (1995): 36–38.

32. For examples see Joe R. Feagin and Melvin P. Sikes, *Living with Racism: The Black Middle-Class Experience* (Boston: Beacon Press, 1994).

33. Henry Giroux, "Are Disney Movies Good for Your Kids?," in *Kinderculture: The Corporate Construction of Childhood*, eds. Shirley R. Steinberg and Joe L. Kincheloe (Boulder: Westview Press, 1998), p. 61.

34. John Newsinger, "US: Me Disney, You Tarzan," *Race and Class* 42 (2000): 78.

35. As cultural critic Henry Giroux stated, "The animal kingdom provide(s) the mechanism for presenting and legitimating social hierarchy,

royalty, and structural inequality as part of the natural order." See Giroux, "Are Disney Movies Good for Your Kids?" ibid., pp. 62–63.

36. For further discussion see Lauren Dundes, "Disney's Modern Heroine Pocahontas: Revealing Age-Old Gender Stereotypes and Role Discontinuity Under a Façade of Liberation," *The Social Science Journal* 38 (2001): 353.

Chapter 5

1. John Leo, "When Life Imitates Video," *U.S. News and World Report*, May 3, 1999, p. 14.

2. Leo, ibid., p. 14.

3. "Hooked on Video Games," *Maclean's*, December 6, 1999, p. 10.

4. Ashling O'Connor, "Eidos Faces U.S. Shooting Lawsuit," *Financial Times*, June 6, 2001, p. 24.

5. "Ending the Blame Game," *Denver Post*, March 6, 2002, p. B6. Leo, ibid., p. 14.

6. Cited in Glenn Gaslin, "Lessons Born of Virtual Violence," *Los Angeles Times*, October 3, 2001, p. E1.

7. Karen E. Dill and Jody C. Dill, "Video Game Violence: A Review of the Emperical Literature," *Aggression and Violent Behavior* 3 (1998) 407–428. Mark Griffiths, "Violent Video Games and Aggression: A Review of the Literature," *Aggression and Violent Behavior* 4 (1999): 203–212. Lillian Bensley and Juliet Van Eenwyk, "Video Games and Real-Life Aggression: Review of the Literature," *Journal of Adolescent Health* 29 (2002): 244–257. Craig A. Anderson and Brad J. Bushman, "Effects of Violent Video Games on Aggressive Behavior, Aggressive Cognition, Aggressive Affect, Physiological Arousal, and Prosocial Behavior: A Meta-Analytic Review of the Scientific Literature," *Psychological Science* 12 (2001): 353–359.

8. Quoted in M. B. Hanson, "The Violent World of Video Games," *Insight on the News*, June 28, 1999, p. 14.

9. Tracy L. Dietz, "An Examination of Violence and Gender Role Portrayals in Video Games: Implications for Gender Socialization and Aggressive Behavior," *Sex Roles* 38 (1998): 425–442.

10. Steven Kent, "Game Glorifies Life of Crime," *USA Today*, December 20, 2001, p. 3D.

11. Kent, ibid., p. 3D.

12. Crispin Sartwell, "Violence and Culture: Breaking the Rules OK in Video Games," Atlanta *Journal-Constitution*, January 9, 2002, p. 14A.

13. Glenn Gaslin, "Lessons Born of Virtual Violence," *Los Angeles Times*, October 3, 2001, p. E5.

14. Quoted in Ken Macqueen, "Killing Time: Video Games Present a Child's Garden of Mayhem," *Maclean's*, April 30, 2001, p. 22.

15. Michael Brody, "Playing With Death," *The Brown University Child and Adolescent Behavior Letter*, November 2000, p. 8.

16. Chris Zdeb, "Violent TV Affects Kids' Brains Just as Real Trauma Does," *The (Montreal) Gazette*, June 5, 2001, p. C5.

17. Michele Norris, "Child's Play? Grand Theft Auto III Provides Video Gamers with a Virtual World of Extreme Violence," *ABC World News Tonight*, July 2, 2002.

18. Lillian Bensley and Juliet Van Eenwyk, "Video Games and Real-Life Aggression: Review of the Literature," *Journal of Adolescent Health* 29 (2001): 244–257. Jeanne B. Funk "Video Games: Benign or Malignant?" *Journal of Developmental and Behavioral Pediatrics* 13 (1992): 53–54. C. E. Emes, "Is Mr. Pac Man Eating Our Children? A Review of the Effect of Video Games on Children," *The Canadian Journal of Psychiatry* (1997): 409–414.

19. M. Winkel, D. M. Novak, and H. Hopson, "Personality Factors, Subject Gender, and the Effects of Aggressive Video Games on Aggression in Adolescents," *Journal of Research in Personality* 21 (1987): 211–223.

20. Craig Anderson and Karen Dill, "Video Games and Aggressive Thoughts, Feelings and Behavior in the Laboratory and Life," *Journal of Personality and Social Psychology* 78 (2000): 772–790.

21. Amy Dickinson, "Video Playground: New Studies Link Violent Video Games to Violent Behavior," *Time*, May 8, 2000, p. 100.

22. For further problems, see Guy Cumberbatch, "Only a Game?" *New Scientist*, June 10, 2000, p. 44.

23. Anderson and Dill, ibid., 22.

24. Anderson and Dill, ibid., 33.

25. Marnie Ko, "Mortal Konsequences," *Alberta Report*, May 22, 2000.

26. Dickinson, ibid., p. 100.

27. Marilynn Larkin, "Violent Video Games Increase Aggression," *The Lancet*, April 29, 2000, p. 1525.

28. Quoted in Charles Arthur, "How Kids Cope with Video Games," *New Scientist*, December 4, 1993, p. 5.

29. Derek Scott, "The Effect of Video Games on Feelings of Aggression," *The Journal of Psychology* 129 (1995): 121–133.

30. Jim Ritter, "Parents Cautioned to Heed Ratings," *Chicago Sun-Times*, May 12, 2002, p. 11.

31. Burhan Wazir, "Adults Only? Violence Makes Games Unsuitable for Children," *The Observer*, December 16, 2001, p. 13.

32. Joe Follick, "Lawmakers: Restrict Sale of Violent Video Games," *Tampa Tribune*, December 25, 2001, p. 1.

33. Follick, ibid.

34. Follick, ibid.

35. David Lightman, "Video Games Sell, Despite Labels," *Hartford Courant*, December 14, 2001, p. A23.

36. Ritter, ibid., p. 11.

37. Norris, *ABC World News Tonight*, ibid.

38. Alex Pham, "Army's New Message to Attract Recruits: Uncle 'Sim' Wants You," *Los Angeles Times*, May 22, 2001, p. A1.

Chapter 6

1. Larry Katz, "Don't Blame Marilyn Manson," *Boston Herald*, April 28, 1999, p. 59.

2. Faye Fiore, "Lawmakers Warn Hollywood to Curb Violent Fare," *Los Angeles Times*, May 5, 1999, p. A32.

3. Jeffrey Jensen Arnett, "Adolescents' Uses of Media for Self-Socialization," *Journal of Youth and Adolescence* 24 (1995): 519.

4. Arnett, ibid., 524.

5. Scott Mervis, "Devil's Advocate: Marilyn Manson Is a Panty-Wearing Soldier in the Battle for the First Amendment," Pittsburgh *Post-Gazette*, May 2, 1997, p. 20.

6. Mervis, ibid., p. 20.

7. Mervis, ibid., p. 20.

8. Marilyn Manson, "Columbine: Whose Fault is it?" *Rolling Stone*, June 24, 1999, p. 23.

9. Max B. Baker, "Armey Urges Reunion to Rethink Planned Marilyn Manson Concert," Fort Worth *Star-Telegram*, March 20, 1999, p. 3.

10. Mervis, ibid., p. 20.

11. Dave Ferman, "Rock 'n' Ratings: Marilyn Manson and Other Lewd, Rude Concert Acts Could Soon Be Rated X," Fort Worth *Star Tribune*, April 19, 1998, Arts 1.

12. James H. Burnett III, "Detractors, Fans Greet Marilyn Manson Here," Milwaukee *Journal Sentinel*, April 26, 1999, p. 1.

13. Burnett, ibid., p. 1.

14. Manson, ibid., p. 23.

15. Ronald K. Fitten, "Trial to Begin for Teen Charged in Triple Slaying," *Seattle Times*, August 24, 1997, p. B1.

16. Ronald K. Fitten, "Loukaitis Jurors Hear Parents, See Pearl Jam Video," *Seattle Times*, September 9, 1997, p. B3.

17. Fitten, "Loukaitis Jurors Hear Parents," ibid.

18. Alex Fryer, "School Violence Pervades Films, Books and Music," *Seattle Times*, April 25, 1999, p. A1.

19. Steve Ritea, "Rink Lands in Civil Liberties Dispute," *Times-Picayune*, July 16, 2000, p. A1.

20. Ritea, ibid., p. A1.

21. Ritea, ibid.

22. Ritea, ibid.

23. Ritea, ibid.

24. A. D., "Eminem Responds," *Rolling Stone*, August 3, 2000, p. 18.

25. A. D., ibid., p. 18.

26. James Delingpole, "Your Children are Rap Victims," *The Spectator*, December 30, 2000, p. 10.

27. Robert Hilburn, "Eminem, On and On," *Los Angeles Times*, May 22, 2002, p. F1.

28. Oliver Wright, "Eminem Fanatic Turned to Violence," *The Times* (London), June 2, 2001.

29. Wright, ibid.

30. Christopher Walker, "Judge Asks to Hear Violent Rap Song," *Ottawa Citizen*, October 23, 2001, p. B3.

31. Walker, ibid., p. B3.

32. "Around the Nation," *Washington Post*, May 3, 1996.

33. Chuck Philips, "Murder Case Spotlights Marketing of Violent Lyrics," *Los Angeles Times*, January 21, 2001, p. C1.

34. Philips, ibid., p. C1.

35. Philips, ibid., p. C7.

36. Philips, ibid., p. C7.

37. "First Amendment Shield For Slayer Raises Concerns," *Los Angeles Times*, January 28, 2001, p. C2.

38. Allison Hope Weiner, Thom Geier, and Brian M. Raftery, "Facing the Music," *Entertainment Weekly*, August 24–31, 2001, pp. 10–13.

39. Weiner, Geier, and Raftery, ibid., p. 11.

40. Weiner, Geier, and Raftery, ibid., p. 13.

41. Weiner, Geier, and Raftery, ibid., p. 13.

42. Weiner, Geier, and Raftery, ibid., p. 13.

43. Jane Caputi and Diana E. H. Russell, "'Femicide': Speaking the Unspeakable," in *Feminist Frontiers*, fourth edition, eds. Laurel Richardson, Verta Taylor, and Nancy Whittier (New York: McGraw-Hill, 1997), p. 421.

44. Christopher Bantick, "Eminem's a Poet But the Oldies Don't Know it," *Courier Mail*, March 6, 2001, p. 11.

45. Suzanne Fields, "Bad Raps: Music Rebels Revel in their Thug Life," *Insight on the News*, May 21, 2001, p. 48. Val Aldridge, "A Load of Rap," *The Dominion* (Wellington), December 16, 2000, p. 19.

46. Terry McDermott, "Parental Advisory: Explicit Lyrics," *Los Angeles Times Magazine*, April 14, 2002, p. 32.

47. McDermott, ibid., p. 12.

48. McDermott, ibid., p. 14. Amy Binder, "Constructing Racial Rhetoric: Media Depictions of Harm in Heavy Metal and Rap Music," *American Sociological Review* 58 (1993): 753–767.

49. Sociologist Bethany Bryson conducted an analysis of musical dislikes using data from the General Social Survey, a nationally representative random household survey, and found strong associations between musical intolerance and racial intolerance. She notes that "people use cultural taste to reinforce symbolic boundaries between themselves and categories of people they dislike. Thus, music is used as a symbolic dividing line that aligns people with some and apart from others." Bryson also observed a correlation between dislike of certain groups and the music associated with that group. Bethany Bryson, "'Anything But Heavy Metal': Symbolic Exclusion and Musical Dislikes," *American Sociological Review* 61 (1996): 884–899.

50. Greg Wahl, "I Fought the Law (and I Cold Won!): Hip-hop in the Mainstream," *College Literature* 26 (1999): 101.

51. McDermott, ibid., p. 14.

52. Tricia Rose, "'Fear of a Black Planet': Rap Music and Black Cultural Politics in the 1990s," *Journal of Negro Education* 60 (1991): 279.

53. Amy Binder points out in her study of over 100 news stories on gangsta rap that in contrast to heavy metal, which is feared for being potentially dangerous for individual listeners, rap's critics have focused on its alleged threat to society as a whole. (See page 754.)

54. Kerri Harrop, Letter to the editor, *Seattle Times*, September 15, 1997, p. B5.

55. Dick Weissman, "Some Thoughts on the Columbine Shootings," *Popular Music and Society* 23 (1999): 29–30.

56. Judy Mann, "The Real Root Cause of School Violence," *Washington Post*, May 28, 1999, p. C11.

57. Richard Corliss, "Bang, You're Dead," *Time*, May 3, 1999, p. 50.

58. Ann Powers, "The Stresses of Youth, The Strains of Its Music," *New York Times*, April 25, 1999.

59. Hilary Rosen, "It's Easy, But Wrong, to Blame the Music," *Billboard*, May 8, 1999.

60. Jann Wenner, "Guns and Violence," *Rolling Stone*, June 10, 1999, p. 47.

61. David E. Nantais, "CDs Don't Kill People," *America*, January 1–8, 2000, p. 15.

62. Nantais, ibid., p. 14.

63. Nantais, ibid., p. 15.

Chapter 7

1. Marilyn Elias, "Selling to Kids Blurs Ethical Picture," *USA Today*, March 20, 2000, p. D7.

2. Stephanie Schorow, "Sales Pitches Strike Out: Advocacy Group Protests Marketing to Children," *Boston Herald*, September 10, 2001, p. 31. Ira Teinowitz, "FTC Opinion Stirs Advertiser Fears; Hands-Off Stance on Violence in Marketing May Invite Legislation," *Advertising Age*, November 27, 2000, p. 4.

3. Schorow, ibid., p. 31.

4. Steven Manning, "Branding Kids for Life," *The Nation*, November 20, 2000, p. 7. Susan Linn, "Sellouts," *The American Prospect*, October 23, 2000, p. 17.

5. Manning, ibid.

6. Manning, ibid.

7. Lisa Prue, "Author: Advertisers Harmful to Children," Omaha *World-Herald*, April 20, 2001, p. 39.

8. Ronald Brownstein, "As Youths are Bombarded With Ads, A Pro-Family Group Counterattacks," *Los Angeles Times*, April 30, 2001, p. A5.

9. Prue, ibid., p. 39.

10. Linda Bortell, "Antidote to Ad Blitz: Spending Time," *Los Angeles Times*, December 9, 2000, p. B11.

11. Tom McGee, "Getting Inside Kids' Heads," *American Demographics* 19 (1997): 53–59.

12. "The Merchants of Cool," *Frontline*, Public Broadcasting System, February 27, 2001.

13. Michael Schudson, *Advertising, the Uneasy Persuasion: It's Dubious Impact on American Society* (New York: Basic Books, 1984), p. 233.

14. Andy Fry, "Just Who are You Kidding? Techniques for Marketing to Children," *Marketing*, October 9, 1997, p. 26.

15. Patrick Barrett, "Are Ads a Danger to Kids?" *Marketing*, September 4, 1997, p. 15.

16. David L. Louden and Albert Della Bitta, *Consumer Behavior: Concepts and Applications*, fourth edition (New York: McGraw-Hill, 1993), p. 153.

17. Reinhold Bergler, director of the Institute of Psychology at the University of Bonn, critiques what he calls "naïve everyday psychology" as employed to explain advertising's alleged effects on children. "There are no mono-causal links between advertising and the effect it has on behavior," he stated in response to the belief that young people are easily manipulated by informed advertisers. Reinhold Bergler, "The Effects of Commercial Advertising," *International Journal of Advertising* 18 (1999): 412.

18. Lucy Henke, "Young Children's Perceptions of Cigarette Brand Advertising Symbols: Awareness, Affect, and Target Market Identification," *Journal of Advertising* 24 (1995): 13–28.

19. Barrett, ibid., p. 15.

20. Kristina Feliciano, "Just Kidding," *Mediaweek*, May 1, 2000, p. 58.

21. Feliciano, ibid., p. 58.

22. Louden and Della Bitta, ibid., p. 154.

23. Fry, ibid., p. 26.

24. Barrett, ibid., p. 15.

25. Jade Garrett, "Are Children an Advertiser's Perfect Audience?" *Campaign*, August 25, 2000.

26. Garrett, ibid.

27. The ads discussed in this section aired during a Saturday morning in March 2000.

28. Barrett, ibid., p. 15.

29. Schudson, ibid., 233.

30. Donna R. Powlowski, Diane M. Badzinski, and Nancy Mitchell, "Effects of Metaphors on Children's Comprehension of Print Advertisements," *Journal of Advertising* 27 (1998): 83–97.

31. Deborah Roedder John, "Consumer Socialization of Children: A Retrospective Look at Twenty-Five Years of Research," *Journal of Consumer Research* 26 (1999): 204. Also see David M. Borish, Marian Friestad, and Gregory M. Rose, "Adolescent Skepticism Toward TV Advertising and Knowledge of Advertiser Tactics," *Journal of Consumer Research* 21 (1994): 166.

32. Tamara F. Mangleberg and Terry Bristol, "Socialization and Adolescents' Skepticism Toward Advertising," *Journal of Advertising* 27 (1998): 11–20.

33. Juliet B. Schor, *The Overspent American: Why We Want What We Don't Need* (New York: HarperPerennial, 1998).

34. Nancy Gibbs et al., "Who's In Charge Here?" *Time*, August 6, 2001, p. 40.

35. Marci McDonald and Marianne Lavelle, "Call it 'Kid-fluence'," *U.S. News & World Report*, July 30, 2001, p. 32.

36. McDonald and Lavelle, ibid., p. 32.

37. Stephanie Schorow, "Sales Pitches Strike Out: Advocacy Group Protests Marketing to Children," *Boston Herald*, September 10, 2001, p. 31.

38. Linda Bortell, "Antidote to Ad Blitz: Spending Time," *Los Angeles Times*, December 9, 2000, p. B11.

39. Daniel Bell, *The Coming of Post-Industrial Society: A Venture in Social Forecasting* (New York: Basic Books, 1976).

40. Kim Campbell, "Deprived of Parent Time? Not Most Kids," *Christian Science Monitor*, April 5, 2000, p. 1.

41. Campbell, ibid., p. 1.

42. Campbell, ibid., p. 1.

43. Betsy Hart, "Kids Need Parents Who Know How to Say No," *Chicago Sun-Times*, August 5, 2001, p. 28.

44. Ann Perry, "Don't Give Your Kids Too Much, Experts Say," San Diego *Union-Tribune*, January 20, 2002, p. H1.

45. Gibbs, ibid., p. 40.

46. John De Graaf, David Wann, and Thomas H. Naylor, *Affluenza: The All-Consuming Epidemic* (San Francisco: Berrett-Koehler Publishers, 2001).

47. Don Oldenburg, "Ads Aimed at Kids," *Washington Post*, May 3, 2001, p. C4.

48. Hart, ibid.

49. Rachel Giese, "Those Gap Kids Ads are Not Alright!," *Toronto Star*, August 17, 2000.

50. Mike A. Males, *Framing Youth: Ten Myths about the Next Generation* (Monroe, Maine: Common Courage Press, 1999), chapter 9.

51. Steven Manning, "Students for Sale," *The Nation*, September 27, 1999, p. 11.

52. See Roy Fox, *Harvesting Young Minds: How TV Commercials Control Kids* (Westport, Conn.: Praeger, 2000).

53. They have since changed names and are no longer involved in educational marketing.

54. Manning, ibid.

55. See Naomi Klein, *No Logo: Taking Aim at the Brand Bullies* (New York: Picador USA, 1999).

56. Ellen Seiter, *Television and New Media Audiences* (Oxford: Oxford University Press, 1999).

57. Scott Donaton, "Why the Kids Marketing Fuss? Here's Why Parents are Angry," *Advertising Age*, October 16, 2000, p. 48.

58. Cindy Dell Clark, *Flights of Fancy, Leaps of Faith: Children's Myths in Contemporary America* (Chicago: University of Chicago Press, 1995).

59. Valli Herman-Cohen, "The Key to Life? It's in a Handbag," *Los Angeles Times*, February 1, 2002, p. E1.

Chapter 8

1. Kathleen Kelleher, "Birds and Bees: Don't Let TV Be Your Teenager's Main Source of Sex Education," *Los Angeles Times*, April 30, 2001, p. E2. Brian Lowry, "Grappling With Teen Sex," *Los Angeles Times*, February 20, 1999, p. A1. Marla Matzer, "Racy Content Rising on TV," *Daily News*, February 10, 1999, p. N1. Deborah M. Roffman, "Dangerous Games; A Sex Video Broke the Rules. But for Kids the Rules Have Changed," *Washington Post*, April 15, 2001, p. B1.

2. Lyn Gorman and David McLean, *Media and Society in the Twentieth Century: A Historical Introduction* (New York: Blackwell, 2003), pp. 36–40.

3. The Motion Picture Production Code, 1930.

4. James E. Côté and Anton L. Allahar, *Generation on Hold: Coming of Age in the Late Twentieth Century* (New York: New York University Press, 1994), chapter 1.

5. For further discussion see Martha Wolfenstein, "Fun Morality: An Analysis of Recent American Child-Training Literature," in *The Children's Culture Reader*, ed. Henry Jenkins (New York: New York University Press, 1998), p. 199.

6. Beth L. Bailey, *From Front Porch to Back Seat: Courtship in Twentieth-Century America* (Baltimore: The Johns Hopkins University Press, 1989).

7. Rickie Solinger, "Race and 'Value': Black and White Illegitimate Babies, 1945–1965," in *Feminist Frontiers*, fourth edition, eds. Laurel Richardson, Verta Taylor, and Nancy Whittier (New York: McGraw-Hill, 1997), p. 282.

8. National Opinion Research Council, General Social Survey (NORC: University of Chicago, 1998). www.icpsr.umich.edu-GSS-index.html.url.

9. Dennis Prager, "Our Kids' Innocence, Unprotected," *Los Angeles Times*, October 1, 2000, p. Calendar 10.

10. Henry Jenkins, "The Sensuous Child: Benjamin Spock and the Sexual Revolution," in *The Children's Culture Reader*, ed. Henry Jenkins (New York: New York University Press, 1998), p. 209.

11. Jenkins, ibid., p. 225.

12. Kaiser Family Foundation, "Sex on TV," full report online: www.kff.org/content/2001/3087SexOnTv.pdf.

13. Peter Kelley, David Buckingham, and Hannah Davies, "Talking Dirty: Children, Sexual Knowledge and Television," *Childhood* 6, no. 22 (1999): 221–242.

14. This study replicated a previous study of sex on television by analyzing 1,114 programs from the 1999–2000 season. Authors sought to address whether the frequency of what they defined as sexual messages were increasing, how sexual messages are presented, and whether the risks and responsibilities of sex are portrayed.

15. For discussion about how audiences create varying meanings from texts and are not simply manipulated by messages, see: David Morley, *Television, Audiences and Cultural Studies* (New York: Routledge, 1992); John Fiske, *Understanding Popular Culture* (London: Routledge, 1989); and Ien Ang, *Living Room Wars: Rethinking Audiences for a Postmodern World* (London, Routledge, 1996).

16. Kaiser Family Foundation, ibid., p. 1.

17. Kaiser Family Foundation, ibid., p. 1.

18. Alan Gutmmacher Institute, *Facts in Brief: Teen Sex and Pregnancy*, 1999 (online: [www.agi-usa.org]).

19. Mike Males, *Framing Youth: Ten Myths About the Next Generation* (Monroe, Maine: Common Courage Press, 1999), chapter 6.

20. Julian Wood, "Repeatable Pleasures: Notes on Young People's Use of Video," in *Reading Audiences: Young People and the Media*, ed. David Buckingham (Manchester: Manchester University Press, 1993), p. 184.

21. Kelley et al., 238.

22. Karen Sternheimer, "A Media Literate Generation? Adolescents as Active, Critical Viewers: A Cultural Studies Approach" (Ph.D. dissertation, University of Southern California, 1998).

23. For elaboration on this concept, see: William Corsaro, *The Sociology of Childhood* (Thousand Oaks, Calif.: Pine Forge Press, 1997), chapter 1. Alan Prout and Allison James, "A New Paradigm for the Sociology of Childhood? Provenance, Promise, and Problems," in *Constructing and Reconstructing Childhood*, eds. Allison James and Alan Prout (London:

Falmer Press, 1997), pp. 7–33. Patricia A. Adler and Peter Adler, *Peer Power: Preadolescent Culture and Identity* (New Brunswick, N.J.: Rutgers University Press, 1998), introduction.

24. Corsaro discusses the concept of "interpretive reproduction" in chapter 2 of the work listed above. He argues that children do not merely reproduce adult culture but re-interpret it to fit their own experiences.

25. Barrie Thorne, *Gender Play* (New Brunswick, N.J.: Rutgers University Press, 1993).

26. Donna Eder, Catherine Colleen Evans, and Stephen Parker, *School Talk: Gender and Adolescent Culture* (New Brunswick, N.J.: Rutgers University Press, 1995), pp. 83–102.

27. Valerie Walkerdine, "Popular Culture and the Eroticization of Little Girls," in *The Children's Culture Reader*, ed. Henry Jenkins (New York: New York University Press, 1998), p. 257.

28. Jenny Kitzinger, "Who Are You Kidding? Children, Power, and the Struggle Against Sexual Abuse," in *Constructing and Reconstructing Childhood*, eds. Allison James and Alan Prout (London: Falmer Press, 1997), pp. 165–189.

29. For further discussion see James R. Kincaid's provocative book, *Child-Loving* (New York: Routledge, 1992).

30. Henry Giroux, "Teenage Sexuality, Body Politics, and the Pedagogy of Display," in *Youth Culture: Identity in a Postmodern World*, ed. Jonathon S. Epstein (Malden, Mass.: Blackwell Publishers, 1998), p. 28. Also see Naomi Wolf's discussion of the virginity fetish in *The Beauty Myth: How Images of Beauty Are Used Against Women* (New York: Anchor Books, 1991), p. 14.

31. Giroux discusses beauty pageants in "Stealing Innocence: The Politics of Child Beauty Pageants," in *The Children's Culture Reader*, ed. Henry Jenkins (New York: New York University Press, 1998), p. 277.

32. Results of the National Campaign to Prevent Teen Pregnancy as reported by Lisa Mascaro, "Sex Survey: Teach Teens To Just Say No," *Daily News*, April 25, 2001, p. N1.

33. Mike Males, *The Scapegoat Generation: America's War on Adolescents* (Monroe, Maine: Common Courage Press, 1996), p. 46.

34. Males, ibid., pp. 47–48.

35. Males, ibid., p. 52.

36. Males, ibid., p. 56.

37. Males, ibid., p. 48.

38. Males, ibid., p. 51.

39. Mike Males, *Framing Youth: Ten Myths about the Next Generation* (Monroe, Maine: Common Courage Press, 1999), 195.

40. Males, ibid., pp. 214–215.

41. In *Framing Youth*, pp. 182–188 Males discusses the connections between poverty and early pregnancy. He argues that underlying fears of teenage pregnancy is fear of young people of color, and that focusing only on pregnancy enables us to avoid talking about race and class. He concludes it is easier to demonize teen mothers and popular culture than to understand why teen pregnancy is so much more likely amongst the poor. The middle-class privileges many Americans take for granted often do not apply to this disadvantaged group, who are less likely to benefit from public education and whose economic prospects, even *without* children, are rather grim. In sum, Males argues that the teens most at risk of becoming pregnant are the same ones we demonize as we refuse to acknowledge the economic and social challenges they face *prior* to becoming parents.

42. Statistics supporting this point from the Centers for Disease Control and Prevention can be found in the introduction of: Dale Kunkel, Kirstie Cope-Farrar, Erica Biely, Wendy Jo Maynard Farinola, and Edward Donnerstein, *Sex on TV: A Biennial Report to the Kaiser Family Foundation 2001* (Menlo Park, Calif.: Kaiser Family Foundation, 2001).

43. Alan Gutmmacher Institute, *Trends in Abortion in the United States, 1973–2000,* 2003.

44. See Debra Boyer and David Fine, "Sexual Abuse as a Factor in Adolescent Pregnancy and Child Maltreatment," *Family Planning Perspectives* 24 (1992): 4–11.

45. Giroux, ibid., p. 28.

46. See Michel Foucault, *The History of Sexuality Volume 1: An Introduction* (New York: Vintage, 1980).

47. For a discussion of this practice in the beginning of the twentieth century see Steven Schlossman and Stephanie Wallach, "The Crime of Precocious Sexuality," in *Juvenile Delinquency: Historical, Theoretical and Societal Reaction to Youth,* second edition, eds. Paul M. Sharp and Barry W. Hancock (Englewood Cliffs, N.J.: Prentice-Hall, 1998), pp. 41–62. Immigrant girls were often considered delinquent if juvenile courts believed they were *likely* to engage in sex—no proof of actual behavior was necessary.

48. Angela Y. Davis, "Outcast Mothers and Surrogates: Racism and Reproductive Politics in the Nineties," in *Feminist Frontiers,* fourth edition, eds. Laurel Richardson, Verta Taylor, and Nancy Whittier (New York:

McGraw-Hill, 1997), p. 375. Also see Mike Males, "Framing Youth," ibid., chapter 6.

49. James Heinz, Nancy Folbre, and the Center for Popular Economics, *The Ultimate Field Guide to The U.S. Economy* (New York: New Press, 2000), pp. 89, 99. Reported data are from 1998.

50. Lisa Belkin, "The Making of an Eight-Year-Old Woman," *New York Times Magazine*, December 24, 2001, p. 38.

51. See Debra Haffner, *Beyond the Big Talk: Every Parent's Guide to Raising Sexually Healthy Teens* (New York: Newmarket Press, 2001). Also see Deborah Roffman, *Sex & Sensibility: The Thinking Parent's Guide to Talking Sense About Sex* (Reading, Mass.: Perseus, 2001).

52. Closing speech delivered at the National Media Education Conference in Colorado Springs, Colo., 1998. Thompson noted that television programs tend to be at least a decade behind in terms of presenting social changes. For instance, in spite of the social turbulence of the 1960s, television programs did not reflect the changing social climate until the 1970s.

53. For further discussion, see Naomi Wolf, *The Beauty Myth: How Images of Beauty Are Used Against Women* (New York: Anchor Books, 1991).

Chapter 9

1. Associated Press, "Internet is Blamed in Death of Altar Girl," *Los Angeles Times*, May 22, 2002, p. A15.

2. Mark McCarthy, "FBI Agent: Web Puts Kids in Peril," *Omaha World-Herald*, March 21, 2002, p. 3B. Karen Thomas, "Instant Message to All Parents: Watch the Kids," *USA Today*, July 10, 2001, p. 3D. Carrie Johnson, "Saving Kids from Online Predators," *St. Petersburg Times*, May 20, 2002, p. 8.

3. Bev Wake, "Luring Children via Internet Should be Illegal, OPP Says," *Ottawa Citizen*, September 4, 2001, p. B6.

4. National Child Abuse and Neglect Data System (NCANDS), "Summary of Key Findings from Calendar Year 2000" (Washington, D.C.: Children's Bureau, Administration on Children, Youth and Families, April 2002).

5. Johnson, ibid., p. 8.

6. Johnson, ibid., p. 8.

7. Wake, ibid., p. B6.

8. "The Danger Lurking in Net Chat Rooms," *Sydney Sun Herald*, July 15, 2001, p. 16.

9. Johnson, ibid., p. 8.

10. Elissa Gootman, "Stepping Up Protection for Youths on Internet," *New York Times*, August 21, 2001, p. B5.

11. "One in Five Teens Approached for Sex Online," *Curriculum Review*, October 2001, p. 5.

12. Associated Press, ibid., p. A15.

13. Associated Press, ibid., p. A15.

14. National Research Council, *Youth, Pornography, and the Internet* (Washington, D.C.: National Academy of Sciences, 2002).

15. Kathleen Kelleher, "With Teens and Internet Sex, Curiosity Can Become Compulsion," *Los Angeles Times*, April 15, 2002, p. E5.

16. Nate Guidry, "Caught in the Web," Pittsburgh *Post-Gazette*, January 30, 2002, p. E4.

17. Karen Thomas, "Instant Message to All Parents: Watch the Kids," *USA Today*, July 10, 2001, p. 3D.

18. Thomas, ibid., p. 3D.

19. Bill McConnell, "'One Click' to Safety," *Broadcasting and Cable*, May 10, 1999, p. 12.

20. Elissa Gootman, "Stepping Up Protection for Youths on Internet," *New York Times*, August 21, 2001, p. B5.

21. Norman Oder, "CIPA Trial Ends with Judicial Skepticism about Overblocking," *Library Journal*, May 1, 2002, pp. 16–17.

22. Oder, ibid., p. 17.

23. David G. Savage, "Ruling Halts Internet Limits," *Los Angeles Times*, June 1, 2002, p. A12.

24. Amitai Etzioni, "Internet Can Be a Safe Place for Kids and for Free Speech," *Los Angeles Times*, June 6, 2002, p. B15.

25. U.S. Census Bureau, *Statistical Abstract of the United States*, Table 1155, "Public Library Use of the Internet: 2000" (Washington, D.C.: Government Printing Office, 2001).

26. Will Manley, "The Manley Arts: Good Fences Make Good Libraries," *Booklist*, November 1, 2001, p. 446.

27. Reuters, "House OKs Plan to Set Up Internet Domain for Children," *Los Angeles Times*, May 22, 2002, p. A33.

28. Marjorie Heins, *Not In Front of the Children: "Indecency," Censorship, and the Innocence of Youth* (New York: Hill and Wang, 2001), p. 257.

29. National Research Council, *Youth, Pornography, and the Internet* (Washington, D.C.: National Academy of Sciences, 2002).

30. Tony Wilhelm, Delia Carmen, and Megan Reynolds, "Connecting Kids to Technology: Challenges and Opportunities," Annie E. Casey Foundation, June 2002.

31. Wilhelm, Carmen, and Reynolds, ibid.

32. Wilhelm, Carmen, and Reynolds, ibid.

Conclusion

1. Irving Janis and Seymour Feshback, "Effects of Fear-Arousing Communications," *Journal of Abnormal and Social Psychology* 48 (1953): 78–92.

2. Todd Gitlin, *Media Unlimited: How the Torrent of Images and Sounds Overwhelms Our Lives* (New York: Metropolitan Books, 2001).

3. Recent data from the Executive Office of the President, Budget of the United States Government, Fiscal Year 2001. Martin Marger, *Social Inequality: Patterns and Processes*, second edition (New York: McGraw-Hill, 2002), pp. 180–183.

Selected Bibliography

Adler, Patricia A., and Peter Adler. *Peer Power: Preadolescent Culture and Identity*. New Brunswick, N.J.: Rutgers University Press, 1998.

Altheide, David. *Creating Fear: News and the Construction of Crisis*. New York: Aldine De Gruyter, 2002.

Ang, Ien. *Living Room Wars: Rethinking Audiences for a Postmodern World*. London: Routledge, 1996.

Arnett, Jeffrey Jensen. "Adolescents' Uses of Media for Self-Socialization." *Journal of Youth and Adolescence* 24 (1995): 519.

Bailey, Beth L. *From Front Porch to Back Seat: Courtship in Twentieth Century America*. Baltimore: Johns Hopkins University Press, 1989.

Barker, Martin, and Julian Petley, eds. *Ill Effects: The Media/Violence Debate*. London: Routledge, 1997.

Bergler, Reinhold. "The Effects of Commercial Advertising." *International Journal of Advertising* 18 (1999): 412.

Binder, Amy. "Constructing Racial Rhetoric: Media Depictions of Harm in Heavy Metal and Rap Music." *American Sociological Review* 58 (1993): 753–767.

Borish, David M., Marian Friestad, and Gregory M. Rose. "Adolescent Skepticism Toward TV Advertising and Knowledge of Advertiser Tactics." *Journal of Consumer Research* 21 (1994): 166.

Bryson, Bethany. "'Anything But Heavy Metal': Symbolic Exclusion and Musical Dislikes." *American Sociological Review* 61 (1996): 884–899.

Buckingham, David. *After the Death of Childhood: Growing Up in the Age of Electronic Media*. Cambridge: Polity Press, 2000.

——. *The Making of Citizens: Young People, News and Politics*. London: Routledge, 2000.

——. "Media Education in the U.K.: Moving Beyond Protectionism." *Journal of Communication* 1 (1998): 33–43.

Buckingham, David, ed. *Reading Audiences: Young People and the Media*. Manchester: Manchester University Press, 1993.

Calvert, Karin. *Children in the House: Material Culture of Early Childhood, 1600–1900*. Boston: Northeastern University Press, 1992.

Calvert, Sandra. *Children's Journeys Through the Information Age*. Boston: McGraw-Hill, 1999.

Clark, Cindy Dell. *Flights of Fancy, Leaps of Faith: Children's Myths in Contemporary America*. Chicago: University of Chicago Press, 1995.

Cooper, Cynthia. *Violence on Television: Congressional Inquiry, Public Criticism and Industry Response—A Policy Analysis*. Lanham, Md.: University Press of America, 1996.

Corsaro, William A. *The Sociology of Childhood*. Thousand Oaks, Calif.: Pine Forge Press, 1997.

Côté, James E., and Anton L. Allahar. *Generation on Hold: Coming of Age in the Late Twentieth Century*. New York: New York University Press, 1994.

Dayan, Daniel, and Elihu Katz. *Media Events: The Live Broadcasting of History*. Cambridge: Harvard University Press, 1992.

Dill, Karen E., and Jody C. Dill. "Video Game Violence: A Review of the Empirical Literature." *Aggression and Violent Behavior* 3 (1998): 407–428.

Eder, Donna, Catherine Colleen Evans, and Stephen Parker. *School Talk: Gender and Adolescent Culture*. New Brunswick, N.J.: Rutgers University Press, 1995.

Felson, Richard. "Mass Media Effects on Violent Behavior." *Annual Review of Sociology* 22 (1996): 103–129.

Fiske, John. *Media Matters: Everyday Culture and Political Change*. Minneapolis: University of Minnesota Press, 1994.

Fowles, Jib. *The Case for Television Violence*. Thousand Oaks, Calif.: Sage, 1999.

Fox, Roy F. *Harvesting Minds: How TV Commercials Control Kids*. Westport, Conn.: Praeger, 2000.

Freedman, Jonathan L. *Media Violence and Its Effect on Aggression*. Toronto: University of Toronto Press, 2002.

Funk, Jeanne B. "Video Games: Benign or Malignant?" *Journal of Developmental and Behavioral Pediatrics* 13 (1992): 53–54.

Gauntlett, David. *Moving Experiences: Understanding Television's Influences and Effects*. London: John Libbey, 1995.

———. "Ten Things Wrong with the Effects Model." In *Approaches to Audiences: A Reader*, edited by Roger Dickinson, Ramaswani Harindranath, and Olga Linné. London: Arnold, 1998.

Giroux, Henry. *The Mouse That Roared*. New York: Rowman & Littlefield, 1999.

——. *Channel Surfing: Racism, The Media, and the Deconstruction of Today's Youth*. New York: St. Martin's Press, 1998.

——. "Teenage Sexuality, Body Politics, and the Pedagogy of Display." In *Youth Culture: Identity in a Postmodern World*, edited by Jonathon S. Epstein. Malden, Mass.: Blackwell Publishers, 1998.

Gitlin, Todd. *Media Unlimited: How the Torrent of Images and Sounds Overwhelms Our Lives*. New York: Metropolitan Books, 2001.

——. "Media Sociology: The Dominant Paradigm." *Theory and Society* 6 (1978): 205–253.

Gittins, Diana. *The Child in Question*. New York: St. Martin's Press, 1998.

Glassner, Barry. *The Culture of Fear: Why Americans Are Afraid of the Wrong Things*. New York: Basic Books, 1999.

Goldman, Robert, and Stephen Papson. *Sign Wars: The Cluttered Landscape of Advertising*. New York: The Guilford Press, 1996.

Griffiths, Mark. "Violent Video Games and Aggression: A Review of the Literature." *Aggression and Violent Behavior* 4 (1999): 203–212.

Gunter, Barrie, and Jill L. McAleer. *Children and Television: The One Eyed Monster?* New York: Routledge, 1990.

Hartley, John. *The Politics of Pictures: The Creation of the Public in the Age of Popular Media*. London: Routledge, 1992.

Heins, Marjorie. *Not In Front of the Children: "Indecency," Censorship, and the Innocence of Youth*. New York: Hill and Wang, 2001.

Heinz, James, Nancy Folbre, and the Center for Popular Economics. *The Ultimate Field Guide to The U.S. Economy*. New York: The New Press, 2000.

Henke, Lucy. "Young Children's Perceptions of Cigarette Brand Advertising Symbols: Awareness, Affect, and Target Market Identification." *Journal of Advertising* 24 (1995): 13–28.

Hine, Thomas. *The Rise and Fall of the American Teenager: A New History of the American Adolescent Experience*. New York: Perennial, 1999.

Hobbs, Renée. "The Seven Great Debates in the Media Literacy Movement." *Journal of Communication* 1 (1998): 16–32.

Hodge, Robert, and David Tripp. *Children and Television: A Semiotic Approach*. Stanford: Stanford University Press, 1986.

Hoffner, Cynthia, et al. "The Third-Person Effect in Perceptions of the Influence of Television Violence." *Journal of Communication* 51 (2001): 283–298.

James, Allison, Chris Jenks, and Alan Prout. *Theorizing Childhood*. New York: Teacher's College Press, 1998.

James, Allison, and Alan Prout. *Constructing and Reconstructing Childhood: Contemporary Issues in the Sociological Study of Childhood*. London: Falmer Press, 1997.

Jenkins, Henry, ed. *The Children's Culture Reader*. New York: New York University Press, 1998.

John, Deborah Roedder. "Consumer Socialization of Children: A Retrospective Look at Twenty-Five Years of Research." *Journal of Consumer Research* 26 (1999): 204.

Jones, Gerard. *Killing Monsters: Why Children Need Fantasy, Super Heroes, and Make-Believe Violence*. New York: Basic Books, 2002.

Kelley, Peter, David Buckingham, and Hannah Davies. "Talking Dirty: Children, Sexual Knowledge and Television." *Childhood* 6 no. 22 (1999): 221–242.

Kincheloe, Joe L. "The New Childhood: Home Alone as a Way of Life." In *The Children's Culture Reader*, edited by Henry Jenkins. New York: New York University Press, 1998.

King, Cynthia M. "Effects of Humorous Heroes and Villains in Violent Action Films." *Journal of Communication* 1 (2000): 5–24.

Kincaid, James R. *Child-Loving*. New York: Routledge, 1992.

Kitzinger, Jenny. "Who Are You Kidding? Children, Power, and the Struggle Against Sexual Abuse." In *Constructing and Reconstructing Childhood: Contemporary Issues in the Sociological Study of Childhood*, edited by Allison James and Alan Prout. London: Falmer Press, 1997.

Krcmar, Marina, and Kathryn Greene. "Predicting Exposure to and Uses of Television Violence." *Journal of Communication* 3 (1999): 24–45.

Lewis, Justin, and Sut Jhally. "The Struggle Over Media Literacy." *Journal of Communication* 1 (1998): 109–120.

Louv, Richard. *Childhood's Future*. New York: Anchor Books, 1990.

Males, Mike A. *The Scapegoat Generation: America's War on Adolescents*. Monroe, Maine: Common Courage Press, 1996.

——. *Framing Youth: Ten Myths about the Next Generation*. Monroe, Maine: Common Courage Press, 1999.

——. "Why Demonize a Healthy Teen Culture?" *Los Angeles Times*, May 9, 1999: M1.

Mangleberg, Tamara F., and Terry Bristol. "Socialization and Adolescents' Skepticism Toward Advertising," *Journal of Advertising* 27 (1998): 11–20.

Medved, Michael. *Hollywood vs. America: Popular Culture and the War on Traditional Values.* New York: HarperCollins, 1992.

Meyrowitz, Joshua. "Multiple Media Literacies." *Journal of Communication* 1 (1998): 96–108.

Morley, David. *Television, Audiences and Cultural Studies.* New York: Routledge, 1992.

Nixon, Helen. "Adults Watching Children Watch South Park." *Journal of Adolescent & Adult Literacy,* September 1999, 12.

Palladino, Grace. *Teenagers: An American History.* New York: Basic Books, 1996.

Potter, W. James, and Ron Warren. "Considering Policies to Protect Children From TV Violence." *Journal of Communication* 4 (1996): 116–138.

———. "Humor as Camouflage of Televised Violence." *Journal of Communication* 2 (1998): 40–57.

Real, Michael. *Exploring Media Culture: A Guide.* Thousand Oaks, Calif.: Sage, 1996.

Rose, Tricia. "'Fear of a Black Planet': Rap Music and Black Cultural Politics in the 1990s." *Journal of Negro Education* 60 (1991): 279.

Schudson, Michael. *Advertising, the Uneasy Persuasion: Its Dubious Impact on American Society.* New York: Basic Books, 1984.

Scott, Derek. "The Effect of Video Games on Feelings of Aggression." *The Journal of Psychology* 129 (1995): 121–133.

Seidel, Ruth. *Keeping Women and Children Last: America's War on the Poor.* New York: Penguin, 1998.

Seiter, Ellen. "Children's Desires/Mother's Dilemmas: The Social Contexts of Consumption." In *The Children's Culture Reader,* edited by Henry Jenkins. New York: New York University Press, 1998.

———. *Television and New Media Audiences.* Oxford: Oxford University Press, 1999.

Sherr, Susan A. "Scenes from the Political Playground: An Analysis of the Symbolic Use of Children in Presidential Advertising." *Political Communication* 16 (1999): 45–59.

Spigel, Lynn. "Seducing the Innocent: Childhood and Television in Postwar America." In *The Children's Culture Reader,* edited by Henry Jenkins. New York: New York University Press, 1998.

Springhall, John. *Youth, Popular Culture and Moral Panics: Penny Gaffs to Gangsta-Rap, 1830–1996.* New York: St. Martin's Press, 1998.

Steinberg, Shirley R., and Joe L. Kincheloe, eds. *Kinderculture: The Corporate Construction of Childhood.* Boulder: Westview Press, 1998.

Sternheimer, Karen. "A Media Literate Generation? Adolescents as Active, Critical Viewers: A Cultural Studies Approach." Ph.D. dissertation, University of Southern California, 1998.

——. "Blaming Television and Movies Is Easy and Wrong," *Los Angeles Times*, February 4, 2001, p. M5.

Thorne, Barrie. *Gender Play*. New Brunswick, N.J.: Rutgers University Press, 1993.

——. "Re-Visioning Women and Social Change: Where are the Children?" *Gender and Society* 1 (1987): 85–109.

Tobin, Joseph. *Good Guys Don't Wear Hats: Children's Talk about the Media*. New York: Teacher's College Press, 2000.

U.S. Department of Education. *Indicators of School Crime and Safety*. Washington, D.C.: Government Printing Office, 2000.

Valkenburg, Patti M., and Sabine C. Janssen. "What do Children Value in Entertainment Programs? A Cross-Cultural Investigation." *Journal of Communication* 2 (1999): 3–21.

Wertham, Frederic. "Such Trivia as Comic Books." In *The Children's Culture Reader*, edited by Henry Jenkins. New York: New York University Press, 1998.

Wooden, Wayne S., and Randy Blazak. *Renegade Kids, Suburban Outlaws: From Youth Culture to Delinquency*, second edition. Belmont, Calif.: Wadsworth, 2001.

Woodhead, Martin. "Psychology and the Cultural Construction of Children's Needs." In *Constructing and Reconstructing Childhood: Contemporary Issues in the Sociological Study of Childhood*, edited by Allison James and Alan Prout. London: Falmer Press, 1997.

Zimring, Franklin E. *American Youth Violence*. London: Oxford University Press, 1998.

Index

ABC World News Tonight, 117, 122
Activism and youth, 55
ADD, 92
Adler, Patricia, 181
Adler, Peter, 181
*Adolescence: Its Psychology and
    Its Relations to Physiology,
    Anthropology, Sociology, Sex,
    Crime, Religion and
    Education* (Hall), 172
Adult authority
    advertisement and, 15, 16,
        149–150, 153–155, 168
    Beavis and Butt-head, 89, 90,
        94–95
    cartoons and, 89–90, 107
    monitoring media culture, 38
    music and, 15, 38
    Simpsons, The, 14, 89, 90, 95–98,
        107
    South Park, 89, 90–93, 94
Advertisement
    adult authority and, 15, 16,
        149–150, 153–155, 168
    brand awareness, 151–152, 159
    children's knowledge and,
        158–159

fear of exploiting children, 147,
    148–160, 241n.17
grown-up appeal and, 156–157
marketing research, 150–153
Media Marketing Accountability
    Act, 10
obesity/eating disorders and, 15
in schools, 162–164
youth independence and,
    155–156
See also Consumption
Advertising Age, 165
Affluenza, 162
Aftab, Parry, 198–199
Aggression
    definition, 80
    video games and, 119–120
    violence vs., 79, 80
"Aggression composite," 80
Aggressive and Violent Behavior,
    111
"Aggressive personalities," 119
ALA (American Library
    Association), 200, 201
Aladdin
    power and, 89, 102
    racism and, 13, 98, 104

sexism and, 103, 104–105,
      106–107
Alberta Report, 120
Alcohol use trends, 54
Alienation
   bullying and, 52, 131, 132
   Columbine High School
      shooting, 52–53
   music and, 15, 131–132, 142–143
   understanding of, 131–132
   violence and, 10
   See also Isolation
Allen, Steve, 2
Altheide, David, 209
American Enterprise, The, 91
American Graffiti, 31
American Library Association
   (ALA), 200, 201
American Pie, 17
American Prospect, The, 148
Anderson, Craig, 118–119
Annenberg Public Policy Center
   study, 12
Annie E. Casey Foundation study,
   204, 205
AOL Time-Warner, 6
Apathy label, 55
Ariès, Phillipe, 27
Aristocats, The, 102, 103
Arizona Republic, 78
Armey, Dick, 130
Arnett, Jeffrey Jensen, 128
*Ask the Children: What America's
   Children Really Think about
   Working Parents* (Galinsky),
   161

Baby Boom children and
   marketing, 30
Baby Bottle Pops, 157

Bad Seed, The, 42
Baez, Joan, 129
Bailey, Beth L., 173
Baker, Jane, 120
Bambi, 86
Bandura, Albert, 68
Barca, Joe, 122
Barrett, Patrick, 152–153
Basketball Diaries, The, 2, 68
Bauer, Gary, 46
Beastie Boys, 140
Beatles, 127, 133
Beauty and the Beast
   power and, 89, 102
   sexism and, 103–104, 106–107
Beauty in films, 105
Beavis and Butt-head
   adult authority and, 89, 90,
      94–95
   role models and, 94–95
   teen alienation and, 14, 107
Becker, Edward R., 200
Behaviorism, 116
Behle, Dee Anna S., 51
Bell, Daniel, 161
Bergler, Reinhold, 241n.17
Berkeley Media Studies Group,
   65
Bianchi, Suzanne, 161
Billboard magazine, 142
Binge drinking, 54
Birth control
   access to, 174
   Comstock obscenity laws and,
      50, 202
Blackboard Jungle, The, 42
Blazak, Randy, 67
Blind date, 179
Blume, Judy, 179
"Bobo doll" experiment, 68

Boston Globe, 78, 80
Boston Herald
  advertisement, 148, 160
  media/violence, 70, 125
Bowling for Columbine, 12, 62
Brain studies (media violence),
    73–74, 117
Brand awareness, 151–152, 159
Brody, Michael, 115–116
Brokaw, Tom, 9
Brown, Jeffrey, 88
Bryson, Bethany, 239n.49
Buckingham, David, 24–25, 81
Buffy the Vampire Slayer, 214
Bullying
  music and, 131, 132
  problem of, 52, 131
Bush, George H. W., 95
Bush, George W., 48, 49, 139

California's Proposition 187, 189
Calvert, Karin, 27–28
Campaign, 153
Caputi, Jane, 138–139
Car culture, 31, 173–174
Careless Whisper (Wham), 127
Cartoons
  adult authority and, 89–90, 107
  animal kingdom/social hierarchy,
    104, 234–235n.35
  children's ability to interpret, 13,
    86
  Disney genre, 89, 98–106,
    233n.15
  fears of, 5, 89–90, 106–107
  role models and, 90–98
  slapstick/comic relief of, 87
  violence in, 85–86, 87–88
  See also specific cartoons
Catholic Legion of Decency, 171

Causal relationships
  cartoons/viewer behavior, 86
  media/real violence and, 3–4
  research and, 79, 81
CDA (Communications Decency
    Act/1996), 200
Censorship
  in free society, 121
  self-censorship (Hollywood),
    6
Center for Commercial-Free Public
    Schools, 163
Center for Media Literacy, 215
Center for Missing and Exploited
    Children, 196
Centers for Disease Control and
    Prevention, 54
*Centuries of Childhood: A Social
    History of Family Life*
    (Ariès), 27
Checkoway, Barry, 55
Chicago Sun-Times
  consumerism, 161, 162
  video games, 122
  youth-bashing, 44
Child abuse
  inadequate attention to, 3
  sexual innocence and, 183–184
  See also Sexual abuse
Child care, 37
Childhood
  descriptions of, 22–25
  diversity in experiences, 23
  fantasy of, 36
  historical changes in, 27–34, 172
  nostalgia for, 32–33, 34–35
  rethinking of, 25–27
  social construction of, 24, 27
  technology changes and, 34–36
  See also Innocence (childhood)

Child Internet Protection Act
        (CIPA/2000), 200–201
Child labor, 28–29
Child Online Protection Act
        (COPA/1998), 200, 201
Children
    adult contact/time with, 43, 161
    contradictory view of, 39–40
    as distinct demographic group,
        30
Cinderella, 99, 103
CIPA (Child Internet Protection
        Act/2000), 200–201
Clark, Cindy Dell, 93, 165–166
Class
    adult media perceptions and,
        37–38
    Beavis and Butt-head, 94–95
    media fear and, 8, 9, 10
    middle-class youth/violence, 67
    Victorian era children and, 28
Cleland, Max, 41
Clinton, Bill
    entertainment industry and, 49
    Internet regulation, 199
    youth violence, 41
Clinton, Hillary Rodham
    advertisement, 148
    Internet crimes, 199
Coca-Cola, 163
College preparation education,
        53
Collins, James, 91
Colonial America
    childhood and, 27–28
    "teenagers" in, 172
Colonialism and films, 99, 101, 102
Columbine High School shooting
    clique structures/outcasts and,
        52–53

lack of predictors for, 123
media-blaming in, 1–2
music and, 125, 130
video games and, 109–110, 112,
        125
youth violence generalization,
        41–42
Comedy Central, 91
Comic books, 8–9
Communication changes, 35
Communications Decency Act
        (CDA/1996), 200
Comstock obscenity laws, 50, 202
Condom use, 54
Consumption
    advertisement and, 16
    critical consumerism, 167
    fear of youth materialism, 148,
        160–167
    following WW II, 30, 161
    shared identity and, 164–165, 166
    Time/CNN poll on, 162
    in U.S., 161–162, 164–167
    See also Advertisement
Coontz, Stephanie, 32
Cooper, Cynthia, 12
COPA (Child Online Protection
        Act/1998), 200, 201
Cop Killer (Ice-T), 141
Corliss, Richard, 142
Correlation statistics, 79
Cosby, Bill, 26
Costello, Elvis, 127
Country music, 140
Covenant with North Carolina's
        Children, 44
Crane, David, 50
Creating Fear: News and the
        Construction of Crisis
        (Altheide), 209

Crimes Against Children Research
Center, 196
Cultural expectations and
childhood, 26
"Cultural pollution," 49, 51
Cumberbatch, Guy, 120–121
Curfew laws, 47, 48
Cyber sex, 198

Daily News, New York, 86
D'Arcy, Jan, 195
Delingpole, James, 134
Denver Post, 2, 78, 79
Desensitization
cartoons and, 88
media violence/brain studies
and, 73–74
violence and, 10
Die Hard, 12
Digimon: The Movie, 165
Dill, Karen, 118–119
Disney-genre films
cartoons, 89, 98–106, 233n.15
colonialism/European power
and, 99, 100, 101, 102
historical truth in, 13, 101,
102
public scrutiny of, 13–14
racism and, 13, 98, 99, 100,
101–102, 104
sexism and, 99, 100, 101,
103–106, 106–107
Disney studio and competition, 6
Dole, Robert, 49
Domino's Pizza, 163
Donaton, Scott, 165
Doom (video game), 109, 120
Dragon Ball Z, 13, 85
Duran Duran, 127
Dylan, Bob, 129

Earth 2000, 55
Eating disorders/obesity, 15
Economic change effects, 7
Education
college preparation and, 53
compulsory education
beginnings, 29–30
corporate-sponsored schools,
162–164
immigrant children and, 29
inadequate attention to, 3, 208
inadequate funding for, 94,
162–164, 209
media literacy, 214–215
"moral education," 48
in poverty areas, 4, 57–58
Educators and media fears,
214–215
Eidos, 110
Eminem (Marshall Mathers),
133–137, 139
England's history of media fear,
8
Entertainment, 19
Entertainment industry
marketing report on, 50–51
political criticism of, 49,
50–51
See also specific media
Entertainment Weekly, 137
Etzioni, Amitai, 200
Eunick, Tiffany, 69–70
Exorcist, The, 42–43
Exxon, 163

Family Research Council, 46
Family violence
inadequate attention to, 3
statistics on, 4
youth violence and, 12–13

Fear
  media fear/public policies, 209–210
  power of, 207, 220
  See also Media fears
"Fear of a Black Planet: Rap Music and Cultural Politics in the 1990's" (Rose), 141
Federal Trade Commission (FTC)
  marketing strategies, 50–51
  violent movies, 12
Feliciano, Kristina, 152
Fellini, Federico, 171
"Femicide," 138–139
First Amendment, 121, 199, 211
Fiske, John, 38
Focus groups, 150–151
Forbes, 122
Forever (Blume), 179
Formanek-Brunnell, Miriam, 33
Frame Works, 44
Freedman, Jonathan L., 63, 232n.53
Freud, Sigmund, 31, 175
Frontline, 151
FTC. *See* Federal Trade Commission

Gaines, Donna, 53, 142
Galinsky, Ellen, 161
Gangs
  politics and, 48
  violence and, 72, 75
Gangsta rap, 141
Garbarino, James, 79
Gazette, Montreal, 73
Geise, Rachel, 162
Gender
  childhood experiences and, 23
  media violence and, 81
  mid–1900s roles, 31
  socialization of boys, 4
  video games and, 110, 113, 115
  violence and, 231n.35
  See also Sexism
General Social Survey
  music/racism, 239n.49
  sex, 178
  voting, 48
Generation React: Activism for Beginners (Seo), 55
Genesis, 127
Gerbner, George, 76
Giroux, Henry, 184
Gitlin, Todd, 63, 73, 210
Godard, Jean Luc, 171
Goldberg, Danny, 50
Gore, Al, 48, 49, 51, 199
Gore, Tipper, 9
Grand Theft Auto III, 113–114, 122
Grease, 31
Great Depression, childhood and, 29–30
"Greatest generation," 9
Grossman, David, 110
"Guilt money," 161
Gun control
  ambivalence towards, 62
  avoidance of discussing, 81
  video games control and, 110
Gun culture
  media violence fear and, 62
  Wal-Mart, 12, 222n.21

Hall, G. Stanley, 172
Halpern, John, 51–52
Hart, Betsy, 161, 162
Hartley, John, 38
Harvard School of Public Health, 86
Hays Office, 171
Hays, Will, 171

Health care
  inadequate attention to, 3
  two-tiered system in, 4
Health insurance, 4
Heavy metal music, 126, 127, 137,
  139
Heins, Marjorie, 49–50, 201
Herman-Cohen, Valli, 166
Herrera, Nestor, 70, 71
"High" culture, 9
Hilburn, Robert, 134
Hip-hop, 141
HIV infection, 185, 186
Hobson, Jane, 151
Homicides
  of children, 196
  statistics on, 65, 66, 67
Homophobia and music, 134–135
Honesty, adults/children, 92–93
Horror films, 82
Houston, Whitney, 133

Ice-T, 141
Imitation assumption, 68–71
Immigrant children and education,
  29, 189
Indecency laws, 50
Individualism in America, 62–63
Innocence (childhood)
  adult views of, 23, 25, 32
  advertisement and, 160–161
  Disney films/parks and,
    100–101
  ignorance vs., 26
  "loss of innocence," 25
  movies and, 171
  sexual innocence, 174–175,
    183–184, 191
  South Park, 14, 107
  in Victorian era, 28

Interactive Digital Software
  Association, 121
Internet
  cyber sex, 198
  development of, 35–36, 194
  fears of, 17, 194–197
  income/race and, 195, 204–205
  information regulation and, 50,
    199–204
  pornography and, 197–199
  two-tiered economy and, 195,
    204–205
Internet blocking software
  as cyber-parent, 194
  problems with, 200, 201
  public funding and, 200–201
  use of, 12, 198
Isakson, Johnny, 51
Isolation
  individual media and, 38
  video games and, 111
  See also Alienation

Janoff, Joshua B., 45–46
Jazz, 129
Jenkins, Henry, 31, 112
Jeremy (Pearl Jam), 132, 142
Jerry Springer, 68, 76, 170
John, Deborah Roedder, 158
Jones, Gerard, 14, 68, 79
Journal and Constitution, Atlanta,
  51
Journalists and media fears, 211–213
Journal of Adolescent Health, 111
Journal of Personality and Social
  Psychology, 118
Journal of the American Medical
  Association
  cartoon violence, 86
  obesity, 15

Jungle Book, The, 99
Justice system
  adult courts and juveniles, 47
  juvenile courts formation, 43
Juvenile offenders
  adult courts and, 47
  politics and, 48
  sentences for, 10
Juvenile violence study, Los
    Angeles, 74–78, 230–231n.33,
    231n.35

Kaiser Family Foundation study
    (sex/media), 176–178,
    244n.14
Kansas City Star
  cartoons, 2, 85
  media violence, 2, 64, 73
Karlitz, Howard, 14
Katz, Larry, 125
Kellner, Douglas, 14
Kellogg's, 163
"Kidfluence," 159
Kids, 184
Kids Say the Darndest Things, 26
"Kids.us," 201
Kilbourne, Jean, 148
*Killing Monsters: Why Children
    Need Fantasy, Super Heroes,
    and Make-Believe Violence*
    (Jones), 14, 68
Kim (Eminem), 136
Kincheloe, Joe, 25
Kitzinger, Jenny, 24, 25
Kline, Stephen, 115
Kohl, Herbert, 114, 122
Kunkel, Dale, 232n.53

Lancet, The, 120
Leo, John, 109

Lethal Weapon, 12
License to Ill (Beastie Boys),
    140
Lieberman, Joseph, 49, 114, 122
Linkletter, Art, 26
Linn, Susan, 15
Lion King, The, 104
Little Mermaid, The, 13, 103
Los Angeles
  crime and poverty, 66
  juvenile violence study, 74–78,
    230–231n.33, 231n.35
Los Angeles Times
  advertisement, 16, 160, 166
  cartoons, 14, 86
  entertainment industry criticism,
    2, 49
  Internet dangers, 196, 197
  music, 125, 140
  politics and youth, 51
  research studies, 78, 80
  video games, 114–115
  youth-bashing, 46
  youth sexuality, 174–175
Loukaitis, Barry, 132
Lowry, Brian, 51, 232n.53
Lunch Box, The, 131

Males, Mike, 185, 186
Manley, Will, 201
Manson, Marilyn, 125, 130–132
Marijuana use trends, 54
Marin, Rick, 91
Marketing, 152
Markey, Edward J., 50
Marsden, Andrew, 153
Master P, 133
Mathers, Marshall (Eminem),
    133–137, 139
Mathews, Jane, 151, 152

Maturity
  delaying of, 34
  historical regard for, 28
McCain, John, 199
McCarthy era, 8, 31
McConnell, Frank, 96
McDermott, Terry, 140, 141
"Mean-world" syndrome, 76
Media Awareness Network, 195
Media fears
  changing times and, 5, 6–7, 38–39
  contemporary fears overview,
    11–18, 39
  educators and, 214–215
  flawed logic of, 2–4
  history of, 7–11
  journalists and, 211–213
  parents and, 216–217
  policymakers and, 213–214
  real problems vs., 3, 4–5, 19
  reasons for, 38–39
  youth perspective on, 217
  See also specific media
Media literacy education, 214–215
Media Marketing Accountability
    Act, 10
Media ownership and, 6, 51,
    210–211
Media violence
  assumption about research,
    78–83
  brain studies and, 73–74, 117
  criticism of movies, 49
  fear of, 61, 62, 63
  imitation assumption, 68–71
  media/real violence link
    assumption, 71–78,
    230–231n.33, 231n.35
  plot device and, 6, 77
  university studies of, 5

  violence increase assumption,
    64–68
Mediaweek, 152
Mellencamp, John, 128
"Merchants of Cool, The"
    (Frontline), 151
Milwaukee Journal Sentinel, 46,
    72, 131
Miscegenation laws, 188
Misogyny
  changing status of women and,
    138–139
  music and, 133–134, 134–139, 140
  in video games, 113
  See also Sexism
Moore, Michael, 12, 62
Mortality rates (children), 27–28,
    32–33
Mortal Kombat, 120
Murray, John, 73, 74, 117
Music
  adult authority and, 15
  age-based identities, 129–130
  alienation and, 15, 131–132,
    142–143
  anti-authority themes, 126
  country music, 140
  fear of, 125–127, 130–132
  functions of, 127–130, 143–144
  group identity and, 128–130
  heavy metal music, 126, 127, 137,
    139
  historical fear of, 9
  homophobia and, 134–135
  industry of, 143
  jazz, 129
  Marilyn Manson, 125, 130–132
  misogyny and, 133–134, 134–139,
    140
  obscenities in, 126–127, 140–141

racism and, 239n.49
rebellion and, 15, 129–130
rethinking fears of, 142–144
swing music, 9, 30, 129
See also Rap music

Nantais, David E., 143–144
National Campaign to Prevent Teen
Pregnancy, 185
National Center for Children in
Poverty, 4
National Center for Youth Law, San
Francisco, 47
National Media Education
Conference (1999), 61
National Research Council, 201
Nation, The, 148
Natural Born Killers, 68
Newsday, 52
Newsinger, John, 102
Newsweek, 91
New York Times, 190, 196
Nightmares, 82
Nixon, Helen, 91
Norris, Michele, 117
North Carolina, Mecklenburg
County, 47
Nostalgia
Disney films/parks and, 100
for past childhood, 32–33, 34–35
past/present school problems,
224n.17
*Not In Front of the Children:
"Indecency," Censorship, and
the Innocence of Youth*
(Heins), 50, 201

Obesity
adults and, 15
advertisement/youth and, 15

Officer and a Gentleman, An,
191
Omen, The, 42–43
Osbourne, Ozzy, 125, 138
Ottawa Citizen, 196
*Overspent American: Why We
Want What We Don't Need,
The* (Schor), 159

Pac-man, 112, 118
Pahler, Elyse, 137–138, 139
Palamountain, Chris, 47
Palladino, Grace, 9, 29–30, 129
Parents
handling media fears, 216–217
support for, 209
time spent with children, 161
*Parent's Guide to Protecting Your
Children in Cyberspace*
(Aftab), 198
Parents Music Resource Center
(PMRC), 9
Patterson, E. Britt, 66
Pearl Jam, 132, 142
Penthouse, 198
People, 19
Pepsi, 163
Piaget, Jean, 158
Pikachu dolls, 156
Pittsburgh Post-Gazette
cartoons, 85, 86
Internet dangers, 198
Marilyn Manson, 130
violence, 64, 85
Plain Dealer, Cleveland, 44
Plato, 8
Playboy, 200
Play functions, 79
PMRC (Parents Music Resource
Center), 9

Pocahontas
European power, 102
historical truth, 13, 101
racism, 98
sexism, 103, 105–106
Policymakers
media fears and, 213–214
senators/representatives
website, 213
Politics
entertainment industry criticism,
49, 50–51
gang violence and, 48
protection of children, 49–50
video games and, 121–123
voting, 48–49, 51, 52
youth action in, 55
of youth-bashing, 47–51
youth issues and, 51–52
Pong, 115
Poverty
consumerist society and, 162
economic changes and, 7
effects on youth, 37, 76, 77
inadequate attention to, 3, 208
Internet accessibility and, 195,
204–205
race and, 32, 33
statistics on, 4–5
teen pregnancy and, 186, 246n.41
youth violence and, 12–13,
66–67, 76, 77
Powers, Ann, 142
Power struggles and popular
culture, 9–10
Prager, Dennis, 174–175
Predator 2, 62
Preparing children, 25
Presidential campaigns, 48
Priest, Judas, 125, 138

Prince, 9
Printing press and power, 9–10
Professional wrestling, 88
Protect Children from Video Sex
and Violence Act (2002), 122
Protection (of children)
advertisement and, 149, 158
dangers of, 25, 28
Internet and, 201
politics and, 49–50
restricting youth and, 50
Psychological Science, 111
Psychology and raising children,
30–32
Puritan ethics, 29

Quest for Fire, 182

Race
childhood experiences and, 23
delinquency fears and, 43
Internet accessibility and, 195,
204–205
poverty and, 32, 33
Racism
in cartoons, 86, 89
Disney genre-films and, 13, 98,
99, 100, 101–102, 104
miscegenation laws, 188
movies and, 13–14, 171
rap music and, 140–141, 239n.53
sex and, 188–189
video games and, 113
Rambo, 12
Rap music
anti-authority themes in, 126
criticism of, 9, 139–141
fear of, 140–141
racism and, 139–141, 239n.53
violence and, 133–134

Reality Bytes, 45
Real World, 170
Reckless Youth, 42
Research
  debate and, 82–83, 232n.53
  media violence/real violence
    link, 78–83, 232n.53
  numbers of studies, 80, 232n.44
  shortcomings in, 79–80, 119–120
  of video games/violence, 111,
    112, 117–121
  violence complexity and, 81–82
Ricki Lake, 170, 179
Road to El Dorado, The, 13, 101
Rock and roll fears, 129, 140
Rocky IV, 73
Roffman, Deborah, 16–17
Rolling Stone, 130, 131, 134, 142
Rosemary's Baby, 42
Rosen, Hilary, 142
Rose, Tricia, 141
Russell, Diana E.H., 138–139

"Safe thrills," 73
San Francisco Chronicle, 62
Sartwell, Crispin, 114
Saturday Night Fever, 182
Sawyer, Forrest, 66
*Scapegoat Generation: America's
  War on Adolescents* (Males),
  185
School shootings
  fears of, 56–57
  music and, 132
  of past, 57
  survey on prevention, 81
  youth-bashing and, 41–42
  See also Columbine High School
    shooting
Schor, Juliet B., 159

Schudson, Michael, 151
Scott, Derek, 121
Seattle Times, 142
Seiter, Ellen, 37–38, 164
Self-censorship (Hollywood), 6
Senate Judiciary and Government
  Affairs Committee, 121
Seo, Danny, 55
September 11, 2001 attacks
  lack of predictors for, 123
  sense of security and, 6–7
Sex
  racism and, 188–189
  social control of, 187–190,
    246n.47
Sexism
  cartoons and, 86, 89
  in Disney genre films, 99, 100,
    101, 103–106, 106–107
  movies and, 13–14, 182–183
  music and, 133–134
  policing female sexuality,
    189–190, 246n.47
  women's objectification in
    media, 180, 182–183
  See also Gender; Misogyny
Sex/media
  fears of teen sexual activity,
    170–172, 184–187, 191–192
  gender and, 179–180
  history of, 171–172
  Kaiser Family Foundation study
    on, 176–178, 244n.14
  plot device and, 6
  television and, 16–17, 176–177
  women's objectification, 180,
    182–183
Sexual abuse
  perpetrators of, 24, 195
  sexual activity and, 186, 187

sexual innocence and, 183–184
statistics on, 195
Sex/youth
adult males and, 185, 186, 187,
197
car culture and, 31, 173–174
childhood and, 174–176,
181–183, 245n.24
increasing freedoms in,
173–174
information and, 175–176, 177,
178, 190, 202–204
music and, 129
peer status and, 179–181, 181,
182, 186–187
premarital sex, 170–171,
173–174, 175
sexual activity trends, 54, 58,
178, 185–187
"Talking Dirty: Children, Sexual
Knowledge and Television,"
178–180
videotaping sex, 16
virginity and, 183–184
Sherr, Susan A., 48
"Shock rock," 126, 130
Simon and Garfunkel, 127
Simpsons, The
adult authority and, 14, 89, 90,
95–98, 107
role models and, 95–98
social criticism in, 96–98
Singer, Dorothy, 73
60 Minutes, 12
Skinner, B.F., 116
Slacker label, 45–46
Slayer, 134, 137–139
Sleeping Beauty, 86
Snoop Dogg, 133
Snow White, 99, 103

Social criticism and The Simpsons,
96–98
Social problems
educators and, 214–215
individual actions, 217–219
journalists and, 211–213
media-blaming and, 210–211,
219–220
parents and, 216–217
policymakers and, 213–214
public policy failures, 37, 208
Socrates, 40
Sopranos, 17
South Park
adult authority and, 89, 90–93,
94
childhood innocence and, 14,
107
role models and, 90–93
violence and, 68, 87
Space Invaders, 115
Spam, 199
Spears, Britney, 133, 183–184
Spock, Benjamin, 175
Sports violence, 77, 117
Spring Break, 170
Springfield, Rick, 127
Springhall, John, 8
Springsteen, Bruce, 127, 128
Squeeze, 127
Stan (Eminem), 134, 135–136
Status quo and media-blaming,
210–211
Stereotypical images
of children, 23, 24
in mass entertainment, 5–6
movies and, 13–14
resentment of, 76
See also Racism; Sexism
St. Louis Post-Dispatch, 80, 81

Stop Teaching Our Kids to Kill
　(Grossman), 110
St. Petersburg Times, 196
Suburban life and childhood, 31
Surgeon General report on
　violence (2001), 12–13
Swing music, 9, 30, 129
"Sword of Berserk," 110

"Talking Dirty: Children, Sexual
　Knowledge and Television,"
　178–180
Tampa Tribune, 122
Tarzan
　colonialism, 102
　power, 89, 102
　sexism, 104
Tate, Lionel, 69–70
Teel, Christopher, 55
Teenage pregnancy
　poverty and, 186, 246n.41
　prevention of, 185
　trends in, 33, 54, 187
Teenagers
　as social creation, 172
　term use beginnings, 9, 30
*Teenage Wasteland: Suburbia's
　Dead End Kids* (Gaines), 53,
　142
Telecommunications Act (1996)
　media ownership and, 6, 51,
　210–211
　politics and, 51
"Television: What Every Parent
　Should Know," 11
Television
　development of, 35
　sex and, 16–17, 176–177
　social climate and, 192, 247n.52
　statistics on watching, 16–17

Theory of cognitive development,
　158
Theory of interactivity, 116–117
Thompson, Robert, 192
Thorne, Barrie, 181–182
Three Stooges, The, 73
Time
　cartoons, 91
　media violence, 86
　spoiled children, 159
　video games, 119, 120
Times-Picayune, New Orleans, 44
Tobacco industry hearings, 50–51
Tooth fairy, 92, 93, 165
Toronto Star, 162
*Truth about Reference Librarians,
　The* (Manley), 201
213 (Slayer), 137

Unemployment of youth, 53–54
Union-Tribune, San Diego, 161
"Urban Chaos," 110
Us, 19
USA Today
　advertisement/youth, 148
　media violence, 78
　video games, 114
U.S. News & World Report, 159

Valentine, 70
Valentino, Rudolph, 171
Viacom, 6
Victorian era, 28
Video games
　as easy target, 5, 113
　gender and, 110, 113, 115
　interactive nature of, 110–111,
　113, 116–117
　misogyny and, 113
　politics and, 121–123

ratings for, 121
reality vs., 115
real violence statistics and, 113
violence and, 109–112, 112–116
violence link research, 14, 111,
    112, 117–121
Village of the Damned, 25
Violence
    aggression vs., 79, 80
    in cartoons, 85–86, 87–88
    inadequate attention to, 83
    increase assumption, 64–68
    Los Angeles study (juveniles),
        74–78, 230–231n.33, 231n.35
    media/real violence link
        assumption, 71–78,
        230–231n.33, 231n.35
    middle-class youth and, 67
    origin of, 81
    poverty and, 12–13, 66–67, 76, 77
    rap music and, 133–134
    risk factors for, 66–67, 123–124
    sociological perspective of, 63,
        66–67
    sports violence, 77, 117
    statistics on, 64–65, 66, 67
    Surgeon General report on
        violence (2001), 12–13
    trends in, 57
    valuing of, 77–78
    wars/resolving conflict with,
        77–78, 88, 117
    in Western culture, 77–78, 87, 88,
        117
    See also Family violence; Media
        violence
Virginity, 183–184
Visual literacy, 35
Vocational training, 53
Volunteer work of youth, 55

Voting
    age and, 48–49, 51
    youth alienation and, 52

Walkerdine, Valerie, 183
Wall Street Journal, 85
Wal-Mart and guns, 12, 222n.21
Warner, Brian, 130
Washington Post, The
    cartoons, 86
    music/violence, 137, 142
    TV sex, 16–17
    youth violence, 10, 42
Waxman, Henry, 50–51
*Way We Never Were: American
    Families and the Nostalgia
    Trap, The* (Coontz), 32
Websites
    Center for Media Literacy, 215
    for senators/representatives,
        213
Weissman, Dick, 142
"Welfare queen," 188, 189
Welfare reform legislation (1996),
    4, 208
Wenner, Jann, 142–143
Wertham, Frederic, 8
Wham, 127
Wild Youth, 42
Wile E. Coyote, 86, 87
Wiles, Doug, 122
*Willie Wonka and the Chocolate
    Factory*, 82
Winnie the Pooh, 86
Wizard of Oz, The, 82
Wooden, Wayne, 67
Workplace shootings, 57

Xenophobia and cartoons, 13,
    89

Young Doctors in Love, 169
Youth-bashing
    history of, 42–43, 44
    in movies, 42–43, 45
    politics of, 47–51
    recent books on, 44
    school shootings and, 41–42
    of today, 44–47

youth alienation and, 51–54
"Youth crisis," 47–48
"Youth, Pornography, and the
    Internet," 202

ZapMe!, 163
Zelizer, Viviana A., 29
"Zero tolerance in school," 48